THE LIVING THEATRE

Books by Elmer Rice

NOVELS

On Trial (novelization of play)   1915
A Voyage to Purilia   1930
Imperial City   1937
The Show Must Go On   1949

PLAYS

On Trial   1919
The Adding Machine   1923
The Passing of Chow-Chow (one act)   1925
Wake Up Jonathan (with Hatcher Hughes)   1928
Close Harmony (with Dorothy Parker)   1929
Cock Robin (with Philip Barry)   1929
Street Scene   1929
The Subway   1929
See Naples and Die   1930
The Left Bank   1931
Counsellor at Law   1931
The House in Blind Alley   1932
We the People   1933
Three Plays Without Words (one act)   1934
The Home of the Free (one act)   1934
Judgment Day   1934
Two Plays (Between Two Worlds and Not For Children)   1935
Black Sheep   1938
American Landscape   1939
Two on an Island   1940
Flight to the West   1941
A New Life   1944
Dream Girl   1946
Seven Plays by Elmer Rice   1950
The Grand Tour   1952
The Winner   1954
Cue For Passion   1959

PAMPHLETS

The Supreme Freedom   1949
Conformity in the Arts   1953

PUBLISHERS

Elmer Rice

THE LIVING
THEATRE

 HARPER & BROTHERS, NEW YORK

CONTENTS

CONTENTS

FOREWORD

In the spring of 1957, I received an invitation from the Graduate School of Arts and Sciences of New York University to conduct a drama course during the forthcoming academic year. I was hesitant about accepting, for I have no academic background and, except for brief spells at the University of Michigan, the Yale School of the Theatre and the University of Colorado's Writers' Conference, I was without experience as a teacher. However, I was assured that there was no formal prescription for the course, and that all that was required was that I draw upon my practical acquaintance with the professional theatre. Given so much latitude, and with more than forty years of theatrical activity behind me, I felt that it was a job I might be able to handle, so finally I agreed to undertake it.

I chose, as a title for the course, Contemporary Theatre. That seemed broad enough to cover anything I might want to talk about—and, indeed, so it proved to be. About seventy students enrolled, and I want to describe the composition of the group, for it has an important bearing upon the genesis of this book. The students were all graduates, ranging in age, I should say, from twenty-five to thirty-five. All were residents of the metropolitan area of New York, many of them natives. While some were undoubtedly taking the course solely in pursuance of the laborious business of accumulating credits for a master's or a doctor's degree, most were intensely, even passionately, interested in the theatre. Perhaps I should say dispassionately interested, for only a few were embarking upon theatrical careers. Many were teachers or prospective teachers (not necessarily of the drama), and the rest were engaged in a variety of occupations, for the most part unrelated to the theatre. As a group I should characterize them as alert, sophisticated, well read and "theatre-wise" (or rather "drama-wise": a distinction about which I shall have a great deal to say). Some had worked with college or amateur theatre groups; all went to see as many current New York productions as their time and money permitted—five to ten plays a year, on the average, I suppose. In terms of knowledge, taste and interest, they belonged in what might be called the top stratum of the theatre-going public.

The course comprised twenty-eight weekly sessions of two hours each. I decided to devote half of each session to exposition and half to discussion. This plan worked out well, for the discussions not only served as a guide to the topical constitution of the course, but revealed the extent to which even this rather exceptional and specialized group of theatre students and theatregoers was unfamiliar with, or misinformed about, the basic nature of the theatre and of the various complex elements that contribute to its structure and operation.

At the very outset, I surprised and even disconcerted the students by telling them that I was not giving a drama study course and that, in fact, there would be little or no discussion of the content or the quality of individual plays. They could not understand how it was possible to discuss the theatre for an entire academic year without analyzing and appraising plays, and it took me several weeks to overcome their skepticism and resistance. But as the course progressed and we warmed to the subject, questions multiplied, discussion became more lively, one thing suggested another, and at the end of the year there were still many aspects that we had not had time to examine.

I do not know, of course, how much the students got out of the year. Certainly they increased their fund of information about the practical workings of the theatre; they revised some of their opinions about its character and functions; and they got rid of some of their misconceptions. But whatever may have been the value of the course to them, it was of great value to me. The process of organizing my factual experiences and of formalizing my thoughts about the theatre gave them a concreteness and a pattern they had not had before. It occurred to me that if all this material were put into readable form it might be useful—or even entertaining!—to those whose interest in the theatre extends beyond mere playgoing or mere play reading. As far as I know, not very much has been written about the theatre as a social institution and about the relationship of its technical and human mechanisms to the projection of dramatic literature. I hope that this book, written primarily because of my own interest in the subject, may make a slight contribution to general knowledge.

It should be made clear to the reader that this is not a scissors-and-paste job—a collage of lecture papers or previously published articles, trimmed to size. The talks were extemporaneous; I did not even use notes. So that while the book is a synthesis of the lectures and discussions, it is written from scratch. Further, since I am not a philosopher or a research scholar, there is little in the book that is theoretical or historical. The facts and (highly debatable) opinions are drawn from my own experiences as a playwright, stage director and producer of plays. That explains, and I hope excuses, my continual use of the first person singular.

ELMER RICE

Stamford, Connecticut
February, 1959

THE LIVING THEATRE

I CREATION AND COMMUNICATION

Whether or not art can be defined, every artist knows—
or would know, if he thought about it—that the artistic im-
pulse is compounded of two elements: a need for self-expression and a desire to communicate what is expressed.

What do we mean by self-expression? Avoiding psychological or philosophical profundities, it can be simply explained
in terms of two colloquialisms. We say that a man "has something on his mind": an agitating idea or image or problem;
we say he "has something he wants to get off his chest":
an exciting emotion, whether joyous or painful. In either case,
he has a sense of constriction and uneasiness; he feels op-
pressed, obsessed even. He wants relief from tension, purgation.
If he cannot get his trouble off his mind or off his chest by
direct action, he must rid himself of it by symbolically ex-
ternalizing it. Thus, literally, he presses it out, or expresses
it.

Now of course all self-expression is not art, even by the
broadest definition. But certainly every work of art reveals
the personality of the artist and gives expression, either in
an overt or in disguised (and often unconscious) form, to his
thoughts and feelings, whether the form be verbal, graphic,
plastic or tonal. By critical standards, the thoughts and feel-

I

ings may be commonplace and banal, the formalization trivial and clumsy. Nevertheless, it may safely be said that when
the last word is written, the last brush stroke applied, the
artist feels relaxed and at ease; the incubus has been exorcised.
More likely than not, he feels pleased with himself too—mo-
mentarily, at any rate.

Yet his self-satisfaction is far from complete, because he
has fulfilled only half his purpose, for his desire to communicate is as strong as his need to express himself. Always, during the process of creation, there is present a hypothetical
(and ideal) spectator or auditor, and when the job is done
the artist hopes that he will materialize. He may shoot his
arrow into the air, not knowing where on earth it will fall;
but he expects the spot to be inhabited.

Stories of artists who toss their manuscripts into the fire or
who ruthlessly slash their canvases, or refuse to permit their
works to be published or exhibited should be examined with
a certain amount of skepticism. If an artist does destroy or
withhold his work, it is probably because it has not fulfilled
his need for self-expression or because he fears disapproval
or ridicule. In either case it is evident that he attaches enormous importance to communication; for if he were concerned only with the act of creation he would not care whether
anyone saw his work or not. It is improbable that any such
artist ever lived. Emily Dickinson allowed only three or four
of her poems to be published during her lifetime. But she
did not destroy the rest. It is not unlikely that she cherished
the secret hope that someday they would appear between
covers, for future generations to marvel at and sigh over—as
indeed they have.

In the main, the processes of creation and of communication are wholly dissimilar. One is the spontaneous and self-
initiated activity of an individual, the other an organized industrial or technological process. In primitive societies this
disparity may not be very evident, but it widens rapidly as

the social texture becomes more intricate and complex; so that in the modern world, the machinery of communication has almost acquired an identity of its own, with a relationship to the artist that is mechanistic rather than organic. Many years ago, the head of a large business organization said to me: "A play or a book or a painting may be a work of art when the artist creates it; and it may be a work of art when he is dead. But while it is being marketed and exploited, it is a piece of merchandise, and must be treated like any other piece of merchandise." Of course, that statement is oversimplified, but there is a large element of truth in it—a truth that is too often ignored by those who write about the arts as well as by those who have had little personal contact with artists.

However, it is not ignored by the artists themselves. Many devotees of the arts believe that if they could be eavesdroppers at a gathering of creative artists they would hear brilliant and penetrating discussions of the theory of art and the problems of craftsmanship. This belief is, I am afraid, a romantic delusion. I have had the good fortune, on many occasions, to be in the company of celebrated practitioners of the several arts, but I have never been fortunate enough to get in on one of those aesthetic discussions. When artists get together they behave in the same way that bankers, college professors, taxi drivers, plumbers, athletes or clergymen do: they gossip about their absent colleagues and they talk shop. Furthermore, their shop talk is, to the outsider, as dull as the shop talk of any other group. It consists largely of grievances: complaints (often justified) about the shadiness of theatrical producers, the cupidity of publishers, the extortions of art dealers, the inefficiency of agents, the incompetence or vindictiveness of critics. (When publishers, producers and dealers congregate, they talk—often with justice—about the unreasonableness, undependability, greediness and ingratitude of artists.)

I offer a few concrete illustrations of the artist's preoccupation with the merchandising of his wares. Many years
ago, while I was director of dramatics at the University Settlement in New York, the acting group wanted to give three
or four performances of one of Bernard Shaw's short plays:
The Shewing-up of Blanco Posnet. Permission was requested,
and finally granted, but only after a long correspondence (conducted by Shaw, in longhand, on post cards) dealing with
terms and conditions. I have never ceased to marvel at the
amount of time and energy expended, by a world-famous
dramatist, on the licensing of a production to an obscure amateur group. In my files are several long letters from Theodore
Dreiser, relating to the problem of collecting royalties on the
Japanese translation of one of his books. On several occasions
when I met James Joyce in Paris, he talked mostly about
the piracy of *Ulysses* (then under the interdiction of the
literary experts of the United States Customs Service) by an
unscrupulous New York publisher, and sought to enlist the
aid of his hearers in obtaining redress. Once, in London, I
was invited to lunch with John Galsworthy, a great idol of
mine. I went with trepidation, afraid that I might be drawn
into literary talk far beyond my depth. My fears were groundless. Galsworthy spent most of the lunch hour lamenting his
apparent inability to write a play that was a box-office success.

Now I do not mean that these men, all in the top rank
of contemporary writers, were lacking in artistic convictions
or interest in the principles of workmanship. But they either
kept their beliefs to themselves or confined discussion of them
to a few intimates, preferring to express themselves through
their work. In general, I should say that the artists who talk
most about the principles of art are those least likely to produce work that endures.

There is nothing deplorable in the artist's fixation upon the
market place. Viewed upon his eminence, or in the perspec-

tive of history, he may appear as a heroic symbol of the aspirations and the creativeness of man. Seen face-to-face he is just another human being, with human desires and human weaknesses. He wants to live—even though Voltaire may not have seen the necessity—and, on the whole, he would rather live well than badly. Since, ordinarily, his livelihood depends upon the sale of his work, his interest in economics is understandable. But there is much more to it than that. Like most other human beings, he wants praise, he wants recognition, he wants the self-satisfaction and sense of security that derive from achievement. The apparatus of communication is therefore of paramount importance to him, for its functioning often determines the nature and degree of response to his product, irrespective of the quality of the work itself. To put it another way, good works of art often fail, bad ones often succeed, for reasons unrelated to their inherent character.

The functioning of the apparatus is important to the consumer of the artistic product too: the reader, auditor, spectator. For cultural patterns and artistic tradition depend as much upon a collective body of appreciators as upon individual artists. Consequently, the conditions that govern the accessibility and availability of works of art are vitally important to society as a whole, and art lovers should understand the mechanics of communication.

There are great variations both in the nature and in the operation of the communicative machinery of the several arts, the most obvious differentiation being between those art forms that communicate themselves directly and those that depend upon interpretation. In the first category are the plastic arts, painting and sculpture (and of course such related handicrafts as ceramics, basketry, textiles and the like). When the artist puts down his brush or chisel his statement is completed. It can be seen for what it is by anyone who looks at it. If, however, the artist wants to reach more people than he can bring into his studio—and he usually does—he must engage in some form of marketing: make arrangements for the display of his work by an art dealer or a museum. (This applies equally to a Picasso, to a Grandma Moses, or to one of the currently fashionable air-brush manipulators.) He is now clearly in the realm of commerce, where he finds himself wrestling with such problems as valuations, commissions, publicity, advertising and the like —matters far removed from artistic creation. Communication, then, is by no means a simple and natural consequence of creation. It entails judgment, perseverance and persuasiveness, as well as business organization and salesmanship. Still, whatever the mechanics of exhibition, the exhibited work communicates itself directly and wholly, exactly as the artist executed it.

When we turn to the literary arts—the novel, the essay, poetry, in fact, any form of writing (excluding for a moment, the drama)—we find a more complex situation. When the author comes to the end of his manuscript, his statement, too, is complete, ready to be communicated, but unlike a painting or a sculpture, it is not yet formally ready to be communicated, unless he is content to pass the script from hand to hand among his acquaintances. To reach a substantial number of his potential readers he must depend upon some procedure for the multiplication and distribution of copies, in other words, some form of publication.

It should be remembered that literature is by far the youngest of the arts. Painting, sculpture, drama, music, the dance, and architecture preceded it by many millenniums. Storytelling is probably almost as old as human speech, but oral narration is not literature, since it inevitably contains the element of impersonation and must therefore be regarded as a form of drama. Literature therefore begins only with the employment of the written word. And for a long, long time after the invention of writing, the communication of literature was restricted indeed, for those who could read were few and they were dependent for their reading matter upon copies of the original literary work made by hand: a slow, laborious and costly process.

With the invention of printing—only five hundred years ago—the status of literature and of the literary artist changed radically. A book could now be duplicated a thousandfold instead of tenfold, and the increased availability of books resulted in an enormous increase in literacy. Publishing, printing and book selling became occupations of ever-increasing importance. Several books have sold nearly ten million copies in the United States alone. In the Soviet Union, where literacy is now almost universal, it is not unusual, apparently, for a book to be read by millions.

The author, then, who wants to communicate what he has written to a wide audience must avail himself of the complex techniques of publication, which entail the use of elaborate and costly machinery, as well as the services of great numbers of highly skilled technicians: paper-makers, type setters, printers, bookbinders and the like. On the editorial side, there is the publisher himself, with his staff of readers, editors and proofreaders; and for the marketing of the finished product, the talents of experts in publicity, advertising and salesmanship are required. Finally, there is the bookseller or newsdealer, another essential link in the chain of communication.

All these processes and relationships, with one important exception, are parts of a complicated technological, economic and social apparatus that has nothing to do with artistic creation. It involves business organization and business judgment, financial management, labor-employer relations and numerous other factors. The introverted novelist, the sensitive poet, the brooding philosopher, who wants his words to be read, must entrust his manuscript to a series of operations over which he has no control, and the nature of which he hardly understands.

The one exception referred to is editorial supervision and here the author has power to exercise his judgment or his will. Editorial suggestions may include cutting, rephrasing, or changes in the basic material. More often than not an author is willing to accept editorial guidance. Sometimes he stands firm and wins the day. Sometimes he yields against his better judgment. Sometimes there is a deadlock and the author elects the alternative of nonpublication.

But books can be published without editorial advice, or without acceptance of such advice by the author. In other words, editing is neither inherent in the communicative process nor essential to it. It pertains to creation rather than communication. In any event, the important point is that once the book has been published, it speaks for itself, communicates directly to the reader. No interpretative mechanism or personality is required; everything is right there on the printed page to be apprehended and appraised. Further, the page will be the same next week as it is today, and (barring physical deterioration) the same ten years from now; and if fifty thousand copies have been printed, the page is exactly the same in each copy. The literary artist, then, like the plastic artist, is able to communicate with relative ease, and without the aid of supplementary and complicating artistic elements.

The other arts—architecture, music and the drama—are in a basically different category—not with respect to creation, but with respect to communication. The architect, the composer, the dramatist, can be said, too, to have finished his creative work when he puts down his pencil, but here the resemblance between him and the poet or painter ends. For an architectural rendering is not a building, a score is not music, and (to a lesser extent) a play script is not a play. To make the artist's statement explicit and fully comprehensible, elaborate interpretative techniques are required.

Architectural projects are not, ordinarily, self-initiated as are other works of art, but are created in response to some specific utilitarian need or demand. Hence, whatever the architect's ideals, tastes or preferences may be, he must always keep in view the predetermined end; in solving his aesthetic problem he must accept the terms prescribed. Even in the rare cases when he is given an entirely free hand—say by an adventuresome or a timid home owner—he must be governed by such considerations as building regulations, zoning laws and cost limitations.

If we assume that, even within these rigorous limitations, the architect is able to make an aesthetic statement that satisfies him, he still is far from achieving communication. The drawings, models, blueprints and specifications constitute merely a *plan* for a building. Its realization can be made possible only by the employment of many hands and many skills. Direct communication is out of the question; for even the most detailed model can do little more than suggest the mass and texture of the finished structure. The progression from creation to communication is slow and intricate.

Until comparatively recent times, architectural works were artistic collaborations, executed by a whole corps of artists —stonecutters, glass-makers, woodcarvers, ceramists—of whom the architect was merely the chief. The Parthenon, Notre Dame de Chartres, the Temple of Heaven in Peking, the Taj Mahal, Angkor-Wat, the viaducts and amphitheatres of antiquity, the palaces and châteaux of the Renaissance—all these are clearly not the product of one artist's imagination or one pair of skilled hands. But with the invention of machinery and the development of technology, individual workmanship and handicrafts have become obsolete, and today the execution of the architect's design is left to crews of mechanics, each specially trained to perform some endlessly repeated industrial routine that requires neither interest in, nor awareness of, the over-all plan.

Architecture, not only because of its permanence and majesty, but because it does satisfy so many basic human needs, is perhaps the greatest of all the arts. Yet it must be recognized that as our society becomes more and more mechanized, the architect finds it more and more difficult to communicate his vision and his soaring aspirations. And without communication, he achieves only half his purpose.

Music again presents special problems of communication. It probably shares with the dance the distinction of being the oldest of the arts; older even than man, for many nonhuman animals engage in rhythmic dancelike movements or produce harmonious sounds. As for man, it is very likely that musical expression, in the form of cadenced shouting or the plangent percussion of two solid objects, preceded articulate speech, as it does with children of pre-speech age. If so, and there was someone within earshot, communication was immediate and direct.

However, when we speak of music as an art, we are not usually thinking of such primitive improvisations, any more than we think of the recitals of the prehistoric bard as literature. For our purposes, music begins with the formalization of musical expression and the invention of some system of notation, just as literature begins with the invention of writing. The composer expresses his musical fantasies by means of arbitrary tonal symbols, just as the author expresses his verbal fantasies by means of arbitrary alphabetical symbols (or by pictographs). In either case, the notations are intelligible only to those who have learned the meaning of the symbols. With literature, of course, it is necessary to understand not only the system of notation, but the *language* employed. Theoretically, then, it would seem that the composer, like the novelist or poet, can convey his meaning to anyone who is familiar with his notational system. But it is not so; for the full understanding of word symbols can be transmitted by the eye, while the full understanding of musical symbols requires the ear, and therefore the symbols must first be translated into sound.

Of course, there are many people who can read music at sight—though compared to those who can read words their number is infinitesimal—and I have known individuals who claim that they can read even a complicated orchestral score and *hear* it as if it were being performed. Surely this is an exceptional talent, far beyond the range of the average music lover, and if the composer had to depend upon such persons for the enjoyment and appreciation of his work his audience would be small indeed. Quite apart from that, the fact is that music is written not to be read but to be performed. Notation is merely a device for formally expressing the composer's creation and for the guidance of those who undertake its communication.

We must now consider an element in the communicative process that differs qualitively from anything we have heretofore discussed: the element of interpretation. Whether the music is vocal or instrumental, solo or concerted, its communication depends upon performers who, unlike linotypists or bricklayers, are not merely trained mechanics or artisans, but are themselves practitioners of artistic skills that are indispensable to the composer.

He is dependent upon them not only for the physical act of communication but for its fidelity; that is, for the extent to which the performance truthfully and artistically projects what the composer has intended to express. Further, the performer can display his technical skill only through the use of an instrument, whether it be his own voice box or a manufactured contrivance. A limited vocal range (or an attack of laryngitis), an untuned piano or a badly constructed violin, may gravely distort the composition. The interpretation may also be affected by climatic and acoustical conditions, by improper groupings of performers, by inadequate rehearsals and by other factors. Ensemble performances almost always require the leadership of a conductor, whose conception of the proper tempo, volume, emphasis and balance shapes and colors the performance, as anyone knows who has heard numerous renditions of a Bach concerto, a Beethoven symphony or a Handel oratorio.

Distinction must be made, too, between different types of musical composition. Opera and ballet, with respect to the problem of communication, are dramatic rather than musical forms, for they comprise such purely theatrical elements as impersonation, movement, scenery, costumes, stage lighting and stage machinery. Hence their performance is governed by the same conditions that govern the performance of plays.

Also, even with nondramatic music, the manner of communication is often affected by the nature of the composition. The simpler the performance requirements, the more direct can communication be between the composer and the listener. A solo composition, whether vocal or instrumental, can be performed, for his own enjoyment, by anyone who has the requisite skill. And two or more can join forces in the front parlor or the rumpus room for the performances of duets, trios, quartets or even more elaborate compositions. But it must not be overlooked that even in this simple situation the interpretative element is indispensable to communication, and the executants play the dual role of performer and listener. As the complexity of the composition increases the difficulties multiply.

It follows that musical works requiring a large number of executants are almost invariably performed in public. And, of course, smaller works have frequent public performances too. So that, to a great degree, musical communication requires not only the services of trained and properly equipped performers, but the organization and use of facilities for public presentation.

The very words public performance suggest two elements we have not yet encountered in our discussion of the other arts. Public implies a collective rather than an individual response; performance implies a place in which to perform. Hence, audience and auditorium: assemblage of a group of receptive persons, and a structure suitable not only for their accommodation but for the disposition of the performers. Even an outdoor concert requires a bandstand and space for the listeners.

Ordinarily the arrangements are considerably more elaborate, and for professional performances to which admission is charged a building adapted to musical rendition is essential, as well as the employment of a whole staff of specialists, who have little or nothing to do with the creation of music or with its performance: ticket sellers, ushers, electricians, piano movers, cleaners, accountants, press agents. These factors, incidental to any sort of public performance, are merely mentioned here, for they will be fully discussed in connection with the communication of drama.

With respect to drama, the essential requirement of communication is simply stated: plays are written to be performed before an audience in an auditorium. While that is true, in the main, of music too, the presentation of drama is so much more complicated that the difference becomes one of kind rather than of degree. Collectively, the performance, the audience, the auditorium and many other elements constitute an institution—it might almost be termed an organism—called the theatre, that is unique. Though it is an instrumentality for the communication of drama, it has an independent social and artistic existence of its own. Its significance can best be expressed by the statement that without the art of the theatre there could be no art of the drama. Therefore an understanding of what the theatre is is mandatory not only for the dramatist, but for the drama lover and drama student (the terms are not necessarily synonymous). To arrive at that understanding, it is necessary to inquire into the nature of drama, and the nature of the theatre, before proceeding to a detailed investigation of the constituent elements of the theatre.

II THE NATURE OF DRAMA

The greatest mistake that the student or teacher of drama can make is to approach it as primarily a literary art. Yet this is a usual approach in college and secondary-school drama courses. It is hard to say exactly why. It may be that the school does not provide facilities for acting plays or opportunities for seeing them acted. It may be a hangover from the Puritan tradition that the theatre is an abode of Satan. Many of our colleges were founded by religious bodies; indeed many of them are still under some form of religious control. Or it may be that those who have had little actual contact with the enacted drama do not fully understand its essential nature and characteristics. Whatever the reasons, the literary approach is not to be commended, for it is constricting and misleading.

This is not to say that literary excellence is not an essential criterion in the evaluation of a play. Of course it is; but it is by no means the only criterion or even the most important. A great drama is almost certainly a great work of literature, but it does not follow that a great work of literature, written in the form of a play, is a great drama. Shakespeare's immortality in the theatre rests upon his dramaturgic skill; his transcendent poetry is a glorious embellishment that may, for example, perish in translation without destroying the dramatic effectiveness of the

14

plays. The same may be said of the wit and brilliant diction of Shaw, who is a first-rate dramatist, a large body of critical opinion to the contrary notwithstanding.

In the dazzling literary world of nineteenth-century England nearly every great poet and novelist wrote, or tried to write, plays: Shelley, Browning, Tennyson, Swinburne, Stevenson, Conrad, George Moore, Hardy. The most conspicuous example is perhaps Henry James, a stage-struck soul, who wrote play after play and deeply mourned his inability to write a viable one. Many of the works written in play form by these masters are imbued with thought, imaginativeness and beauty; yet they are not suitable for stage presentation. They are aptly called "closet dramas": works to be read and enjoyed in the privacy of one's study. Their unsuitability for the stage is attributable to their authors' lack of understanding of the nature of drama or to their inability to master stage technique. In the preface to a volume of his published plays, Lord Dunsany—surely a "literary" dramatist—has this to say: "Believing plays to be solely for the stage, I have never before allowed any of mine to be printed until they had first faced from a stage the judgment of an audience to see if they were entitled to be called plays at all."

The essence of drama is not words but action. Plays are written to be enacted. In Aristotle's classic definition, a tragedy (that is, a play) is an imitation of an action. The word tragedy itself means literally a goat-song, which refers, apparently, either to an ancient religious ritual in which a goat was sacrificed, or to the goatskins which the performers wore. (There is an extraordinary modern play by Franz Werfel called *Bock Gesang* or, in English, *Goat-song*.) Comedy means a festivity with music and dancing or a festal procession. A revue is a re-seeing, that is, a re-enactment of topical incidents. Such words as act, play, show and spectacle put the emphasis upon doing and seeing; so do director, producer, actor, performer and mime (a favorite word of Max Beerbohm's, when he wrote dramatic criticism for the

Saturday Review). Scene, stage and theatre all refer to a building or structure designed for performers, and spectators and audience indicate that people come to see and to hear.

In fact, words are not even necessary for the creation and communication of drama. Children at a very early age use dolls or toy animals for the re-enactment or imitation of their own experiences: parental discipline, eating, sleeping or almost any bodily activity. The appeal of pantomine, puppet shows, mummery and pageantry is universal, and these forms of dramatic action are enjoyed by the illiterate as well as by the preliterate. "Dressing up" has a universal appeal too: assuming the guise of some observed or imagined character and simulating the character's activities. Primitive peoples who do not even possess a written language engage in and enjoy all sorts of dramatic activities: puberty, purification, marriage and death rites, ceremonial enactments of hunting, warfare, the crop cycle and propitiation of the gods. In more developed societies such elaborately staged spectacles as ballets and bullfights attract large and eager audiences, and the celebration of the mass, often a highly spectacular ceremony, is deeply moving to multitudes of communicants to whom the verbiage employed is unintelligible. Or take an illustration of a wholly different sort: silent movies, an enormously popular form of dramatic representation. True, explanatory subtitles and suggestions of dialogue were often flashed upon the screen, but appreciation of the films did not depend upon these literary aids, and in the best of the silents they were used sparingly or not at all. Charlie Chaplin and Mickey Mouse conquered the world without words of tongue or pen.

Even when words are a vital part of the dramatic creation, a spectator may derive considerable enjoyment from it without understanding the language. Here we see a fundamental difference between literature and drama, between books and plays. If one knows the play, one can follow it readily enough in a completely unfamiliar language. Thus I have been able to enjoy performances of *Othello* in Turkish, *Hamlet* in Serbo-Croatian and in Uzbek, *Oedipus Rex* in Greek, and *The Lower Depths* in Japanese, though I know hardly a word of any of these languages. Acquaintance with the text made it possible for me to follow the action without difficulty and I was greatly interested in the characterizations, the styles of acting, the staging and other details of performance. But if I were presented with a translation into any of these languages of *David Copperfield*, *Main Street* or *Crime and Punishment*, I could do no more than stare blankly at the printed page. Given a brief story synopsis, the alert spectator can pursue the thread of even an unfamiliar play. Many opera-goers understand very well what is happening on the stage and, in substance, what the performers are singing about, though they could not understand the words even if the singers succeeded in making them intelligible.

All this is not to say that the text of a play cannot convey to the reader some sense of its dramatic impact. Of course it can, and the better-written the text, and the more perceptive and imaginative the reader, the greater the effect. Rarely if ever, though, can it produce the same effect as a fine stage performance. We can read Hamlet's soliloquies or Antony's funeral oration and grasp their meanings, their revelation of character and the music of their measures, but how much greater is our emotion and our aesthetic pleasure when we hear the words pronounced by a fine actor! To read in a stage direction such indications of mood as "savagely" or "tearfully" is surely not the same as to sit tensely in one's seat while a player strides the boards in simulated rage, or to be moved to tears oneself by the apparent distress of a beautiful actress.

Moreover, the things that happen in a play usually create a greater impression than the things that are said. In the theatre it is indeed true that actions speak louder than words. A witticism or verbal quip will seldom provoke as much laughter as an incongruous confrontation of characters or a physical embarrassment, known in theatrical circles as situation laughs or sight gags. To read in the text of a play that a character sits on his hat or on a freshly painted bench, or that he loses his trousers or falls down an open trap door, is not likely to elicit more than a faint smile, yet the representation of these accidents can produce roars of laughter. The mere sight of a performer's red nose, shambling gait or ill-fitting clothes brings forth chuckles that no mere description could. An evil-visaged actor's stealthy movements across a dimly lighted stage, to the accompaniment of ominous sound effects, may rouse an audience to a pitch of excitement and terror than can hardly be indicated by the descriptive text.

Many, many years ago, I saw the famous William Gillette in a dramatization of Conan Doyle's detective stories called, appropriately enough, *Sherlock Holmes*. In the climactic scene of the play the mastermind of Baker Street, pursued by the sinister Professor Moriarty, takes refuge in the Stepney Gas Chamber. Warned of the approach of the Professor, he looks about for some means of escape, and then, as the door opens, he quickly puts out the lights. The stage is in complete darkness; nothing is visible except the glowing end of the cigar Holmes has been smoking. We cannot see Moriarty and his confederates enter but we can hear them. "Follow the cigar!" shouts Moriarty. There is excited movement, then curses, followed by the switching on of the lights. Then we see that the wily Holmes has placed the cigar on the sill of one window and made his escape through another. It may all sound rather ridiculous, but it would be impossible to exaggerate the effect it had upon the audience. Shivers and exclamations of apprehension were followed by relief that expressed itself in delighted laughter and sustained applause. I saw the play in 1911, and all I remember of the text is what I have quoted; but I shall never forget the lean and agile Gillette in his deer-stalker's cap, or the excitement of that scene.

A more orthodox illustration is provided by the familiar knocking-at-the-gate scene in *Macbeth*. In Act II, Scene II, after the bloodstained Macbeth, fresh from the murder of Duncan, has refused to do the necessary business of implicating the sleepy grooms, Lady Macbeth, scornful of his infirmity of purpose, takes the dagger and leaves him alone in the dimly lighted courtyard while she goes off to do the job herself. Then there occurs in the text the stage direction: "Knocking within." This is repeated three times in the ensuing fifteen or eighteen lines that bring the scene to a close. During that time Lady Macbeth returns, now bloodstained too. Presently, the pair exit as the knocking continues.

It is dramatic enough in the reading, but the full effect can be understood only when one sits in the theatre watching those two desperate figures in the cold predawn light, he already overcome with guilt and remorse, she hysterically intent upon the consummation of the crime. Then comes the knocking upon the locked gate of the castle; the inchoate fears of Macbeth and the cold disdain of his wife are punctuated by the repeated pounding. Who is there? Will the guilt be discovered? The words convey all that, of course, but they are immeasurably enhanced by the visible and audible situation. No one who has merely read the play can be aware of the intensity of this celebrated scene when it is enacted. It should be noted, too, that Shakespeare, the master dramatist, having built up the tension to an almost unendurable degree, now relieves it by introducing the clownish porter. What he says is not particularly comic, but as he gabbles on, oblivious to the insistent knocking, the terror abates and we are glad that we are able to breathe again and to laugh again.

A somewhat similar effect of mounting tension is achieved in Galsworthy's *Justice* without a single word being spoken. The play, which is a bitter and ironic polemic against the inflexibility and inhumanity of the criminal law, deals with a clerk named Falder, who commits a petty theft to further an illicit love relationship. He is tried, convicted and sent to prison. In Act III, Scene III, we see him in his prison cell. The text first describes the cell in considerable detail, then Falder's behavior in the "fast-failing daylight": his restlessness, nervousness, inability to concentrate, his futile attempts to learn what is going on outside. Aimlessly, he picks up a tin lid, then suddenly drops it— "the only sound that has broken the silence." The text continues:

There is a sharp tap and click; the cell light behind the glass screen has been turned up. The cell is brightly lighted. Falder is seen gasping for breath. A sound from far away, as of distant, dull beating on thick metal, is suddenly audible. Falder shrinks back, not able to bear this sudden clamour. But the sound grows, as though some great tumbril were rolling towards the cell. And gradually it seems to hypnotise him. He begins creeping inch by inch nearer to the door. The banging sound, travelling from cell to cell, draws closer and closer; Falder's hands are seen moving as if his spirit had already joined in this beating, and the sound swells till it seems to have entered the very cell. He suddenly raises his clenched fists. Panting violently, he flings himself at his door and beats on it. The curtain falls.

The writing here is graphic and cannot fail to stir the emotions of the sensitive reader. But anyone who saw John Barrymore's performance of the play can testify that no mere reading could produce one-tenth the effect that his interpretation did. His prison garb and prison pallor, his haunted look and jerky, unco-ordinated movements created immediately an atmosphere of intense suffering, augmented, of course, by the dismal cell, the crepuscular light, the unearthly silence. As the scene progressed, and one watched the aimless movements of this frenzied caged animal, one became increasingly taut and constricted. The clatter of the tin lid abruptly breaking the silence, the flashing on of the cell light, abruptly dispelling the darkness, jangled the already overcharged nerves. Then the distant pounding began, and as the sound came nearer and nearer, and the distraught prisoner fought harder and harder to control his hysteria, the emotional load became almost unendurable; the falling curtain left the spectator spent and breathless. All this was accomplished without the use of a single line of dialogue or any other literary device: it was sheer drama, projected entirely in terms of action.

A contrasting but analogous example is afforded by J. M. Barrie's *Peter Pan*. The play is charmingly written, but no reading can convey the effect produced by a stage performance. The most astute reader could hardly visualize the character of Peter, as I have seen it variously portrayed by such brilliant actresses as Maude Adams, Eva Le Gallienne, Jean Arthur and Mary Martin. Further, the audience is ordinarily composed largely of children, many of whom would be incapable of reading the text or even of following it if it were read aloud to them. In the theatre they follow with enchanted attentiveness. The dialogue has great appeal, of course, but the main interest is visual: the Indians; the pirates; the villainous Captain Hook, with his prehensile hand; his implacable enemy, the crocodile that has swallowed the alarm clock; Peter's detachable shadow; the mischievously dancing light that is Tinker Bell; and Nana, the faithful nurse-dog. Barrie's first reference to Nana is illuminating. After describing her, he says: "The cuckoo clock strikes six and Nana springs into life. This first movement of the play is tremendously important, for if the actor playing Nana does not spring properly, we are undone." While this is tongue-in-cheek, it nevertheless indicates the dramatist's awareness of the importance of performance. The excitement of Peter's flying cannot be conveyed by words, especially when he soars out over the audience itself. And when the dimming light warns us that the poisoned Tink is dying and Peter, addressing the audience, says, "Do you believe in fairies? Say quick that you believe! If you believe, clap your hands!" the nature of the response establishes a kind of communication that is rarely achieved by any artist.

I hope I may be forgiven for using my own play, *Street Scene*, as another illustration of the nonliterary aspects of the drama. (In fact, I intend later to tell in detail the story of the production of this play, for it illustrates in many ways the relationship between the drama and the theatre.) The entire action of the play takes place in front of a New York brownstone tenement house.

The setting in itself makes a visual impression that the textual description can only suggest. The elapsed time is a night and a day during a typical early-summer New York heat wave. There are more than fifty characters in the play, and during most of the action they come and go incessantly. There are, in the dialogue, many references to the excessive heat, but these do not suffice for the creation upon the stage of the *atmosphere* of heat, which is essential to the play. The production of the desired effect required the use of a multitude of visual devices: not only such stage properties as ice-cream cones and fans, but the appearance and attitude of the actors. Thus each member of the cast, by his or her flimsy, or even scanty, attire, by languid movement and irritability of manner, contributed to the general impression of devastating heat. The play opened in the middle of a severe winter, yet so convincing was the illusion of heat that many people, upon leaving the theatre, were startled by the cold outside. This was exactly the feeling that I wanted to communicate when I wrote the dialogue and the descriptive text, but for the full accomplishment of my purpose the appurtenances of the stage and the skill of the actors were necessary.

What has been said is neither intended to discourage the reading of plays nor to minimize the importance of the drama in world literature. Great enjoyment and great enlightenment may be derived from the reading of great plays, and the dramatist, like any other writer, finds pleasure in seeing his work between covers. But no true dramatist writes solely, or primarily, for the library. All the while he is writing he dreams of his play coming alive upon the stage, sees his characters in motion and hears them speaking his lines. Incidentally there is a great difference between reading a play before one has seen it and afterwards. The later reading, reinforced by memories of the production, brings out values not previously realized. Even though a playwright is not writing for a particular actor, he usually has some concept of what his characters should look like and sound like. Some playwrights (and I am one of them) begin by making rough ground plans of the stage settings, in order to keep the movements of their characters within the limits of visibility and the stage area. Some go further and manipulate miniature figures to simulate the physical action. Others dictate their dialogue, or speak it aloud as they write it, so that they may have some notion of how it falls upon the ear.

The playwright who understands his craft never loses sight of the fact that in order to communicate what he has created he is dependent upon an elaborate apparatus which comprises not only physical, mechanical and organizational elements but artistic interpretative assistance. This apparatus is called the theatre, and without it there could be no art of the drama.

III THE NATURE OF THEATRE

As we have noted, the word theatre, in its narrower sense, means a place for the performance of plays, literally a seeing-place. At the very minimum, it contains two distinct and fairly large areas: one for the performers, the other for the spectators. Ordinarily, however, and particularly in advanced societies, a theatre consists of considerably more than these two indispensable elements. It is usually a structure of some sort—not necessarily roofed over—that is especially adapted for dramatic presentations. Since both seeing and hearing are requisites to the enjoyment of a play, attention is usually given, in the construction of the building, to acoustical requirements; and there is usually a raised stage, in order that the performers may be more visible. Also, since a performance usually lasts for two hours or more, it is customary to provide seats for the spectators. If the building is entirely enclosed, or if night performances are to be given, some system of artificial lighting must be installed. Besides such basic requirements, there is nearly always some sort of scenic investiture, either permanent or changeable; storage space for scenery and properties; dressing rooms for the performers; and, except in outdoor or so-called arena theatres, a curtain between the stage and the auditorium. In most modern theatres there will also be found mechanisms for the moving of scenery and the control of lights; lounges and lavatories; a lobby with a box office; and sometimes bars and refreshment rooms. In the area that is called backstage there may be a green room (a lounge for the actors), rehearsal space and workshops.

When we use the term theatre we ordinarily mean a structure intended primarily for the performance of plays, whether it be an antique outdoor theatre, such as may still be seen in an excellent state of preservation at Epidaurus, or a modern metropolitan theatre, equipped with all sorts of technological devices, such as the Grosses Schauspielhaus in Berlin. But plays may be presented in all sorts of places not intended for theatrical use at all. I have seen *Jedermann* performed in the public square before the Cathedral of Salzburg, an unforgettable performance, with the cathedral façade as a scenic background and voices calling from all the neighboring church steeples. Also at Salzburg I saw the Max Reinhardt production of *A Midsummer Night's Dream* in the Reitschule, an old riding academy. (The Provincetown Theatre in New York was once a stable, and if you sat beside the wall you could see the iron rings to which the horses had been tied.) I have seen *The Winter's Tale* in front of a hedge in Regent's Park in London; an operatic performance of *Mefistofele* in the ruins of the Baths of Caracalla in Rome; a ballet in the courtyard of Edinburgh Castle; a striking production of *Hamlet* on the battlements of the ancient walled city of Dubrovnik; *Murder in the Cathedral* on the green before the Abbey Church of Tewkesbury; a puppet shadow play in the garden of a private residence in Peking; high mass on Christmas Eve in San Marco in Venice. (In characterizing the mass as a theatrical performance, I am not facetious or irreverent. We have seen that the drama is a development of old religious rituals. This particular performance, with the glorious mosaics of the church as a setting, with its costumes, incense, dramatic lighting, music, rhythmic movement, trained performers, poetical and emotional text, and responsive audience, had most of the concomitants of a stage production.) Besides these, I have seen innumerable theatrical performances in tents, cellars, school auditoriums and gymnasiums, hotel ballrooms, stadiums and barns; in fact, in the United States, barn has almost become a synonym for a summer theatre.

But whether indoor or outdoor, whether simply or elaborately equipped, a theatre, in this simple sense of a viewing place, is indispensable for the communication of drama. The nature and degree of communication is affected directly by many factors pertaining to the theatre that have nothing whatever to do with the content of the plays presented or the artistic aims of their authors. In large cities the mere geographical location of the theatre may determine the extent of attendance. A theatre centrally located, accessible to a bus line or a subway station and to adequate parking facilities for private cars, will almost certainly attract larger audiences than a theatre lacking any or all of these conveniences, irrespective of what play is being produced. Bad acoustics or sight-lines, uncomfortable seats or inadequate heating or cooling systems tend to keep away people who might otherwise come.

So far we have used the word theatre only in its narrower and more literal sense. It has far, far wider scope and connotation, comprising all the phases and mechanisms of play production. We mean something very different when we say *the* theatre than when we say *a* theatre. *The* theatre is not limited to the physical viewing place. It includes the multiple techniques required for the organization and projection of a dramatic presentation, the numerous and varied personnel, both artistic and technological, engaged in the application of these techniques, and the audience. In the aggregate these constitute an institution that is not only cultural but social; one that has an identity and a history of its own and is in many ways independent of the art of the drama.

The essential characteristic of the theatre—professional or amateur, commercial, subsidized or academic—is that it is a collective enterprise, in contrast to the dramatic art, which is almost wholly individualistic. The importance of this distinction cannot be overemphasized because it is at the root of all the problems that are peculiar to the communication of drama. The collective nature of the theatre is apparent in at least three respects.

In the first place, plays are written to be performed in the presence of a collective entity—the audience. Books, pictures, statues are addressed to the solitary reader or viewer; music may be performed and enjoyed by one or two individuals. But plays are written to be communicated to a numerous group gathered in one place at one time. The organization and assemblage of the group call for a special set of procedures, and the difference between a collective response and an individual response is not only one of degree, but one of kind. This temporal and physical collective assemblage makes it imperative that the play, both in creation and in performance, be immediately apprehensible. There is no lingering, no turning back. The audience must move forward with the performers, and what is not instantly grasped is forever lost.

Secondly there can be no direct communication between the dramatist and his audience. The projection of his play entails the skills and services of a director and actors, designers of costumes and scenery, stagehands, "front-of-the-house" employees and managerial executives. All these must be co-ordinated in the carrying out of an organized plan. Individualism must both express itself and be, to a large extent, subordinated to the over-all scheme. This creates relationships, and often conflicts, that are professional, economic and personal. The possible permutations are as infinite as the moves in a chess game, and the outcome is as unpredictable.

These two collective characteristics of the theatre—the audience and the executants—produce a third: its public nature. Other works of art may be enjoyed not only by individuals, but in private. Failing a publisher or an exhibitor, a poem or a painting may be passed from hand to hand. Or, if it is considered subversive or indelicate, and hence socially unacceptable, it may be read or displayed in a locked room behind drawn blinds. But the essence of a dramatic performance is that it is public. It is practically impossible to keep secret an activity that demands the facilities and the number of participants required for the showing of a play. The theatre by its very nature is out in the open. This, of course, makes it subject to many forms of public scrutiny, influence, supervision and regulation, covering matters that are fiscal, political, religious, social or governmental by nature and have little or nothing to do with the drama as an art, e.g., taxes, building laws and fire prevention; racial exclusion or segregation; Sunday laws; regulation of child labor; political affiliations of personnel.

The theatre then can truly be said to have a form, an identity and a life of its own. In a sense it seems to exist for the purpose of serving the drama, but sometimes it is not easy to say which is servant and which master. Paintings and books are sometimes neglected at the time they are created, and long afterwards are resurrected and appreciated. But a play that is unperformed quickly falls into an oblivion from which it is seldom rescued. The theatre as an institution has had a long, long life, with ups and downs like those of a stock-market graph: jagged when seen at short range, gently undulant when viewed in perspective. Not can it be said that these fluctuations correspond exactly with variations in the aesthetic excellence of the drama, that the theatre flourishes most when dramaturgy is at its peak or vice versa. In the long history of the theatre there have been relatively few periods of brilliant dramatic writing, but, with a few gaps, the theatre has a history of continuing popular appeal. Its deviations are more likely to be attributable to extraneous factors of a political, social or economic nature. In fact, a survey of the comtemporary theatre in various countries indicates that its form and function are often determined by the state of society and the cultural climate.

IV THE THEATRE AND THE SOCIAL ENVIRONMENT

How the theatre is shaped and developed by the social environment can be demonstrated quickly by looking at two countries that are almost at the extremes of the industrial and, in the modern sense, cultural scales: Mexico and Germany.

In describing the nature of the theatre in Mexico, we must exclude Mexico City, which has closer links to European and American culture than to that of its native Indian population. Here the theatre can hardly be said to have any distinguishing characteristics, being in the main imitative and derivative. This in itself indicates the relationship between the state of culture and the state of the theatre.

Mexico is almost entirely a country of villages whose population is preponderantly Indian, with only a slight foreign admixture. Conquered by the Spaniards in the sixteenth century, the inhabitants were forced to adopt the language and religion of Spain. Today Spanish is the official language and Roman Catholicism the official religion. But the language of pre-Conquest Mexico survives in place names and in the contemporary idiom, and the church ceremonies are tinctured with pagan ritual and pagan belief. The economy is largely agrarian and still predominantly based on handicrafts. Except for a few large cities, the social and cultural unit is the village.

The theatre, therefore, is a village affair, a communal enterprise known as the fiesta, in which the entire population usually participates either as performers or as spectators. Often these fiestas take on the aspect of a fair, lasting for several days, and combining with the theatrical performance a market, religious observances and various forms of diversion. Each village has its own annual fiesta peculiar to itself, but it may also engage in more general celebrations of saints' days or important historic events. Usually the dramatic feature of the fiesta is performed by a group of villagers who specialize in the skills of dancing, singing or playing musical instruments. These skills are frequently handed down from father to son, so that the performers have almost a professional status, though of course performing is merely an avocation with them. Many of them have great theatrical talent and perform most artfully.

The dramas are simple and naïve: enactments of incidents in the lives of the saints or of Christ. A favorite one is the conversion of the Moors by St. James. This was introduced by the Spanish priests, who saw that the Indians could not be cured of their passion for dancing and singing, and so, instead of attempting to suppress the horrid pagan rites, transmuted them into more seemly and orthodox dramatic presentations. Other dramas are similar to the medieval mystery and miracle plays, with a strong emphasis upon the supernatural and plenty of devil-dancing.

One popular historic fiesta deals with the victory of the Mexicans over the French. A typical village performance begins with a horseback procession of the principal characters, followed by a pitched battle between detachments of French, Spanish and Indian soldiers. This goes on for a large part of the day and ends at dusk with a solemn funeral of the French dead, including Napoleon.

In Oaxaca I saw a specially staged performance, in the little plaza in front of the local agricultural school, of another very popular fiesta. This treated of the conquest of the Aztecs by

Cortes. The story element was slight; the interest lay in the music, the gay costumes, the gyrations of the performers. The musicians used reeds and gourds and a few more modern stringed instruments. The attire was eclectic, to say the least: a hodgepodge of Renaissance Spanish and native Indian, with modern improvements and improvised embellishments that employed vivid feathers, flowers, bits of mirror and brightly colored cloths. In many of the fiestas the performers wear masks representing animals, evil spirits or religious and historic characters.

One aspect of the Oaxaca enactment I found very interesting and significant. The principal character in the play, after Cortes and Montezuma, is the Indian slave girl, Malinche, who became the mistress of Cortes and who reputedly aided him in conquest of the Aztecs. This *femme fatale* and her inevitable confidante— for the exigencies of the drama are universal—were played by little girls of eight or nine, splendidly caparisoned and properly self-important, but hardly able to keep pace with the long-legged men with whom they were obliged to dance. There were two good reasons for this incongruity. The first was that the mores did not permit adult women to appear in theatrical performances. Secondly, the dance-play is a stylized and symbolic representation, and any suggestion of an actual sexual relationship, such as the presence of a grown woman would have provided, would be regarded as an unwelcome intrusion of realism.

It is apparent that theatre of this sort can flourish only in a pre-industrial society, among people who are rooted in the village and deeply imbued with tradition. As industrialized urban centers multiply and villagers are drawn to them by better means of transportation and opportunities for employment, the village unity and the heritage of skills will be weakened, and gradually the machinery of mass communication—movies, radio, television —will push the fiesta into obsolescence. It is a familiar social process, with profound aesthetic and psychological implications.

In Germany we find an almost totally different type of social structure and a totally different type of theatre. Instead of an agrarian handicraft economy, with a population sparsely spread over a wide area, we have a populous nation cramped for living space, crowded for the most part into numerous large cities, and mainly dependent for its livelihood upon industry and commerce.

Culturally, too, the contrast is striking. Though the emergence of Germany from paganism and barbarism was relatively late, and is still not complete (witness the music-dramas of Wagner and the fulminations of Hitler), the influences of the Roman Empire and later of the Renaissance made themselves felt and eventually transformed the semi-savage culture of Germany into one that is comparable to that of her more advanced neighbors. Unlike the placid, conservative Mexicans, the Germans are ambitious, dynamic, resourceful, and highly emulative, as is manifest in the extraordinary economic recovery that swiftly followed the disastrous defeats of World Wars I and II. The will to power and the almost religious worship of learning resulted in a high rate of literacy and an astonishing degree of assimilation and even of creativeness in all the sciences and all the arts. By the seventeenth or eighteenth century Germany occupied a respectable place in Western culture. Her enterprise, natural resources and urbanized population made her adoption of industrialism inevitable, and by the end of the nineteenth century she had advanced to the status of a great world power.

It is obvious that such a social situation is highly conducive to the establishment of a theatre: numerous cities, inhabited by a population with the leisure and the economic means to demand and enjoy organized and sophisticated entertainment and edification. The emphasis on education and the importance placed upon the acquisition of knowledge, often for its own sake, resulted in widespread presentation of the classics of dramatic literature: Greek and Elizabethan plays as well as the lofty, but sometimes ponderous, works of such native writers as Goethe, Schiller and Lessing. Whether or not the production of these plays reflected aesthetic cravings or merely a compulsion for the ingestion of intellectual fare is beside the point. The fact is that the German theatre offered a greater variety of important world dramas than did any other country. Shakespeare's plays in excellent translation were constantly performed; Ibsen and Strindberg were widely acclaimed; Shaw was recognized in Germany when England and America were still turning up their noses at him—for example, *Pygmalion* had its world première in Germany. Public interest in theatregoing and first-rate fare combined to develop an audience that was alert, responsive and dramatically literate. Here again we have a most important determinant of the state of the theatre, at a given time and place, which has little relation to the quality of the plays being written contemporaneously. Modern German drama is certainly not superior to that of England, France and the United States, but its theatre is, or was prior to World War II, decidedly so. With the exception of the Soviet Union, there is no country in which the theatregoing public is more avid. In 1947 I received a letter from a German refugee friend who had returned to Hamburg. He wrote: "We are living in cellars and starving, but there are seven repertory theatres in operation."

Furthermore, to a greater degree than anywhere else in the world, the German theatre reflects the modern passion for technology. (The Soviet Union should perhaps be excepted; however, the technical advances in the Russian theatre are largely German-derived.) Many German theatres, in their seating arrangements, playing areas, stage machinery, facilities for projection and lighting systems, are far ahead of the outdated playhouses of England and the United States. (David Belasco told me many years ago that he had made several trips to Germany for the sole purpose of studying the improved methods of stage lighting.) All these theatrical arrangements and devices are invaluable accessories to the playwright and assist the task of communication.

Technology may also be accountable for the development in Germany of what may be called the cult of the *régisseur*, which attaches as much or more importance to the manner in which a play is done as to the substance of the play itself. Nowhere has this cult been more prevalent than in Germany, though latter-day examples may be found in other countries, including the United States. Frequently the director overshadowed the dramatist, and the public went to see a production rather than a play. To many students of the drama the names of Max Reinhardt, Bertolt Brecht and Erwin Piscator are more familiar than those of Georg Kaiser, Walter Hasenclever, Ernst Toller and Fritz von Unruh. Perhaps directors deserved the greater recognition but if that is true it is convincing evidence of the inherent effectiveness of the theatre.

The political conditioning of the German theatre is also of great interest and significance. For one thing, it accounts for the multiplicity and relative independence of regional theatres throughout Germany. It should be remembered that though ethnically and linguistically its unity goes back many centuries, Germany did not come into being as a political entity until late in the nineteenth century. Prior to that time it had been a sort of loose federation of autonomous kingdoms, dukedoms, principalities and free cities of varying size and with individual characteristics. There had been no capital city for all Germany; even with its elevation to that rank, Berlin remained, emotionally, to most Germans merely the capital of the Kingdom of Prussia. The majority of non-Prussian Germans still have the same sense of resentment and of cultural superiority about the Prussians that the Croats have about the Serbs or the Ukrainians about the Great Russians. Dresden, Munich, Weimar, Leipzig, Frankfort and other cities all had their claims as centers of a particular culture. Neither their political subordination to Prussia nor the subsequent substitution of republican for monarchial government diminished local pride or affected the existence of established cultural institutions.

Therefore the theatres created by petty rulers in the seventeenth, eighteenth and nineteenth centuries—partly in imitation of the court theatres in more advanced countries (notably France), partly because of the rivalry of neighboring princelings, partly as evidence of the sovereign's enlightment and patronage of culture—survived the creation of the empire, two world wars, Hitler's Reich and the partition that followed World War II. Happily so, for many of these theatres, founded by kings for their own aggrandizement, continue to flourish under the administration of state and municipal governments and provide throughout Germany a network of individually operated playhouses well equipped to carry on the tradition of a vital theatre. So we find in Germany a degree of decentralization and variety which cannot be matched in England or in the United States, where nearly all professional theatrical activity originates in London or in New York.

In another sense, political upheavals have profoundly affected the German theatre. Germany's defeat in World War I created an economic stringency which limited the expenditure for theatrical productions and put a premium upon ingenuity in devising effective productions at low cost. This condition may have contributed to the rise of the cult of the *régisseur*. More importantly, the disillusionment and despair that followed defeat created a revolution in dramatic technique and the sudden eruption of a short-lived but vigorous movement known as expressionism. Since the resultant plays were chaotic, episodic and fantastic, demanding new styles of scenery, direction and acting, the theatre was called upon to devise means for the communication of these plays.

An even more striking example of political influence is the devastating effect of the Hitler regime upon the German theatre. Hitler's rabid xenophobia resulted in exclusion from the theatrical repertory of plays by foreign authors, particularly modern dramatists with liberal ideas, whose plays had previously been very popular in Germany. Further, his racial policies drove out of the theatre and out of Germany many Jewish actors, directors, designers and other workers who had made brilliant contributions to the stage and whose loss was almost irreparable. The theatre went into a state of decline; it was given over mainly to the production of dull expositions of Nazi philosophy, produced in a mediocre fashion by the sadly depleted personnel. With the fall of Hitler there came a demand for the revival of the theatre. Many refugees returned, but many had died in exile or had had their morale impaired by the hardships they had endured. Attempts were made to re-establish the old artistic standards, but the twelve-year gap has not been easily spanned, especially since the younger generation had not been trained to carry on the tradition. It will take time to restore the German theatre to its former vigor and excellence.

A word should be said about the fate of theatre workers who are expelled from their native lands. I met many of the refugees who came to the United States in the Hitler years. Their lot was pitiable. Language, of course, was the chief handicap. The actors, even though they spoke English, could hope only for parts that required a European accent. The directors were even worse off, for there are radical differences in production technique between the German and the American theatres, and what producer would be rash enough to entrust the direction of a play to a foreigner uninitiated in the ways of the American stage? German-born playwrights could hardly hope to master the American idiom sufficiently to enable them to write in English; and if they wrote in German, the alien nature of the material and the difficulty of finding a competent adaptor made the chances of production almost negligible. The exiled painter and composer could go on painting and composing, unimpeded by language barriers; the novelist could be published in Switzerland (like Thomas Mann, for example) and read wherever German was understood. But the playwright, divorced from his performers and his audience, had no outlet for his art.

While each country has its peculiar kind of theatre, the pattern throughout Western and Central Europe is not greatly dissimilar to that of Germany, particularly with respect to nation-

ally or municipally supported theatres, which are usually out-
growths of what were once court theatres. In some cases the
original building may still be seen in an excellent state of preservation, like the eighteenth-century theatre of the Swedish kings
at Drottningholm and the exquisite little theatre of the Empress
Maria Theresa at Schönbrunn. The Comédie-Française is, of
course, the lineal descendant of the theatre of Molière; and royal
and imperial opera houses may be found here, there and everywhere. Many of these monuments of the past are still in active
use, but it is regrettable that so many of their structural features
have been retained in modern theatre buildings. As we shall see,
theatre construction has failed to keep abreast with advances in
the technique of building.

Between the extremes of Mexico and Germany there are
many gradations. Every country has cultural peculiarities which
are reflected in its national theatre. Even if I were acquainted at
first hand with them all, I would not feel that a description of
each were necessary. However, there are two countries, Japan
and Russia, which present such striking features that it seems
profitable to examine them in some detail.

V THE THEATRE IN JAPAN

To make fully understandable the complexity of the Japanese theatre and its place in Japanese society would require historical and ethnological explorations that are beyond the scope of this book and beyond the capability of its author. All that I shall attempt is a brief description of its diverse forms, some comments on the relationship of these forms to the social and economic development of the country, and an appraisal of the art of the theatre as it exists in Japan today. What follows is based upon visits to Japan in 1936 and in 1957, conversations with Japanese playwrights, critics and actors, and a certain amount of rather superficial reading.

In examining any aspect of Japanese life it must be remembered that the emergence of Japan as a modern nation occurred only a century ago. Prior to the advent of Commodore Perry, in the middle of the nineteenth century, Japan was a self-contained isolated country, cut off from and hostile to Western influences, with an agrarian economy and medieval and feudal social institutions. In a hundred years it has transformed itself into one of the world's foremost industrial and commercial nations. The process of Westernization continues at an ever-accelerating pace. Modern Tokyo, except for the Imperial Palace and some humbler outlying districts, has a striking resemblance to Detroit. Lanterns have given way to neon lights; the roaring traffic takes its lethal toll; the charming traditional dress has been replaced by garments off the department store rack. You can't hop on a bus or operate a typewriter in a kimono, the office girls tell you. English has become a second, almost a mandatory language; handicrafts are succumbing to the relentless inroads of the machine; baseball is as popular as it is in the United States, and if you sit in a bar you can watch the games on TV. The camera craze is bewildering, not to say harassing; there are soda fountains, quick-lunch counters and night clubs. The educational system has been modified in accordance with Western ideas, German rather than American, I am inclined to think. Democratic political institutions are being introduced, and some improvement is being made in the status of women.

But transformations in the emotional and psychological life of the individual do not keep pace with changes in the material world. The substitution of a girdle for an obi does not necessarily alter deeply ingrained patterns of feeling and of behavior. Even in Western countries where the progression from feudalism to democratic industrialism has been evolutionary in nature, extending over a period of several centuries, it does not follow that the acquisition of an electric dishwasher destroys the belief that thirteen is an unlucky number or that Adam is the father of the human race.

In Japan the process of change was not evolutionary but revolutionary. There was no transitional period, no opportunity for gradual adaptation. In terms of material development Japan was centuries behind the Western world; if the gap was to be closed it had to be done summarily. And it was. Industrialism and Westernization were imposed directly upon the old feudalism without interval for adjustment. It is not surprising, therefore, to find old customs and beliefs existing side by side with the most up-to-date techniques and attitudes.

Let me give one personal experience by way of illustration. In Kyoto I was invited to the home of a prominent citizen on the occasion of a traditional annual ceremony. Once a year the star Vega crosses the Milky Way, and, according to legend, this represents the reprieve of an errant lover who is permitted to traverse briefly the barrier that separates him from his beloved. The fleeting reunion was being celebrated by my host and a group of friends, men and women, who, clad in traditional dress, were squatting on cushions, facing each other across a long narrow table on which was spread a white cloth that represented the Milky Way. What they were doing was writing little seventeen-syllable poems dealing with the fate of the star-crossed lovers and handing the compositions across the table to each other. I was told that all the men were important industrialists or bankers as well as members of the House of Peers. Yet they performed this allegorical ritual with the utmost earnestness and gravity; it was obvious that they were deriving great aesthetic and emotional satisfaction from their participation in it. As I watched them I tried to visualize the members of the board of directors of General Motors or of a committee of the United States Senate and their wives engaged in a similar ceremony, composing sonnets, perhaps, commemorative of the tragic love of Tristan and Isolde; but my imagination was unequal to the task.

This sort of contradiction is to be found in every phase of Japanese life, so it is not surprising to see in the Japanese theatre striking contrasts between the old and the new. At one end of the scale is the No Theatre, which antedates by centuries any established theatrical institution of the Western world, and at the other end flashy modern entertainments that are very similar to the stage shows at New York's Radio City Music Hall, complete with Rockettes and disappearing orchestras. In between are many forms of theatre that mix the traditional and the modern, the East and the West.

The No Theatre, with its repertory of about two hundred and fifty plays, has existed for some six hundred years. It is a peculiarly Japanese institution; there is nothing resembling it anywhere else in the world. It represents in a high degree a distillation of all the magical elements of the theatrical art, as distinguished from the literary elements of the drama. The effect of a performance upon a spectator who, like myself, understands no word of Japanese and has no emotional links with the subject matter of the plays, is quite overpowering. The décor, costumes, music, dance movements, gestures, facial expressions, vocal effects, groupings and timing combine to create an aesthetic whole that is elevating and moving beyond description.

The theatre itself is immediately pleasing to the senses and to the emotions. The spectators sit on two sides of the stage, which is merely a rectangular platform of highly polished wood with a canopy supported by four poles. The scenery, if it can be so called, is, like everything else, formalized and traditional: a screen or backing on which is vividly depicted a twisted pine tree. There are no properties and no appurtenances except cushions for the musicians and singers, who remain seated upon the stage throughout the action, and perhaps a small supplementary platform or two. A long narrow runway is used by the actors for their entrances and exits and often for part of the action. This device is also much used in the Kabuki theatre, and I have seen it employed too in American burlesque houses. As in the early Greek theatre there are two principal actors. The first usually plays the female roles; he is also the only one who wears a mask. There are many types of masks, quite beautiful in their simplicity and clean modeling, each representing a different type of character. The costumes are rich and exquisitely harmonious. The music is provided by several varieties of small drums and high-pitched flutes. The chanting of the chorus is supplemented by the musicians, who utter staccato syllables which have the effect of intensifying the crucial moments of the play.

According to a booklet issued by the official tourist agency of Japan, there are six kinds of No plays, quaintly enumerated as the god piece, the battle piece, the wig piece or the woman piece, the lunatic piece and the revenge piece, the earthly piece and the last piece—that is, the after-piece. A performance usually consists of several plays drawn from these different categories.

In the performance I saw there were three plays, the principal one being *Funa-Benkei*, or *Benkei in the Boat*, a frequently performed "earthly piece," which means that it is supposed to deal with actual persons and is therefore relatively more realistic than the purely lyrical or fantastic plays.

My program contains a complete synopsis of the play, enumerating twenty-four scenes—scenes in the French sense of the term, referring to the entrance or exit of a character. It is too long to quote in full, so I shall give an abbreviated version as it appears in the tourist agency's booklet:

This play has two scenes. The first is the scene in a fisherman's hut by the sea in the neighborhood of Amagasaki, and the second is on the open sea. (The "scenes" are, of course, wholly imaginary, since there is no curtain, and no change of background or properties.) In the first scene Shizuka, a dancing-girl and Hōgwan Yoshitsune's lover (the First Actor), is the heroine. She came as far as this seaside place in order not to lose sight of the Hōgwan, who was escaping to the Western provinces. Thinking it a pity that Hōgwan's resolution had been shaken through his reluctance to part from her, Chief Retainer Benkei (the Second Actor) is anxious about his master and advises him to send her back to town. The Hōgwan is compelled to take his advice. Resenting Benkei's heartlessness, she unwillingly gives her consent to part from the Hōgwan. At the farewell feast Shizuka dances sorrowfully and then makes her exit.

When the dance is over, Benkei, encouraging his fellow-samurai, enters a boat (a stage property is used) and they choose the Hōgwan as their captain. Suddenly the weather becomes bad. The wind blows hard and the waves rise. All pray to the gods for help. Just then the ghosts of the people of the Heike clan who have been ruined by the Hōgwan, advance from the open sea to fall upon the boat. The ghost of Taira-no-Tomomori (the First Actor again plays this role) is at their head brandishing a halberd in the air, and comes to assault the Hōgwan. The fighting begins. By praying to the gods Benkei is just able to drive back the ghost, who vanishes into the distant waves.

This outline of a thin story, lacking in unity and in character development, gives little promise of an exciting dramatic presentation. It is quite probable that there are verbal beauties and emotional overtones in the text, but these, of course, were entirely lost upon me, and I could respond only to the actual physical performance. Nevertheless, I found it one of the most beautiful and stirring dramatic productions that I have ever seen. It is one thing to read "Shizuka dances sorrowfully and then makes her exit," and quite another to see the dance and the exit superbly performed by a disciplined actor to the accompaniment of the plaintive music and the anguished cries of the musicians. The poignancy of this episode induced a sense of spiritual elevation that is indescribable. The reference in the synopsis to a storm at sea does not even remotely suggest the illusion of a raging hurricane produced upon the stage by the mounting tempo of the musicians and singers and the tensed bodies of the actors. The spectator is keyed up to a pitch of excitement and of emotional involvement that is heightened by the sudden terrifying apparition of the dead Taira-no-Tomomori and the ensuing combat between him and Hōgwan, a stylized ballet executed with incredible skill. After this thrilling climax the play comes to a rapid close, leaving the spectator with a sense of profound participation in a noble experience, eloquent proof of the magical power of the theatre.

It should be noted that in this play the part of Hōgwan, the mighty warrior, was enacted by a ten-year-old boy, just as in the Mexican fiesta the courtesan was played by a little girl. As far as I know there are no cultural ties between Japan and Mexico, yet the same psychological and aesthetic reasons govern the use of this convention. In each case, one partner in the central sexual relationship is played by a child in order to emphasize the fact that the love element is symbolic and not literal and realistic.

Because of its austerity and aesthetic economy, its archaic content and form, the appeal of the No theatre is pretty much limited to persons of refined and sophisticated taste, just as in the theatre of the West performances of the Greek classics attract only small and select audiences. At the next level of the curiously stratified Japanese theatre is the Kabuki. It too is a traditional theatre, originating in the seventeenth century, some three hundred years after the beginnings of No, but it has a wide popular appeal and is perhaps the most important type of theatre in Japan today. The Kabuki is an adaptation and, in the literal sense of the word, a vulgarization of the No. Its elements are the elements of No: music, augmented by the use of the samisen and other stringed instruments; masks for the principal actors; stylized dances; plays based upon legendary and historical material, though the repertory has been greatly increased and modernized; and enactment of the female parts by the leading actors of the troupe. Kabuki was founded by a woman, and at first female performers were utilized, but they were soon banned on moral grounds and ever since the cast has been entirely male.

Physically the Kabuki playhouse differs radically from the No. The runway is used—in fact, a great deal of the action takes place upon it; it can represent a verandah, a street, a mountain road or what not. But in other respects there is little resemblance. The Kabuki theatres are modern and spacious, with large balconies and sometimes boxes. The stage is of the proscenium type, equipped with a curtain and up-to-date stage machinery. The twisted-tree backdrop is sometimes used, but most of the plays employ elaborate scenery and properties. The playing areas are vast and have enormous built-in revolving stages which can accommodate two or more large and complicated sets simultaneously, unlike the cramped pie-slice scenes to which the inadequate supplementary turntables of American theatres are restricted. A backstage visit at the Kabuki arouses in the American author or director mingled feelings of admiration and envy.

Besides the use of all this stage paraphernalia—scenery, properties, sound and lighting effects—there is a general broadening and jazzing-up of the performances. Musical or comic interludes, pageantry and spectacular episodes are freely introduced. The result is lively, colorful and diverting entertainment, easily appreciable by the mass audience for which it is designed. This is not to say that Kabuki is deficient in artistic excellence. On the contrary, the décor and costumes are tasteful, the stage direction is excellent and the acting is of a high order.

Acting is a greatly honored profession in Japan. There are actors who proudly trace back their stage heritage in unbroken succession for many generations. When the actor has no son of his own he adopts one, who assumes the name of his foster-parent. Many of these family names are famous in Japanese theatrical history and well known to every theatregoer. I am fortunate enough to be able to count among my friends Ennosuke Ichikawa, one of the great Kabuki actors, descendant of a long line of famous performers. Ichikawa is the family name, but actors are popularly known by their given names. It is a curious custom of the Japanese—disconcerting at first to the uninitiated foreigner—for the audience to express its approval of a well-acted scene, not by applause but by shouting the name of the performer. Ennosuke is an actor of great skill and versatility, who plays both male and female parts and appears also in modern plays and in motion pictures.

Besides these traditional types of theatre there is a flourishing contemporary theatre, comprising both productions of modern plays, Western as well as Japanese, and entertainments of the revue or variety genre. The performances of modern plays are very much like our own, except for the superiority of Japanese stage equipment. The Japanese are amazingly well acquainted with contemporary Western dramatic literature, particularly that of the United States. Many plays are borrowed, to put it euphemistically, and presented with scrupulous fidelity. I have photographs of the Japanese production of *Street Scene,* which in setting, costumes and grouping is, at first glance, indistinguishable from the American production. The difference is discernible only when one sees the Oriental features of the actors with the aid of a magnifying glass. Contemporary native plays are numerous. I have no way of judging their quality or significance, but I have been told that, with a few exceptions, they are not particularly notable.

As I have said, the revue type of entertainment may be compared to, and was probably inspired by, the Radio City Music Hall shows: a hodgepodge of popular songs, ballet, vaudeville and circus turns, gingerbread decoration and eye-filling spectacles, augmented by short plays of a farcical or romantic nature. And though there is no accompanying motion picture the performance goes on for hours and hours.

It is not only in respect to stage facilities that Japanese theatres are superior to ours. In comfort and convenience the popular playhouses put ours to shame. They are roomy, clean and well lighted, and contain large and attractive lounges and promenades, restaurants, snack bars, soda fountains, booths offering books, candy and toys, and even beauty salons. In these establishments whole families can, and do, spend an entire day in enjoyment and relaxation.

Two other unique aspects of the Japanese theatre should not be overlooked. One is the curious type of theatrical organization known as the Girls' Opera Companies. As the name indicates, these are troupes of performers composed entirely of young women. The best-known is the Takarazuka Company, which derives its names from its place of origin, the famous "Pleasure Center" situated between Kobe and Osaka. Here there is school in which the girls are trained and a theatre where they give performances, presumably as part of their course of training. They also give performances in Tokyo and other cities and are enormously popular. The Hollywood movie *Sayonara* has some very good shots of this company, as well as of the Kabuki. The favorite performers are those who enact the male parts.

They affect masculine haircuts and masculine dress and have an ardent following of fans, mostly women. Once when I was staying at the Imperial Hotel in Tokyo I was drawn to my window by a commotion outside. The street was filled with a milling crowd of women who were shouting and pushing as they tried to get at one of these boyish girls who stood in the stage door of the theatre opposite. It took a strong cordon of police to make a lane for her through the crowd and get her into a taxi.

Mention must also be made of the famous Bunraku puppets of Osaka. This type of theatre is about the same age as Kabuki and closely related to it. The puppets are beautiful and amazingly intricate creations; they are about two-thirds human size and each must be operated by two puppeteers. But though the operators are clearly visible, one soon forgets their presence, so lifelike and pleasing are the movements of the puppets. Unfortunately this highly specialized and rather esoteric form of the theatrical art has, like the shadow plays of China, seen its best days and is in a state of decline.

All in all, the Japanese theatre is diversified, popular and, at its best, highly artistic. In accordance with the economic development of Japan, it is big business, too. The construction of splendid playhouses and the production of elaborate spectacles demand huge capital expenditures, so it is not surprising to find that several large syndicates are in control of the theatres and of the various types of theatrical productions that have been described. They also control the production and exhibition of motion pictures, a flourishing industry, and probably now radio and television.

Before turning to the theatre in Russia I feel that I should say something about the Chinese theatre, of which I have had some experience. But I do not find it easy to relate it to the social state of China, probably because I do not understand that state, so about all I can say is that to me the Chinese theatre is, like almost everything else I saw in China (this was in 1936), very confusing. Many years ago I saw the famous Chinese actor Mei

Lan-fang perform in New York. I was greatly impressed by the skill of his disciplined movements, similar in many ways to the art of the No actors, or the Indian dancer Uday Shankar. But seeing a Chinese actor in a kind of recital program designed for Western audiences is quite different from seeing the performance of a play in China.

The Chinese theatre, like the Japanese, is compounded largely of traditional elements: legendary material and stylized methods of presentation. There are, however, some important differences. The Chinese plays are operatic in form, and, as in Western opera houses, the chief interest of the audience seems to be in the rendition of certain passages that are presumably arias, though their musical quality is not evident to the untutored Western ear. Masks are not used; instead there are various standardized types of heavy make-up, which to the informed spectator immediately identify the character as the wicked uncle or the heroic general. Costumes are lavish to the point of gaudiness, but there is no scenery as in the Kabuki, and the properties consist of plain chairs and tables which are manipulated by stagehands in full view of the audience to represent—and very convincingly, too—a wall or a temple or a cart. There is an American play, *The Yellow Jacket,* which effectively portrays the technique of Chinese stage production.

Accustomed as I am to the exquisite control of the plastic elements in Chinese painting and to the minute perfection of Chinese handicraft, I was doubly bewildered by the performance of Chinese plays as I saw them in Peking and in Shanghai. Not only were the theatres uncomfortable and badly arranged, with cramped and inadequately lighted stages, but the whole atmosphere, both onstage and out front, was chaotic. The audience seemed to be paying little attention to what was happening on the stage. People kept coming and going or engaged in lively conversation. Children ran up and down the aisles and sometimes peeped out from the wings. Food venders hawked their wares and flung hot towels to their replete customers. Occasionally some element in the stage performance seemed to engage the attention of the audience and there was a momentary flurry of approval, followd by a reversion to general conversation.

On the stage a group of untidy musicians smoked and chattered when they were not busy producing a cacophonous din with percussion and shrill wind instruments. There is a most amazing contrast between the delicate and moving music of the Japanese stage and the ear-splitting racket of the Chinese. The actors wandered on and off the scene without dramatic effectiveness, and, as far as I could make out, without dramatic motivation. When they were not on scene, or while the stage-hands were shuffling the chairs and tables about, the performers strolled upstage, where they stood yawning or picking their teeth or noses. As a keen admirer of the Chinese people and of Chinese art and culture, I came away with a feeling of boredom, disappointment and puzzlement.

Perhaps I was unlucky in my choice of performances, and I certainly do not pretend that I have made an adequate or fair appraisal of the Chinese theatre. But what I saw of it in Peking and in Shanghai, as well as in the Chinese quarters of New York and San Francisco, and in the course of a recent visit to Hong Kong, leads me to believe that the generally loose structure of Chinese societal life (I am speaking, of course, of pre-Communist China!) was not conducive to the high degree of organization that an effective theatre demands. If I am right, this is another example of the relation of the state of society to the art of the theatre.

VI THE THEATRE IN THE
SOVIET UNION

The relationship between the theatre and the social situation is more evident in the Soviet Union than anywhere else in the world. The contemporary Russian theatre can be understood only when it is viewed in the light of the existing political structure and dominant political philosophy. Everyone knows, of course, that the theatre, like every other institution in the Soviet Union, is completely under state control. But the belief common among Americans that the theatre is employed solely as an instrument for the dissemination of Communist propaganda is mistaken and highly misleading. It ignores the very important and complex historical, social, cultural and artistic features that make the Soviet theatre fascinating and significant. In attempting to describe and to evaluate some of these characteristics, I shall draw largely upon firsthand observations made in the Soviet Union during two fairly long visits—ten weeks in 1932, and a month in 1936—in the course of which I traveled widely, saw a great variety of theatrical entertainment and met many leading theatrical personalities. It may seem that my material is dated, but current articles about the Russian theatre and conversations with recent visitors convince me that there has been little substantial change in its function and character.

Let me begin with a few analogies and some general remarks about the background of the contemporary scene. Like Japan, Russia did not become an industrial nation until very late. What little industrial development there was in the nineteenth century was largely confined to the Leningrad (then St. Petersburg) area. (One of the many fallacies of Karl Marx is his prediction that the social revolution would occur first in the most advanced capitalist countries, with large industrial populations—that is, England and Germany. But the revolution actually occurred in a country where the economy was predominantly agrarian and the proletarian population relatively small.) Large-scale industrialization did not begin until the 1920's, almost a decade after the revolution; but when it did begin it proceeded, and continues to proceed, at a pace that is almost incredible. The immediate result was the mushroom growth of cities and the urbanization of millions of peasants. In the course of a seven-day trip from Moscow to Manchuria I saw from my train window great industrial centers springing up on the Siberian steppes; and during a visit to a modern housing project in Moscow I met tenants who had just moved in from log huts with dirt floors. A by-product of this truly revolutionary process was an expansion of the theatre unique in the history of the world.

But if the industrial history of Russia is in some respects similar to that of Japan, its cultural history is almost wholly different. Japan in its isolation had a highly developed indigenous culture, and the sudden introduction of the completely alien culture of the West had baffling and incongruous consequences. Russia, on the other hand, a "dark" country, largely inhabited by illiterate serfs, had a very low state of culture. However, it was linked geographically and commercially with what many Russians called "Europe," and its cultural influences were mostly European, mainly French and German. The theatre, like the other arts, had a slow and inauspicious start and was almost entirely derivative. It was not until the nineteenth century that there developed in Russia a native theatre worthy of serious consideration. Its emergence was due principally to the creation of a body of plays of superlative quality by such brilliant writers as Lermontov, Pushkin, Ostrovski, Turgenev, Gogol, Tolstoi, Gorki, Andreyev and Chekov. It was, of course, one aspect of a general cultural awakening. Many of these writers also produced superb novels, and a dozen composers created symphonic and operatic music of the highest order.

Development of the arts of the theatre kept pace with the development of dramatic and musical composition. Theatres were established in the provincial cities as well as in Moscow and St. Petersburg. The techniques of acting, dancing and singing were perfected and skilled practitioners began to appear. The Moscow Art Theatre, established in 1898 by Konstantin Stanislavski, and long identified with the plays of Chekov (the curtain still bears, or did in 1932, a representation of a sea gull), became world famous; so did the magnificent ballet troupe of Serge Diaghilev that included the unforgettable Nijinski, Pavlova, Massine, Lopokova and Bolm; the clever and vastly entertaining revue company of Nikita Baliev, and the Yiddish Artef Theatre.

So at the outbreak of the revolution in 1917 there already existed in Russia a distinctive and vital theatre with a brilliant personnel of directors, actors and dancers and a varied repertory of plays, ballets and operas, Western European as well as Russian. This was the base upon which the existing Soviet theatre has been erected, a fact that it is important to remember when we study its nature and its place in Soviet society.

Since the Soviet theatre is entirely regulated and supported by the Kremlin, its extraordinary proliferation and diverse activities may properly be regarded as a direct outgrowth of governmental policy. But this policy has at least three impor-

tant facets which can be roughly classified as political, psychological and cultural. Each is distinct, yet all are interrelated.

Everyone is familiar with the Communist slogan "Art is
a weapon." In the Soviet Union it is much more than a slogan; it is an essential part of governmental policy. The Russian revolution entailed far more than a change in the form
of government. It revolutionized everything: economics, social and personal relationships, moral standards, education, living habits, religious attitudes. The actual participants in the
overthrow of the Czarist regime were a small fraction of
the Russian population, and they were for the most part
motivated by a longing for "bread and peace" rather than by
the fanatical adherence to the Marxist dialectic that animated
their leaders. Therefore, when the mechanics of the transfer
of power had been performed, the handful of Communists
who headed the new government were faced with the task
of making their revolutionary social and economic program
acceptable to a vast population that was mostly illiterate and
largely apathetic or hostile. Coercion could be and was used,
but conversion was more effective. Hence propaganda on a
titanic scale became the order of the day. But the implements
of propaganda were limited. There were relatively few schools,
and many of the teachers had been swallowed up in the mael-
strom of revolution. Newspapers were scarce too, and news-
print, and so were readers. But there were a good many
theatres and innumerable buildings that could be used as theatres; there were experienced actors and directors and, as there
are everywhere in the world, many eager aspirants. The Bol-
shevik propagandists, like their opposite numbers in the American advertising industry, quickly grasped the fact that one
picture is worth a thousand words. For the youngsters, correct ways of thinking or behaving could be driven home far
more readily by the entertaining enactment of illustrative
episodes than by the stammering of ill-qualified pedagogues.
For adults there were more complex parables designed to
stimulate industriousness, patriotic fervor, or hatred of the

class enemy. There was no shortage of writers, many with talent, to supply the required dramatic material. Some had a strong sense of vocation and ardently believed what they wrote; others were quite willing to follow the party line, even in its most bewildering meanderings, and to turn out plays that demonstrated the dangers of foreign intervention, the moral obligation to spy upon one's neighbor or parent, or the dire consequences of misusing agricultural implements. But while it is undoubtedly true that almost every play written in the Soviet Union since the revolution deals with some phase of Communist philosophy or Communist policy, it is decidedly not true that the Soviet theatre is given over entirely to propaganda and that it can be dismissed as insignificant and worthless. On the contrary, the Soviet theatre as a whole is socially and artistically one of the most interesting in the world, for propaganda is only one of its functions, and one that tends, I believe, to diminish in importance with the increasing indoctrination and sophistication of the theatregoers. Nevertheless, wherever art is subject to political control it is stunted and distorted, and the playwright's obligation to make his work subserve the policies of the government has reduced the Soviet drama to a deplorable state of dullness and puerility.

The theatre, as distinguished from the drama, has been affected to a far lesser degree. The writer's enforced conformity destroys his creativeness, while all that is demanded of the performing artist is abstention from antigovernmental activities or heretical utterances. Since most theatre workers are not ardently politically minded, outward orthodoxy imposes no great hardship upon them, and they are able to practice their skills with little or no restriction. So that unlike regimes (e.g. Nazi Germany) whose discriminatory racial or religious doctrines operate against the theatrical personnel and debase the theatre as well as the drama, the Soviet government strikes at the drama but encourages and fosters the theatre.

To recognize this distinction is not, of course, to condone the destructive aspects of Soviet policy.

Besides its usefulness as a political forum, the theatre serves as a means for providing relaxation and entertainment for the hard-pressed population. The rapid pace of industrialization, with its emphasis upon machine tools and war matériel, has made heavy demands on the energies of the workers, without giving them much in the way of physical comforts or usable goods. Better times are always just ahead, and progress has undoubtedly been made; but its rate is slow, and promises are not enough to allay discontent and spur people on to greater efforts. So, not for the first time in history, absolutism is made more palatable by the provision of bread and circuses. There have been times in the Soviet calendar when circuses have been more plentiful than bread. The theatre is an important part of the government's social program, and it enjoys a popularity that is unmatched anywhere in the world. The extent of theatrical activity and the number of theatres are almost beyond belief. A friend of mine, the well-known Soviet dramatist Alexander Afinegenov—he was killed in an air raid on Moscow—told me that one of his plays was in the repertory of *four hundred* theatres! And this was more than twenty years ago. How many theatres there are today, I do not know. But I do know that with the growth of population and the development of new communities, more and more theatres are added. In 1932 I visited Stalingrad, once the sleepy little Volga River town of Tsaritsyn, which was being transformed into a great industrial center. In process of construction were not only factories, dwellings, schools and hospitals, but a theatre, a movie palace and a circus, all considered integral and essential units in a social and economic complex.

This is a familiar pattern throughout the far reaches of the Soviet Union from the Baltic to the Pacific, from the White Sea to the Caspian. Regional theatres have been organized in remote and wholly non-Russian areas, among peoples who prior to the revolution had no written language or fixed habitations: Kirghiz, Turkomans, Mongolians. Under the comprehensive and co-ordinated national theatre program the great metropolitan theatrical troupes tour the provinces in the summer months, while the regional theatres perform in Moscow and Leningrad. I saw performances in Russian, Turkish, Yiddish, Georgian, Ukrainian and Uzbek. I found the Turkish performance particularly instructive, not only in itself—the play was *Othello*, effectively acted, but with great violence —but for its demonstration of the way in which the theatre reflects revolutionary social changes. The performance took place in Baku, a predominantly Turkish city, and here were Moslem women appearing on the stage and others sitting unveiled and apparently quite at ease among the spectators. Another illuminating incident was described to me by Maurice Hindus. To celebrate the opening of a theatre in a new industrial town in the Urals, one of the leading Moscow companies was brought on. Aware of the fact that the audience was composed mostly of recently urbanized peasants who had never seen a play, the director chose for performance a broad sure-fire farce. During the first act there was not a laugh, and when the curtain fell the actors were bewildered and in despair. But the local manager saw the light. Stepping before the curtain he told the audience that if it laughed at what the actors did and said, they would not be offended. The rest of the performance was a howling success.

So popular is the theatre and so great the demand for seats that for most of the productions I saw I was able to get tickets only through the kindness of influential acquaintances. The theatres, most of which operate on a year-round basis, are sold out for months in advance, usually to organized groups: on one night to the workers at a steel plant, on the next to the employees of the Finland railroad station or a certain branch post office. All the theatres are run on the repertory system. In Moscow, where there are perhaps thirty theatres, each with an extensive repertory, the theatre-goer in the course of a season can choose among hundreds of productions of almost every sort: plays, operas, ballets, old and new, Russian and foreign, serious and comic, trivial and meaningful.

The Soviet leaders recognize the importance of the theatre not only as a weapon in the arsenal of propaganda and a tran-quilizer for the discontented, but as a transcendent medium for cultural communication. This passion for the arts is also an inheritance from prerevolutionary Russia. Anyone who is familiar with Russian literature of the nineteenth century knows how bitterly the intellectuals deplored their country's cultural lag and how they strove for national enlightenment. The same fervor animates the autocrats of today, for in spite of the orthodox homage accorded to the proletariat and the rewards bestowed upon individuals for exceptional industrial produc-tivity, it is achievement in the arts and sciences that delights them and makes them swell with pride. Witness, for example, the universal interest and proficiency in the nonproductive activity of chess. Forty years ago two-thirds of the population was illiterate. Today illiteracy has been almost wiped out. Education is compulsory and intensive. Books are published in editions that run into the millions, e.g. Dickens, Balzac, Steinbeck. The ever-multiplying theatres are filled to overflow-ing and they offer a variety of fare that would do credit to any country.

Even if we go to the extreme of writing off as completely worthless every play that has been written in the Soviet Union since the revolution, we must recognize that in pro-duction many of these plays afford opportunities for brilliant displays of the arts of acting, stage directing and designing that make them theatrically fascinating in spite of inept content or weak dramatic construction. What is far more important is that the theatre is given over largely to the production of classics, foreign as well as Russian.

The repertory of ballet and opera includes the best of the Western compositions as well as the works of Tchaikovski, Borodin, Rimsky-Korsakov, Moussorgski, Prokofiev and Shostakovich. In the limited time at my disposal I concentrated on the native works, many of which are seldom performed abroad. In Moscow I saw *Eugene Onegin* and the stirring dances from *Sadko* and *Prince Igor*. In Leningrad I saw a fine performance of *Khovantschina*, and at the Musical Studio of the Moscow Art Theatre a delightful presentation of Moussorgski's charming and funny *Fair at Sorochinsk*. It was so exquisitely sung and acted that I used a precious evening to see it a second time. Also at the Musical Studio I saw a miniature production of a musical version of Sholokov's successful novel *And Quiet Flows the Don*. Later I saw the same work performed at an outdoor theatre said to seat twenty thousand, in the Park of Culture and Rest, Moscow's great amusement park. It was a production which would have gladdened the heart of Cecil B. DeMille, truly supercolossal and hyper-mammoth, with a great parade of lumbering farm wagons, a wedding feast with hundreds of celebrants, and riproaring cavalry charges. This contrast illustrates one of the most fascinating features of the Soviet theatre: a dramatic work is sometimes presented simultaneously in productions that are completely different in style. While I was in Moscow, Ostrovski's ever-popular play, *The Storm*, was being done at the Maly Theatre as a mid-nineteenth-century period piece, while at the same time Meyerhold, then at the height of his fame as a director, was giving it a bewildering "constructive" interpretation. In Odessa, I saw an uncut production of Tchaikovski's ballet *The Swan*. To me it seemed interminable and the music unendurably saccharine, but the audience was enraptured. A contemporary ballet with a Chinese setting, *Red Poppy*, I found very dull indeed. But though I sought out works by Russian composers, I could have seen operas by Bizet, Wagner, Strauss, Massenet, Verdi, Puccini and so on, all popular and, I was told, generally very well performed.

Besides Ostrovski, other prerevolutionary Russian dramatists were well represented in the Soviet theatre: Pushkin,
Gogol, Tolstoi. But I was unable to see any play by Chekov,
whose plays, though not prohibited, were looked down upon,
perhaps because of their preoccupation with the personal problems of the bourgeoisie. I remarked to a Russian acquaintance
that there seemed to be more Chekov produced in New York
than in Moscow. "Oh, I know," he replied, "Chekov is the
American national hero." And when I asked Ernest, my alert
twenty-one-year-old guide, what he thought of *The Three Sis-
ters*, which he said he had seen, he answered: "Well, it was
all about three women who lived in the country and wanted
to go to Moscow. Why didn't they get on the train and go?"

Plays by contemporary British, French, German and American dramatists are also produced, particularly plays that deal
with the malaises of bourgeois society. Eugene O'Neill, Lillian Hellman, Arthur Miller and other American playwrights
are well known. Bernard Shaw and Oscar Wilde are very
popular too. To what extent, if any, the plays are modified in translation to conform to Communist dogma I do
not know.

The classics of world drama are widely produced: Sophocles, Shakespeare, Molière, Schiller, Ibsen. Undoubtedly, the
average Soviet theatregoer is better acquainted than his American counterpart with the plays of Shakespeare, at least in
production. In my crowded days in the Soviet Union I saw,
besides the production of *Othello* already referred to, two
productions of *Hamlet* in Moscow, one by a visiting troupe from
Uzbekistan, the other by the celebrated Vachtangov Theatre.
Each demonstrated a different phase of the Soviet approach
to the theatre. The Uzbek production was crude and dull,
as might have been expected from people who had only recently emerged from nomadism and had no theatrical background whatever. I met the director of the play, a Russian,
after the performance and asked him why, instead of attempting something as ambitious as *Hamlet*, he did not have

his inexpert company present simple plays that were related to their own range of experience. He shook his head and replied: "First they must be thoroughly grounded in the traditions of the theatre. Only when they have absorbed its principles will they be qualified to interpret properly the life around them." Whether or not one agrees with this theory, it certainly indicates that the Russians take their theatre seriously.

The Vachtangov production, which had all Moscow buzzing, was one of the most extraordinary and provocative stage representations that I have ever seen anywhere. It was, if you please, nothing less than a Marxist interpretation of the play! As one entered the theatre, an exhibit in the spacious lobby prepared one for the performance. Engravings and photographs demonstrated that at various times productions of the play have emphasized its romantic, philosophical, psychological or melodramatic aspects; sometimes Hamlet has even been portrayed as a woman. Why not, then, in a Socialist state, a Marxist interpretation?

So we learn that the central problem of the play is: Who is to be king of Denmark? And the unfolding drama becomes a struggle for power between Hamlet and Claudius, who appears as a figure almost equal to Hamlet in importance. Incidentally, this gives the Fortinbras scenes a new significance and makes his triumphal entrance at the end a logical solution of the problem. Throughout the play, incident after incident stresses the political nature of the conflict. When Hamlet delivers the "To be or not to be" soliloquy, he puts on his head the Player King's pasteboard gilt crown, and so his question appears to concern itself with whether or not he is to be king of Denmark. Again, when Polonius comes to the king to tell him of Hamlet's letter to Ophelia, the scene is laid in a portrait painter's studio. The king, crowned, sceptered and majestically robed, stands imposingly upon a dais while the painter works away. Polonius enters and as the scene progresses the king, forgetting that he is being painted, steps down from the platform, clad only in tights! It is seen that the splendid robe and all the paraphernalia of the kingly office are being held up by servitors. The symbolism is obvious: divested of his royal pomp and servile retinue a king is just an insignificant little man in long underwear.

Described in print all this may sound ridiculous; and so it might have seemed in the theatre if the production had been commonplace or inept. But the performance, which lasted for five hours, was superb in every particular and fascinating from beginning to end. Every part was splendidly acted; there was incidental music by Shostakovich; the costumes were borrowed from the Kremlin's historical treasure house; a great staircase, placed at various angles on the vast stage, served as the central motif of the principal scenes; there were countless bits of unexpected and effective business: the king entering on a beautiful milk-white horse and hiding in a hollow tree to eavesdrop on Hamlet and Ophelia; Hamlet coming down the staircase with the body of Polonius over his shoulder and halfway down dropping it into the moat; Ophelia played not as mad but as drunk. All these theatrical elements aroused the spectator to a pitch of excitement, amusement or indignation that no reading of the text could produce. I was deeply touched when Ernest, my young guide and constant theatre companion, to whom Shakespeare had been only a name, suddenly seized my arm in the middle of the second act and said: "You know, the man who wrote this play is really a great dramatist!" Surely, the Bard was never paid a sweeter tribute.

Eugene Vachtangov, director of the theatre in which this *Hamlet* was performed, was one of three *régisseurs* who had studied under Stanislavski at the Moscow Art Theatre and had broken away to found their own theatres—all, of course, with the encouragement and support of the Soviet regime. The other two were Vsevolod Meyerhold, whose theatre also bore his name, and Alexander Tairov, impresario of the Kamerny (Chamber) Theatre.

Each of these directors had his own philosophy and his own

technique of play production, so that if a given play were
to be done simultaneously at all four theatres (a hypothetical
but not altogether impossible occurrence) the performances
would have differed radically. The famous Stanislavski Method,
worshipfully adopted by New York's Group Theatre and
its offspring the Actors' Studio, may be described as completely naturalistic; the total identification of the actor with
the part he is portraying. Anyone who has seen performances
by the Moscow Art Theatre, whether in the Soviet Union
or in New York, Paris or London, has been impressed by the
enormous fidelity to life displayed in even the most minor
characterizations. This ability to depict living characters imparts great interest to even the dullest Soviet play. In one
play called *Bread*, which dealt with the collectivization
of agriculture, there was a scene in which a Communist functionary mounted a stump and delivered a long harangue to
a group of semi-hostile peasants. None of them had a word
to say, yet so great was the art of the actors that each, by
the way he stood or moved or listened, was able to create
a distinct and recognizable character. Again in a play, the
very name and plot of which I have forgotten, a group of
soldiers called to the front bade farewell to their wives or
sweethearts. No words were audible, yet each pair expressed
in a different way the sorrow of parting, with a totality
of effect that was wholly convincing and deeply moving. And
a dramatization of *Pickwick Papers* ended with a Christmas
celebration that was as jolly and uproariously funny as anything I have ever seen on the stage.

At the Vachtangov the naturalistic method was not in
use. The acting was somewhat formalized and stylized, to a
degree that might be called mildly expressionistic; that is to
say, it did not limit itself to realistic portrayal but contained
a strong element of commentary, often satiric. Tairov's productions at the Kamerny inclined toward sentiment, romance
and fantasy, strangely out of keeping, I thought, with the

prevailing philosophy of materialism and "social realism." Yet his theatre was very popular and could not have existed, of course, without official approval. Meyerhold, at the time of my visits, was in high favor with both the intellectual avant-garde and the government, which was planning to build a new theatre for him, though shortly afterwards his star waned rapidly. I was unable to understand the reason for his popularity. To me his noisy, cluttered and shapeless productions and the mechanistic contortions of his actors seemed wholly lacking in either aesthetic or emotional appeal.

Even more "advanced" was the Realistic Theatre, the creation of Nicolai Okhlopkov, who seceded from Meyerhold, as Meyerhold himself had seceded from Stanislavski. Why it was called the Realistic Theatre I cannot imagine, for nothing could have been more remote from what is ordinarily regarded as realism. A note in the program describes the method and aims of the theatre:

The Realistic Theatre has broken away decisively from the so-called "box-stage" and replaced it by a new system of "acting-platforms," which are placed right in the middle of the auditorium. Having freed the actor from the old "box-stage" and having surrounded him with a new and unusual "scenic atmosphere," having placed him in direct contact with the audience, the theatre was compelled to recognize that the old methods of acting technique were no longer valid. Hence the striving of the theatre to achieve a new technique and to widen the range of methods of expression. The new structure of the spectacle has also altered the role of the audience and has made it an active participant in the action.

The reader will recognize this as the sort of "arena" stage that is now coming into general use in little theatres and experimental theatres throughout the United States. The play I saw at the Realistic Theatre was called *Aristocrats*. It dealt with the prison camps of the Arctic Circle, which were surprisingly depicted as benevolent institutions for the regeneration of social outcasts. The spectacle was indeed new as to its structure. A considerable part of the action was performed by a group of young men clad in sky-blue tights, who might roughly be described as stagehands. If a character in the play was required to sit at a table, two of these youths appeared and, kneeling before him, held taut a piece of cloth that denoted the table. A skiing scene was depicted by having a young woman squat motionless on skis while one of the supers waved a pine bough back and forth to indicate her progress down a wooded slope. When a snowstorm was called for, a half-dozen young men cavorted about the stage tossing up handfuls of torn paper. It was hard to reconcile this effete and esoteric ritual with the subject matter of the play and with the iron realities of a dictatorship of the proletariat.

This brief description of different types of theatre in the Soviet Union by no means gives a complete picture of the variety, liveliness and cultural importance of the Soviet theatre as a whole. There is much that is dull or pointless, of course, but all in all, there is no other country in the world where the theatre is so active, so diversified, so well organized, so high in its professional standards and so well attended. It is indeed regrettable that the indigenous drama is not on the same high level.

A discussion of the Soviet theatre must include some observations on its organization and on the economic and professional status of its personnel. Actually the two things are interrelated, for the permanence of theatre companies and the subsidization of the theatre by the government guarantee to the theatre worker continuity of employment and continuity of training: in other words, economic security and progressive professional advancement. There is no job-hunting for the Soviet actor, designer or stage technician, nor is his employment affected by box-office success or failure. He is a member of a going concern that provides him with food, lodging, medical care, paid vacations, and, more important still, the opportunity to perfect himself in his craft and to engage uninterruptedly in that teamwork which is so essential to the art of the theatre.

Thanks to the friendliness of the management of the Kamerny Theatre, I was able to learn something about its typical organizational setup. Though by no means the largest of the Moscow theatres, it had a permanant staff of several hundred. These included actors, musicians, apprentices, scene designers and builders, stagehands, seamstresses, management and service personnel, cooks, waitresses, laundresses. Production plans were comprehensive and long-range, and, as I have indicated, performances were booked for a whole season ahead. Plays were studied and rehearsed for months, sometimes for a year or more. The young beginners were able to learn from masters of their crafts and, as their talents developed, to participate more and more in the activities of the organization. Recent reports, however, indicate a modification of the policy of complete subsidization. How this will affect the status of the workers, and indeed the Soviet theatre as a whole, it is too soon to predict.

By comparison with the West, wages in the Soviet Union are low, comforts few, and restrictions upon personal liberty onerous. But practitioners of the arts are held in high esteem. Public recognition and governmental honors are lavishly bestowed upon them. Some are even provided with cars and country houses (dachas). I visited the charming house of my friend, the playwright Afinegenov, situated in a pine forest not far from Moscow. It had a garage, a tennis court and many other conveniences that few Soviet citizens are able to enjoy. Of course all this, like most things in the world, had its price. Conformity was the price, and for the artist, the individualist who yearns to express himself in his own way, it was perhaps too high a price. But it is a price that Western artists often pay too: the Hollywood writer who turns out, to order, what the movie mogul thinks the public wants; the actor whose television contract requires him to promote the sale of soup or soap. Of course, the important difference is that in a democracy the artist usually has a choice; under a dictatorship he has none.

Thus in the Soviet Union, as in every other country, the particular state of politics, economics and culture imparts to the theatre its own distinctive form and attributes.

VII THE THEATRE IN ENGLAND

In its origins and development, the English theatre is quite similar to the theatres of the nations of Central and Western Europe. Since its history is well documented and readily available, no detailed survey is required here. But a few general observations may be useful, particularly as a preliminary to the examination of the American theatre, with which the remainder of this book will be largely concerned. Further, there are a few special circumstances that differentiate the English theatre from those of the countries that have already been discussed.

So far we have seen that the theatre has been conditioned to a great extent by social, political and cultural factors that often have little relationship to the existing state of the art of the drama; sometimes, indeed, the state of the drama is directly influenced by the form of the theatre. In England we find that for once the reverse is true and in one respect, at least, the theatre has been vitally affected by the drama.

I refer, of course, to the astounding body of dramatic literature created by the group of dramatists generally known as the Elizabethans, though many of their plays were written in the reign of James I. In the late sixteenth century the English drama, theretofore quite undistinguished, burst into a blaze of glory which finds a parallel only in the drama of Periclean Athens two thousand years earlier, and which has been unequaled since.

This literary outpouring was not accidental. It was a direct product of the Renaissance, which took a century or so to work its way northward and westward from Italy to England. The revival of learning, the rediscovery of classical art and literature, the development of new creative techniques and the invention of printing combined to give impetus to new achievements in the arts. In England these cultural factors were greatly augmented by the liberalization of political institutions, the Protestant Reformation, new scientific theories, and, most of all, the discovery and exploration of the New World, in which English mariners played a leading role. After the long sleep of the Middle Ages, Western European man was waking up and flexing his muscles. Widening horizons and an ever-expanding firmament produced new dreams, new visions, new fields of activity. The world was no longer a circumscribed disc but a shining orb spinning in space, and man sat on the top of it, monarch of all he surveyed. It is not surprising that his exultation and sense of emancipation found expression in a glorious outburst of creativeness. Collectively the Elizabethan plays are a paean in praise of man: his majesty, his dignity, his imaginativeness, his adventuresomeness, his prowess, his almost godlike attributes. When the individual fails or is defeated it is because of error or weakness, not because of lack of potentiality or any defect in the order of things. The Elizabethan drama is vibrant with affirmation and vitality; it is exuberant, eloquent and passionate. Its heroes and villains are drawn to a scale larger than life. Its loves and hates, triumphs and despairs are cosmic in scope. No wonder the presentation of these plays drew large and enthusiastic audiences to the theatres in which they were presented; no wonder so many of them have survived the centuries that have seen a progressive shrinkage in the stature of man.

It is unnecessary to enumerate the twenty or fifty playwrights who made greater or less contributions to the totality of

Elizabethan drama. As with the painters of the Italian Renaissance, the great masters had their disciples and their imitators, and
often the journeyman and secondary works were of high quality. But of course, in all the brilliant galaxy, the bright, particular star of Shakespeare shines out above the rest. (A professor of sociology once spent a long, long evening trying to convince me that Shakespeare could not be in a class by himself.
All facts and phenomena, he assured me, could be plotted in a
statistical curve, the apex of which—e.g. Shakespeare—would be
only relatively higher than its immediately adjacent units. Lacking the scholarship to grasp this significant truth, I clung stub-
bornly to the belief that Shakespeare *is* in a class by himself;
and this biased opinion governs what follows.)

Not much is known about Shakespeare and there are some
who doubt that he wrote the plays generally attributed to him.
But whether he wrote them or they were written by Francis
Bacon, the Earl of Oxford, Queen Elizabeth I or, as someone
has suggested, another playwright by the same name, is important only to academic specialists. What is important to every
lover of literature and of the theatre is that some towering genius
wrote thirty-odd plays, universally known as the plays of
Shakespeare, which comprise some of the greatest poetic and
dramatic compositions ever created. We know that Shakespeare
was an actor and a theatre manager, presumably a stage director
too, and we may be sure that his plays were written primarily to
be performed in the theatre and not to be read as literature.
If proof is needed it can be found in the negligent manner in
which the texts were preserved and in the fact that there was no
adequate publication until after Shakespeare's death.

Performed they certainly were, and they have been continuously performed for more than three and one-half centuries.
These performances have built up what may be called a Shakespearean tradition, which is the unique characteristic of the English theatre. Of course, the plays of Marlowe, Jonson, Webster,
Kyd and other contemporaries have been kept alive too, but it is

interesting to speculate whether this survival is attributable to their intrinsic merit, great as it often is, or merely to the fact that they have traveled down through the ages on Shakespeare's coat tails.

In the course of the centuries both the English theatre and the plays of Shakespeare have undergone many vicissitudes. The theatres were often closed during epidemics of the plague, and under Cromwell's rule all theatrical performances were strictly prohibited. As we shall see when we discuss censorship, that wayward child, the theatre, has frequently incurred the disapproval and castigation of its mother, the church. When the Stuarts were restored, the theatres immediately reopened, to the great delight, among others, of Samuel Pepys, an ardent theatregoer, whose diary describes many Shakespearean productions.

The plays themselves were often "adapted"—that is, mutilated—to please latter-day tastes by such theatre managers, actors and playwrights as William Davenant (reputed to be Shakespeare's son), John Dryden and David Garrick. In the early nineteenth century Thomas Bowdler published an edition of Shakespeare from which "those words and expressions are omitted which cannot with propriety be read aloud in a family." Bowdler has been immortalized by the addition to the English language of the verb "bowdlerize," defined by the Shorter Oxford English Dictionary as: "to expurgate by omitting or altering words or passages considered indelicate; to castrate."

But in spite of all handicaps and impediments, the long record of Shakespearean performances is a bright strong thread that runs through the history of the English theatre, profoundly influencing it and giving it much of its present-day color and interest. There are a number of reasons for this. Shakespeare's transcendent literary quality has made him the best-known and most widely read dramatist in world literature. His plays are read for pleasure by millions of adults and perhaps with less pleasure by almost every school child. There is hardly a school or college in the English-speaking world that does not at some·

time stage a play by Shakespeare. Because familiarity with Shakespeare's work is regarded as an essential part of our cultural heritage there is always an audience ready-made for attendance, voluntary or obligatory, at performances of Shakespearean plays. It is, except in rare cases, not a mass audience; but it is in every generation a continuing one, and its existence is a constant incentive to the production of the plays, for one of the chief determinants of the choice of plays to be presented is of course the taste of the potential audience.

Another chief determinant is the opportunity that the plays afford for a display of the skill of the interpretative artists in the theatre. Here the plays of Shakespeare excel. No other dramatist has created as many characters that are what is known in the profession as "good acting parts." Hamlet, Lear, Iago, Shylock, Falstaff, Richard III, Lady Macbeth, Ophelia, Portia, Ariel, Juliet, Rosalind, and fifty other major parts have attracted and taxed the skill of all the brilliant, and all too many dull, actors of the past three hundred years. And there is not a play that does not contain a half-dozen highly actable minor roles: a clown, a saucy wench, an eloquent nobleman, a treacherous scoundrel. Not surprising, for many of these parts were written specifically by Shakespeare for the acting company of which he was a member. I have never yet met an actor with a real vocation for the stage who was not eager for a chance to play Shakespeare; everyone has heard the theatrical cliché: "They all want to play Hamlet."

For the scenic designer and stage director, the loose structure and multiple scenes of Shakespeare's plays, so greatly at variance with the prescribed Aristotelian unities, present fascinating challenges. The use of scenery, which was practically unknown in the Elizabethan theatre, and the evolution of radically different types of stage have created problems of representation, interpretation and stage movement that make heavy demands upon the ingenuity of those charged with the responsibility of production. It should also be noted that Shakespeare's plays have inspired the composition of many operas and of much incidental music of high quality.

The continuity of Shakespearean production, the preoccupation with the histrionic interpretation of the plays and the difficulties of staging have necessitated the establishment of special methods of training and the development of special techniques. This is particularly true in our time, for the modern actor, accustomed to imitating contemporary colloquial speech and ordinary everyday behavior, is simply not qualified to do justice to Shakespeare. The delivery of his lines, rather archaic in their vocabulary and ineffably beautiful in their poetic construction, calls for a clarity of diction and a sweetness of tone than can be acquired only through expert training and assiduous effort. Shaw, in his amusing one-act play *The Dark Lady of the Sonnets*, depicts Shakespeare snooping about and jotting down colorful snatches of overheard conversation. No doubt the daily speech of Elizabethan times was richer and more picturesque than ours, but if Shakespeare's dialogue is a literal recording of it, his ears were sharper than those of his contemporaries. The action and movement of the plays too—the dueling, the courtly ceremonies, the dancing, singing and dumb show—call for instruction in fencing, calisthenics and other forms of body training to impart grace and agility.

As a result, then, of the strength and persistence of the Shakespearean tradition, most English actors, while not innately more talented than their American counterparts, are better trained. Their speech is purer and they comport themselves more easily upon the stage. Plays of very slight substance indeed often succeed in England because of the delight that the audience takes in their skillful performance.

An even more important by-product of the Shakespearean tradition has been the establishment of acting companies dedicated to the performance of Shakespeare's plays, brilliantly exemplified at present by the Shakespeare Memorial Theatre at Stratford-on-Avon and by London's Old Vic Company and its affiliate in Bristol. These excellent companies keep alive all the plays of Shakespeare, not only as dramatic literature, but as exciting theatre. Though they attract large audiences, they are not in the ordinary sense, self-supporting or profit-making, but are subsidized partly by philanthropic contributions and partly by the generosity of the performers. Nearly all the great stars of the English stage make occasional appearances at Stratford or at the Old Vic for salaries that are far below what they can command in the commercial theatre. The affectionate pride with which the Shakespearean companies are regarded by intelligent theatregoers and theatre workers is perhaps the most distinctive and admirable feature of the contemporary English theatre.

In the late seventeenth and early eighteenth centuries there was another brief upsurge in English dramatic writing, usually referred to as the Restoration drama, though most of the plays were written in the reign of William and Mary. These "comedies of manners" by Congreve, Wycherley, Vanbrugh, Farquhar and others, while far inferior to the greatest plays of the Elizabethan era, were characterized by a perfection of speech and an elegance of manners that again demanded exceptional skill in the performers; and the survival of many of these plays upon the English stage has been another factor in the training of actors.

After this brilliant flurry the English drama, except for the brief interlude of Sheridan, sank into a long decline. It is a most remarkable fact that between the death of Sheridan early in the nineteenth century, and the emergence of Henry Arthur Jones and Arthur Wing Pinero near its close—a period that produced many of the greatest poems, novels and essays in English literature—there was hardly a play written that is worthy of more than historical notice.

Yet, as often happens, the English theatre in this dramatically arid era expanded and prospered. It is not hard to explain: the thirst for theatre is constant and insatiable, and even when there are no worthwhile plays to be seen people go to the theatre to see actors perform. So in England the nineteenth century was the heyday of the actor and more particularly the actor-manager, for many of the leading players had their own companies and chose, or even commissioned, plays in which they could appear effectively. As has been indicated, there were always performances of Shakespeare and of the Restoration dramatists. There were also sporadic, and almost invariably unsuccessful, performances of the "closet dramas" of the great contemporary poets and novelists. But in the main the stage was given over to lurid melodramas, treacly romances or bombastic blank-verse dramas upon classical themes: in other words, contrived pieces that gave the actor-manager opportunities to display his personal charms and his bag of histrionic tricks.

In the late nineteenth century the art of the drama came to life again in England, suddenly and brilliantly. But this revival will be described later in connection with the general European movement of which it was a part. In dealing with the English theatre, as with those previously discussed, I have not attempted to present a complete picture. My aim has been to emphasize the unique characteristics and to examine their causes and effects.

The retarded state of the theatre in the English-speaking colonies (now autonomous members of the British Commonwealth) illustrates the dependence of the theatre upon political, cultural and even geographical factors. Vast recently settled and sparsely populated countries like Canada and Australia are not likely areas for the establishment of distinctive and vigorous theatres. Urban centers are few and far apart, preoccupation with the tasks of taming the new land leaves little time or inclination for cultural activities, and, most of all, the colonists are still bound, not only politically, but emotionally and psychologically, to the mother country. Whatever theatre there is, therefore, tends to be derivative and tributary.

Canada, because of its geographical location, is in some ways more closely linked to the United States than to England, and theatrical activity has been restricted mostly to the appearance of English and American touring companies in the larger communities, and the performance of English and American plays by resident stock and amateur companies in the smaller ones. There has been no native Canadian drama to speak of, and while many fine contemporary actors are of Canadian birth, most of them have made their careers on the English and American stages, where the opportunities are greater. There are signs, though, that as Canada grows and becomes more self-sufficient, economically and culturally, she will develop a significant theatre of her own. Most impressive is the successful establishment of the Shakespearean theatre at Stratford, Ontario. Though modeled on the English Memorial Theatre, it has a distinctive quality of its own and can rightly be regarded as a healthy, indigenous product.

In Australia and New Zealand the conditions peculiar to colonialism are much the same as in Canada. The state of the theatre is much the same too: occasional tours by English and American companies and productions, not usually of very high quality, of foreign plays by local companies. As in Canada, the most highly gifted performers are likely to seek their fortunes elsewhere. Recently in Australia there have been written some plays dealing with regional themes, a few of which have been successfully performed throughout the British Commonwealth. This is certainly a hopeful sign, but it is too early to determine whether Australia will develop a vigorous native drama and as a consequence a distinctive national theatre.

There is little to be said about South Africa, the remaining English-speaking dominion, except that here the social situation is complicated by the fact that the colonial white population is largely *non*-English-speaking and the preponderantly native population is subjected to shameful indignities and denied participation in the cultural life of the country. These conditions aggravate the handicaps that colonialism imposes upon art, and so it is not surprising that there is in South Africa no theatre worth talking about.

At the risk of incurring the wrath of Irish patriots, I shall conclude this chapter on England with a brief examination of the Irish theatre. For in spite of ethnic differences and political antagonisms, Ireland was until very recently part of the British Empire, linked to England geographically and economically and to a great extent culturally. In fact, the Irish theatre, prior to the great Irish revival of the late nineteenth century, was as dependent upon England for its theatrical fare as were Canada and Australia. And the dramatic masterpieces created during that revival were, after all, written in English and constitute a vital and enduring chapter in English literature. (Attempts to resuscitate a dead language in a world already bedeviled by a confusion of tongues are as unlikely to succeed in Ireland as in other newborn countries. Even if they do, it is not probable that there will be a resultant enrichment of dramatic literature.)

Nowhere did the nineteenth-century movement reach a higher level or produce plays of more universal significance. This is hard to account for. Ireland is a rather isolated country, with a small and diminishing population and unfavorable economic conditions. While it is rich in cultural traditions and has produced many brilliant intellects, the general level of education is relatively low. The cultural life is centered largely in Dublin, a charming city, with a lovely eighteenth-century visage, but hardly a metropolis or a world capital. Indeed, it is something of a provincial backwater.

Yet in poetic beauty, imaginativeness, insight and theatrical effectiveness it would be hard to match in any country of the contemporary world the plays of J. M. Synge, Lady Gregory, W. B. Yeats, Lord Dunsany, Lennox Robinson and Sean O'Casey. (I do not include Bernard Shaw, Oscar Wilde and St. John Ervine, who are usually identified with the English theatre.) The work of these dramatists is indubitably and vividly Irish in character. Its themes are drawn from Irish legend, from the everyday life of the Irish people and from the events of the unforgettable Easter rebellion. The milieux are Irish, the characters are Irish and, most important of all, the rich musical language, often employing quaint forms of dialect, is unmistakably Irish. Yet these plays are as much a part of world culture as are the archaic sculptures of the Acropolis Museum or the Dutch genre paintings of the seventeenth century.

Associated with the works of these dramatists are the two Dublin theatres in which they were first and repeatedly performed: the world-famous Abbey Theatre and the somewhat less well-known Gate Theatre. In fact, these theatres may be said to owe their existence chiefly to the great outpouring of dramatic literature that began in the 1890's and flowed on for two decades or more. To meet the theatrical requirements of the drama these playhouses, although small, inadequately equipped and financially restricted, had to improvise production methods and to develop actors who were capable of portraying the complex and colorful characters and of doing justice to the cadenced lyrical speech. They succeeded admirably. The productions at the Abbey and at the Gate delighted the aesthetes of Dublin and drew theatre-lovers from abroad. On its tours the Abbey company was acclaimed by American audiences—and sometimes pelted with vegetables by Irish patriots who took exception to some of the portrayals of Irish life. Some of the best actors succumbed to the financial lure of America and remained behind to become ornaments of the American stage, a defection that contributed to the decline of the Abbey Theatre. Here once more we see economics at work in the theatre.

Sad to relate, the glory of the Irish theatre was short-lived. It was a brilliant meteor that flashed suddenly across the theatrical horizon and then faded quickly away. The great writers for whose works it served as a medium of communication are either dead or inactive and they have had no comparable successors. Worse yet, their works are neglected or frowned upon, largely for politico-religious reasons. National independence has not brought to Ireland greater liberalism in the arts or a new impetus to creative effort. Theocratic influences have greatly restricted artistic expression in the Republic. Recently, what promised to be a very interesting drama festival in Dublin had to be called off because official, or quasi-official, objection to some of the works that were to be performed prompted the withdrawal, by way of protest, of still other works and the resultant collapse of the whole enterprise. In Ireland as elsewhere, censorship is the bane of art. The Irish theatre struggles on as best it can, thanks to the devotion of those who cherish its great achievements, but today it cannot be regarded as occupying a very important place in the world theatre.

VIII THE AMERICAN THEATRE: BEGINNINGS

Our summary view of the theatre in Mexico, Germany, Japan, China, the Soviet Union and the British Commonwealth has, I hope, established the fact that it is not only a medium for the communication of drama but an important social institution, whose structure and functions are determined by a great variety of factors, most of which have little or nothing to do with the drama as a literary form. This applies, of course, to the American theatre as well; and its peculiar features will be the subject of a detailed examination, based not merely upon observation but upon long participation in its activities.

Historically, the American theatre falls roughly into four periods: (1) colonial; (2) from the Revolution to the Civil War; (3) from the Civil War to World War I; (4) post-World War I; that is to say contemporary. The emphasis upon wars is partly a convenient device for demarcation, but, as will be seen, the wars also strongly influenced the development of the theatre.

The colonial period may be quickly dealt with. In general, it follows the pattern of the other British colonies. A population composed largely of adventurers and social outcasts was spread sparsely along the fringe of a vast unexplored continent. Occupied with establishing settlements and providing means of livelihood, and often with defending themselves against the hostile aborigines, the early settlers had neither time for nor interest in the arts, particularly not the art of the drama, which demands so much organization. Hence the first century or so of colonization was almost wholly devoid of theatrical activity.

By the middle of the eighteenth century the population had risen to about three million, urban centers had been established, social conditions were becoming stabilized and the country was beginning to prosper. As is true everywhere among city dwellers with money, leisure and a certain amount of sophistication, a demand for organized entertainment developed, and so theatres began to be erected and operated by enterprising individuals eager to profit by satisfying the popular demand. The fare provided in these theatres (principally in Boston and Philadelphia, for New York had not yet emerged as the great American metropolis) was, as in all colonies, almost entirely derivative: visiting companies from the mother country or native imitations of the English stage.

One extremely important fact must be stressed at the outset of any study of the American theatre. It had no ecclesiastical, courtly or governmental origins; it is entirely the product of business enterprise, and during the two centuries of its existence it has in the main been dominated by business enterprise. I do not minimize the important contributions that have been made by groups and individuals animated solely by love of the theatre. In fact, I shall have a great deal to say about them. But they are subordinate to the central fact of business control.

Thus we are introduced to new factors in the theatre: the profit motive and the businessman. No one who fails to grasp their significance can hope to understand the American theatre. I am not suggesting that the theatre in other industrial countries is not largely dominated by commercial interests. But these developed gradually as economic conditions changed, whereas the American theatre had its late beginnings in an era in which commercialism was already ascendant, and was therefore commercial from its very inception.

I do not use the word "commercial" in a pejorative sense but only to distinguish what might be called a primarily economic motivation from a primarily artistic one. It is not a question of being mercenary. A dramatist or actor may be a shameless money-grubber, just as a theatrical producer may be a high-minded idealist. What is important to us here is that the nature of the relationship of each to the theatre has a profound effect upon the nature of the theatre itself.

There have been few artists who have not had to occupy themselves with making a living, and usually they want to live as well as possible. Sophocles must have had some means of livelihood and so must the priests who performed the rituals from which the Greek drama sprang. The participants in the medieval mystery and morality plays were probably artisans for whom acting was an avocation, as are the dancers in the Mexican fiestas or the performers of the Passion Play at Oberammergau. Throughout the centuries dramatists and the interpreters of drama have been paid, in one way or another. Shakespeare and Molière were presumably good men of affairs, and undoubtedly there were others. But until very recent times playwrights and actors have had a rather thin time of it—most of them still do, even in the United States, where the successful few make huge fortunes—yet they cleave to the theatre, either because their desire to express themselves in its terms transcends all other considerations or because they are hapless victims of that most incurable form of madness: stage fever.

Not so the businessman. He may be a lover of the theatre, a discerning critic of dramatic literature, a connoisseur of acting, costuming and lighting; yet what draws him into the theatre is his expectation or hope of reaping financial profit from the presentation of dramatic works. He may also be a stage director or an actor, but in that case he is merely serving in a dual capacity. Indeed he must make a profit, for he can continue to function only as long as his money, or somebody's money, holds out. Therefore he cannot be governed solely by artistic considerations. In fact, his activities are executive rather than artistic: he provides a theatre for the production of plays, and he engages and pays the large and varied personnel that play production demands. In the professional theatre he may be said to be almost indispensable, for the dramatist must depend upon him to supply the machinery of production and the actors must depend upon him for payment. It is obvious then that what is seen in the theatre is determined by the judgment of a person who must be primarily concerned with the monetary aspects of his undertaking. This anomalous and contradictory situation is responsible for a very confused state of affairs in countries, notably the United States, where the theatre is largely under commercial control; and to an even more confused state of thinking among theatregoers and theatre students who are unfamiliar with the actual workings of the theatre.

At any rate, whatever theatre there was in America at the time of the Revolution was under the control of businessmen. With the achievement of independence the American theatre began to expand and develop, and during the next seventy-five years, until the outbreak of the Civil War, there was an enormous increase in the extent and the complexity of theatrical activity. Again the social and economic reasons are apparent: ever-increasing prosperity and rapid growth of population centers, two conditions essential to the existence of a flourishing theatre. The westward movement of the populace, the Louisiana Purchase, the annexation of Texas, and the California Gold Rush added vast areas to the nation and created new cities remote from the Eastern seaboard, eager to welcome theatrical touring companies and able to pay for them.

Independence had its psychological effects too. It created a desire on the part of the newly minted citizenry to show the world that it was aware of the existence of the arts and took pride in its capacity to support them. The level of literacy and of

education was rising, too, and an American literature was beginning to develop, though not yet, as we shall see, in the art of the
drama.

Theatres sprang up everywhere, not only in the well-established cities of the East but in the ramshackle settlements of the
Wild West. Many of these are now ghost towns, but in some of
them the theatres still may be seen. (In Central City, Colorado,
the old playhouse is now the scene of a summer drama festival.)
Stock companies were established in the larger cities, often under
the direction of actor-managers like Lester Wallack and Augustin
Daly, whose theatres in lower Manhattan were still in use in
the early years of the twentieth century. The leading stars of
the English stage found it worth their while to make extended
tours of the new republic, and, with some exceptions, were
greeted with acclaim. Meanwhile, America was developing stars
of its own, notably Edwin Booth and Edwin Forrest. Sometimes
there was intense rivalry between English and American actors,
with popular partisanship on each side. The bitter personal feud
between Forrest and the famous English actor Charles Macready
actually developed into a political situation that had terrible
consequences. So violent was the feeling on both sides that, as
one contemporary publication put it: "The question became not
only a national but a social one. It was the rich against the
poor—the aristocracy against the people; and this hatred of
wealth and privilege is increasing all over the world, and ready
to burst out whenever there is the slightest occasion." Placards
appeared reading: "Workingmen, shall Americans or English
rule in this city?" Alarmed, Macready wanted to call off a performance of *Macbeth* scheduled for the Astor Place Opera
House on the night of May 10, 1849. But he was persuaded to
go on. The theatre was surrounded by a strong force of police,
but they were unable to control the mob of twenty thousand
demonstrators. Troops were called out, and when they were
attacked with paving stones they fired upon the crowd. The
performance went on, to the accompaniment of breaking glass

and musket fire. At the end, Macready, disguised, was smuggled out of the theatre. The casualties were twenty-two killed and a large number wounded. It is evident that people took the theatre seriously.

Little need be said about the plays that were performed during this period. In general the American theatre aped the English. Shakespeare's plays were the chief stock-in-trade of the American star performers and of the English visitors. Contemporary works were likely to be turgid verse-plays dealing with the heroes of antiquity, or sometimes with noble savages, or romantic melodramas and crude comedies. There were some attempts by American playwrights to use native themes and characters, but few have survived or are even worth mentioning. As in England, the theatre was prospering, but the drama was in the doldrums. It is extraordinary that an era that produced writers as distinctively American and as world famous as Melville, Cooper, Irving, Emerson, Thoreau, Hawthorne and Poe did not bring forth a single dramatist whose work can be seriously regarded either as good drama or as good literature. The dramatic awakening in America was to come, but even when it did it was thirty years later than in Europe.

IX THE AMERICAN THEATRE: GROWTH

The development of the American theatre in the half-century between the close of the Civil War and the entry of the United States into World War I is so complex and so exciting that one hardly knows where to begin or what to emphasize. Before any description is attempted, however, it would be well to consider some of the social and economic changes in American life that contributed to the expansion of the theatre.

The industrial revolution which transformed the economy of England in the first half of the nineteenth century was late in reaching America. Prior to the Civil War the energies of the young nation were largely occupied with physical expansion. The major economic activities were the settlement of new areas, the development of the country's incredibly rich natural resources and the attendant enterprises of commerce and transportation.

But the defeat of the Southern Confederacy, which unified the nation and brought to an end the long wasteful years of sectional strife and warfare, the taming of the land and the disappearance of the frontier, and the construction of the first transcontinental railroad opened the way for a surge of industrial development that in a few decades was to make the

United States one of the leading industrial powers of the world.

The effects of this general transformation upon the theatre are readily discernible. With the multiplication of factories, mines and railroads, and the complex organizations necessary for their management, old urban centers grew and new ones sprang up throughout the land. There was a great expansion of population too, both through natural increase and through an ever-swelling tide of immigration. The demand for more and more laborers to keep the wheels turning, coupled with the political disturbances, crop failures and other economic stringencies that plagued Europe, resulted in an influx of millions from the Mediterranean countries, Scandinavia, Ireland, and the Russian, German and Austrian empires. By 1914, when the outbreak of war abruptly cut off the stream, the annual number of immigrants was in excess of a million and a half.

This mass immigration did more than merely increase the population. In many ways it changed the character of American civilization. For one thing, the new arrivals were mostly young, vigorous and adventuresome enough to risk the uncertainties of life in an alien country, and they gave the American bloodstream a new infusion of vitality, enterprise and optimism. Also they modified the ethnic composition and cultural patterns of the nation. Though there had been non-British elements among the first settlers—Dutch, Swedish, French and Spanish—the population had been predominantly of English extraction and the culture almost entirely of English derivation. This was now altered drastically. Cities began to take on something of the flavor of the homeland of their new inhabitants: Scandinavian in St. Paul and Minneapolis; German in Milwaukee, St. Louis and Cincinnati; Irish in Boston and Providence. New York, the chief port of entry, had, a few decades ago, almost as many "foreign" quarters as there are nations in Europe, plus some Middle and Far Eastern ones. Not so long ago it was said that only about one in three of

New York's inhabitants could claim that both his parents were of American birth.

The effect upon the theatre was immediate. For example, large German and Italian populations, steeped in musical tradition, created a demand for the performance of operas and other musical works. In the larger cities dramatic performances were given in the mother tongues of the as yet unassimilated immigrants. Within my own memory there were in New York flourishing German, Chinese, Italian and Yiddish theatres. Foreign folkways and customs, songs and dances, and religious beliefs and practices created regional peculiarities that were later to be utilized in dramatic writing and theatrical performances, or were woven into the general cultural pattern itself. Members of various nationalities appeared upon the stage and portrayed characters from their native lands. After the liberation of the slaves, the Negro influence upon the American theatre, as well as upon the other arts, became more and more important and contributed greatly to the evolution of a distinctively American culture. In vaudeville, burlesque and revues there were Irish, German, Negro, Jewish and Swedish comedians who employed the dialects and poked fun at the quaintness and gaucheries of their compatriots. These performances were in the main good-humored and without malice, and it is to be deplored that in recent years the misguided zeal of nationalistic "pressure groups" has compelled the discontinuance of this form of harmless and amusing satire. The absorption of foreign words and idioms into the language and peculiarities of pronunciation had their effects upon the American vocabulary and American speech, and these striking modifications were reflected in the writing and delivery of stage dialogue, which diverged more and more from its original English model. (In recent years, a curious reverse process has been evident. The popularity of American plays and movies has resulted in the incorporation of many Americanisms in the dialogue of the British drama.)

There were plenty of alert businessmen who were ready to meet the ever-growing demand for theatrical entertainment. By the end of the nineteenth century two great syndicates, operated respectively by the Shubert brothers and by Klaw and Erlanger, were building and managing nation-wide chains of theatres. Here we must take note of a curious geographical fact that has had a profound and decidedly unhealthy effect upon the development of the American theatre. In the mid-nineteenth century New York had become by far the largest and richest city in the United States, and also its greatest center of culture. Like London, Paris and Vienna, it attracted great numbers of gifted persons who sought theatrical careers, and it became almost the sole place of origin for the production of new plays or, for that matter, for the organization of any sort of fresh theatrical activity. Unlike London, for example, it is not located in the center of a small area, readily accessible to the majority of the population. On the contrary, it is on the eastern seaboard of a country that measures three thousand miles from east to west and half that distance from north to south. Only a small part of the population lives within easy distance of New York, and relatively few of those living outside the metropolitan area can afford the time and money required for a round of the New York theatres—at least there were few before the age of aviation. Consequently the plays had to be brought to them, and this accounts for the prevalence of theatres throughout the country and for the development of New York, not only as a play-production center, but as a great play-distribution center.

At the turn of the century there were perhaps forty "first class" theatres in New York—that is to say, centrally located and commercially operated playhouses, seating from eight hundred to fifteen hundred persons, in which plays were performed by companies of professional actors. For the most part the theatre owners were also actively engaged in play production; sometimes they were directors or even co-authors.

Some of the most successful producers of the period—e.g., David Belasco, Charles Frohman, A. H. Woods, Charles Dillingham, George M. Cohan, William A. Brady—found it both convenient and profitable to own theatres in which they could house their own productions.

The ordinary procedure in play production, which has undergone very little change, was to organize and rehearse the acting company in New York and then to "try out" the play in one or more nearby cities for a week or two before opening in a New York theatre. The purpose of this preliminary tour was to accustom the actors to appearing before audiences as well as to get audience reactions, which sometimes prompted revisions in the text of the play or even changes in cast.

If the play was well received in New York it ran continuously as long as the weekly revenue exceeded the cost of operation—in other words, the length of the run was determined by the play's financial success, which did not always correspond with its artistic success or even with its popular appeal. If the play had a New York run of any considerable duration, the company would be sent on tour at the conclusion of the New York engagement. Usually, however, if the play was a great success a second company was organized and sent to Chicago or Boston or the Pacific Coast while the original production was still running in New York. Outstanding successes sometimes had as many as six or seven companies simultaneously touring the country. This will give some idea of the extensiveness of theatrical activity in the United States.

By way of illustration, I shall give the route of a typical touring company which performed a play of mine called *On Trial*. The play ran in New York during the entire season of 1914-15. The following season the New York company, known as the Eastern company, went on tour, and so did two other companies, known as the Central company and the Western company. (This was not an easy play to tour, for it had a cast of about twenty-five and five sets of scenery.) Here is the itinerary of the Western company, which had previously played for eighteen weeks in Chicago:

Week ending:

August	28th	Sioux City and Des Moines
September	4th	Des Moines
	11th	Milwaukee
	18th	Minneapolis
	25th	St. Paul
October	2nd	Duluth
	9th	Wausau, Eau Claire, Red Wing, Rochester, Mankato, Sioux City
October	16th	Sioux City, Lincoln, Omaha
	23rd	Denver
	30th	Salt Lake City
November	6th	San Francisco
	13th	San Francisco
	20th	San Francisco
	27th	Los Angeles
December	4th	Los Angeles, San Diego, Bakersfield, Modesto, Fresno, Sacramento
	11th	Oakland
	18th	Ogden, Cheyenne, Pueblo, Colorado Springs
	25th	Trinidad, Wichita
January	1st	Kansas City
	8th	Kansas City
	15th	St. Louis
	22nd	Terre Haute, Indianapolis
	29th	Cincinnati
February	5th	Middletown, Louisville
	12th	Lexington, Nashville, Birmingham
	19th	New Orleans
	26th	Houston, Galveston, San Antonio, Austin
March	4th	Waco, Dallas, Fort Worth, Oklahoma City
	11th	Oklahoma City, Tulsa, Muskegee, Fort Smith, Little Rock, Hot Springs

	18th	Memphis, Atlanta, Athens, Augusta, Savannah
	25th	Columbia, Anderson, Greenville, Spartanburg, Charlotte, Greensboro
April	1st	Petersburg, Richmond, Newport News, Norfolk
	8th	Hagerstown, Cumberland, Johnstown, Altoona, Wilmington

At the same time the other two companies were engaged in comparable tours in other sections of the country. In the light of present-day theatrical conditions in the American theatre this is truly astonishing and I place so much emphasis upon it because it demonstrates concretely a diffusion of professional theatrical activity that will never be seen again. A shrinkage began in the 1920's and has continued at a rate that is disheartening and alarming, both to those who strongly desire the widest possible dissemination of good theatre and to those who are professionally engaged in theatrical activities. It is years, decades perhaps, since a touring company has visited many of the cities named above, and it is doubtful if more than one in a hundred of their inhabitants has ever seen a play professionally performed.

In the outlying districts of New York and in the nearby suburbs there were a number of theatres in which the New York companies performed immediately after the conclusion of their Broadway engagements. During most of my childhood and youth I lived in upper Manhattan and did much of my early playgoing at the two Harlem theatres, operated by the rival syndicates, where the latest successes could be seen fresh from Broadway.

Besides the touring companies that appeared in plays currently or recently in New York, there were other itinerant companies that performed plays of perennial popularity, many of them dramatizations of successful novels. Innumerable troupes roved the land in various versions of *Uncle Tom's Cabin*. Other favorites were *East Lynne, Shore Acres, Ben Hur, The Old Homestead* and *Mrs. Wiggs of the Cabbage Patch*.

Often well-known actors devoted most of their professional lifetimes to appearances in a single play. Among those I saw in my youth were Joseph Jefferson in *Rip Van Winkle*, David Warfield in *The Music Master*, William Gillette in *Sherlock Holmes* and James O'Neill (Eugene O'Neill's father) in *The Count of Monte Cristo*. There were numerous Shakespearean companies, too, that toured the country year after year, with occasional visits to New York, notably those headed by E. H. Sothern and Julia Marlowe and by Robert B. Mantell.

Nor is this the whole story. For in addition to the touring companies there were in many cities (amounting at one time to about 150) permanent resident companies known as stock companies. These local troupes, often operating on a year-round basis, usually offered a different play every week. The performers were drawn largely from local talent, and the companies often developed local stars with large popular followings. Many of these stars afterwards went on to fame on Broadway or in Hollywood. But in spite of their regional organization and operation, these theatres, too, were tributary to New York, for with few exceptions the plays they performed were the established New York successes of previous seasons. The combination of local stars and modest admission prices attracted considerable audiences and many of these theatres were highly successful. To put it as mildly as possible, the standard of production was often modest too. But not always; some of these theatres had first-rate directors, and their skill was reflected in the excellence of the productions. In general, the stock companies were fine training schools for actors, since an actor, in order to play twenty or thirty different parts in the course of a season, had to develop great versatility and technical skill. In fact, until comparatively recently almost every important actor in the theatre or in the movies had had most of his early training in stock companies.

Other very lively and widespread forms of theatrical activity were burlesque, vaudeville and the spectacles offered by touring troupes like Buffalo Bill's Wild West Show. How vividly I remember the stagecoach robberies, the fights between United States regulars and yelling, half-naked Indians in war paint, the enactment of Teddy Roosevelt's charge up San Juan Hill, and the scaling of the Great Wall of China by the allied troops in the Boxer Rebellion!

Many writers have celebrated vaudeville and mourned its passing. And indeed it was a highly skilled and highly enjoyable kind of theatre. It was by no means confined to trained seals and sleight-of-hand artists. Its performers included a great number of talented and expert actors, dancers, singers and instrumentalists, who developed "routines" that were little masterpieces of timing and technique, and whose material, which included musical and dramatic playlets, was often excellent.

Burlesque, too, before it specialized in scatological jokes and the unveiling of the female form (commonly known as strip tease; though it was H. L. Mencken, I believe, who perferred to call it ecdysis) was a genial form of family entertainment on a rather simple level: a sort of potpourri of broad humor, spectacle and song and dance. As with the stock companies, many subsequently famous actors, particularly comedians, began their careers in burlesque.

Burlesque and vaudville, like the "legitimate" theatre, had rival syndicates and competing chains of theatres or "wheels." This competition, though basically commercial, was not without some interesting artistic results, for each group strove to improve the quality of its productions in order to take business away from its opponent. So that if, for example, Klaw and Erlanger announced the booking of John Drew in their theatre in Kansas City for a certain week, the Shuberts would arrange to have Mrs. Fiske play at *their* Kansas City house during the same week. And so it was with the vaudeville headliners and top stars of burlesque. It was competition that was to prove disastrous in the end, but for a time it stimulated and developed theatrical activity to a degree never before known.

All in all then, the theatre, collectively, with its scores of

New York productions every year, its far-ranging touring companies, its widespread performances of Shakespeare and Gilbert and Sullivan, dramatized novels and old-time favorites, its local stock companies, its spectacles and circuses, its big-city opera houses, its great burlesque and vaudeville circuits, offered a variety of theatrical entertainment that appealed to every taste and was within the limits of almost everybody's budget. It is not surprising that in this period Americans were a nation of theatregoers. In every community there were many people of modest means who went to a theatre as often as once a week. Clearly, the last vestiges of colonialism were fast disappearing and the American theatre was establishing itself as an autonomous, individualized, colorful, prosperous and socially important institution.

So far in our discussion of this period we have examined only the expansion and diversification of theatrical activity. But paralleling this development and even more significant was the first flowering in America of the art of the drama. We have seen that prior to the Civil War almost nothing was written worth discussing. But with the postwar emergence of the United States as a world power, Americans developed a native pride and a self-awareness that were increasingly expressed in the arts, particularly the literary arts. American playwrights of considerable ability made their appearance and began to make use of native material. At first the plays they wrote were homespun dramas or melodramas of rural life or extravaganzas based upon metropolitan foibles. Not much can be said for them as literature, but what makes them important is their emphasis upon American settings and American characters and most of all upon American speech. But by the 1890's a large group of playwrights was actively turning out plays that were far in advance of the naïve and mechanical works of their immediate predecessors. For twenty-five years the plays of these writers occupied a more and more dominant place in the American theatre and gave it an increasingly national flavor.

To the literary critic or the sophisticated theatregoer of today, most of these plays would seem contrived, crude, two-dimensional and even puerile. But if they do seem so it may be largely because both their themes and their manner of expression have been relegated to the movies and to television, and the standards by which the American theatre is judged today are far, far higher than they were fifty years ago. As a matter of fact, many of the dramatists of the period ended their careers as successful Hollywood writers.

However, I think it would be a great mistake to dismiss this large body of work as unworthy of notice or to underestimate its importance in the development of American drama. I may be influenced by the fact that I saw and enjoyed so many of the plays and was personally acquainted with so many of the authors. But, on balance, I think it can be fairly said that they paved the way not only for the works of Eugene O'Neill and his contemporaries but for the popular recognition of that work.

It would not be hard for the caustic critic to demonstrate that among the recurrent themes of these plays were truculent and adolescent chauvinism and isolationism; celebration of the hardihood and the innate nobility of the frontiersman and the rough diamond; the turning of the worm or the triumph of the underdog, though without social implications; the glorification of American aggressiveness and dubious business practices; the taming of the philanderer or of the domineering male by a sly little puss; the successful struggle of female chastity against the most alarming temptations (or, if unsuccessful, the swift and condign punishment that ensued); the canonization of motherhood; the justification of faith and the confounding or conversion of the irreligious; and, in general, the comeuppance of the sinner, the criminal and the nonconformist.

It is really quite extraordinary that, at a time when all Europe was seething with a great renaissance of dramatic literature and America itself had produced novelists of such perceptiveness and literary excellence as Stephen Crane, Henry James, Edith Wharton, Ellen Glasgow and William Dean Howells, and with such heretical social convictions as Jack London, Frank Norris and Upton Sinclair, the theatre was given over largely to clichés, banality and mediocre writing. There were a few playwrights—Percy Mackaye, William Vaughan Moody, Louis Kaufmann Anspacher and Langdon Mitchell—who were mildly acclaimed for the quality of their writing; but they shone only by comparison and their work has shown no great power of survival.

But the staleness and triviality of the themes were offset in large measure by the freshness and liveliness of the material. The unmistakably American character of the plays can be illustrated merely by listing a few titles, picked at random: *Rose of the Rancho, The Girl of the Golden West, Forty-five Minutes from Broadway, He Came from Milwaukee, The Squaw Man, Mis' Nelly of N' Orleans, The County Chairman, The College Widow, The New York Idea, The Grand Army Man, Alabama, Arizona, In Mizzouri, Get-Rich-Quick Wallingford, The Warrens of Virginia, It Pays to Advertise, The Gold Diggers, The Chorus Lady, George Washington Jr., The Great Divide.*

Here we see for the first time the effective use in the theatre of the special zest of American history and American regionalism, American folkways and American enterprise. The plays were peopled with American characters drawn from every level of society and every way of life, often authentically, though superficially, depicted. The "melting-pot" aspect of America, treated in a play by that name by the English dramatist Israel Zangwill, was not ignored. It manifested itself in the flavorsome speech of the characters of recent foreign ancestry and touched upon the tragic and comic implications of racial and ethnic conflicts and misunderstandings. In the use of all this new and vivid material, many of the playwrights displayed great technical skill and a shrewd knowledge of the resources of the theatre. Today the very names of most of these writers, so popular forty or fifty years ago, are forgotten; and their plays are unproduced and unread, except perhaps as historical exercises or as horrid examples of how not to write for the theatre. But they gave pleasure to millions of theatregoers and their contributions to the American theatre should not be minimized.

A few of the outstanding authors of the time deserve at least passing notice. Most colorful and perhaps most popular of all was George M. Cohan. He was not only a playwright, but an actor, singer, dancer, lyric writer, composer, director, producer and theatre owner. Semiliterate and almost completely uncultivated in speech and manners, he had, in his personality and in his work, an infectious quality that endeared him to the theatregoing public and to his professional colleagues. He was the idol of all the actors until he took sides against them when they went on strike in 1919. The ensuing bitterness endured until the very end of his long life. The key to his work and to his success may be found in two aphorisms attributed to him: "Always have them laughing when you say good-by" and "The American flag has saved many a bum show." Known as the Yankee Doodle Boy, he was the prince of flag wavers and a master of sentimental and lighthearted farce-comedy. He could not adapt himself to the demands of a more sophisticated generation, and his popularity waned, but not his fame, which is perpetuated by a statue erected in Times Square, his lifelong haunt.

Almost equally famous was David Belasco. Like Cohan, he was a director, producer and theatre owner, but he wrote a whole series of very successful plays, most of them collaborations or dramatizations of novels or foreign plays. It would be hard, I think, to find much merit in anything he wrote. But he had an uncanny sense of what is called showmanship, and he developed a kind of meticulous realism in his productions that never failed to fascinate the literal minded.

A man of no intellectual attainments whatever and without any real taste, he assiduously created an image of himself as a dreamer and an aesthete.

By contrast, Clyde Fitch was a man of genuine taste and sensitivity. He was prolific, versatile and enormously successful. At one time, he had four hits running simultaneously on Broadway. He wrote not only historical and romantic plays, but plays that attempted to deal seriously with personal and psychological problems. But again the treatment was superficial and the writing, though by no means crude, could hardly be called distinguished. It is doubtful if his plays would bear revival in the contemporary theatre. At any rate, I know of no recent attempt to revive them.

Another fantastically successful playwright was Avery Hopwood. A man of intellect and wit, he devoted himself to the writing of farces with such titles as *Up in Mabel's Room, Getting Gertie's Garter, The Demi-Virgin* and *Ladies' Night (in a Turkish Bath).* His plays had long runs in New York, and some of them had seven or eight companies on tour. After amassing a fortune of many millions of dollars, he came to his end in the waters of the Mediterranean. He is remembered chiefly for his endowment of dramatic activities at the University of Michigan, his alma mater.

Finally, I feel that some mention should be made of Augustus Thomas, an imposing figure, celebrated as an after-dinner speaker and an active worker in the Democratic Party, and often referred to as the "dean" of American playwrights. After a series of dramatizations of various states of the Union (Arizona, Alabama, Missouri) he turned to writing pseudo-psychological melodramas, which in those pre-Freudian days impressed critics and audiences with their apparent profundity. But I think that the success of the plays can properly be attributed to the skillful use of tried-and-true theatrical devices.

These few examples should suffice to give the reader a cross section of the state of the drama at the outbreak of

World War I. Some of the writers of the period were active in the theatre for many more years. Owen Davis, for example, wrote some three hundred plays, ranging from such melodramas as *The Gambler's Daughter* and *Her First False Step* to serious plays like *The Detour*, the Pulitzer Prize-winning *Icebound*, and the excellent dramatization of *Ethan Frome*. But most of the dramatists of this period were eclipsed by the postwar emergence of a new school of playwrights, whose infusion of new ideas and new techniques into the theatre amounted almost to a revolution. Before we examine this new movement, however, it is necessary to look at what was happening to the drama in Europe during the late nineteenth and early twentieth centuries.

X THE DRAMATIC RENAISSANCE
IN EUROPE

The French Revolution and the industrial revolution, both occurring in the late eighteenth century, inaugurated a series of sweeping changes that affected all the Western world and eventually the entire world. In fact, the nineteenth century may properly be called a century of revolution, for no other century has so radically altered the social, political, economic and intellectual life of man. The overthrow of the Bourbons, followed in quick succession by the upheavals of the Napoleonic era, the widespread uprisings of 1848, and the unification of Germany and of Italy, brought about the introduction of new political philosophies and institutions, as well as new uses and alignments of political power. The mechanization of industry changed the structure of society as nothing else had ever done. This era of political and social changes was also the era of a new colonialism. The need of industry for new markets and new sources of raw materials resulted in annexation of large areas in Asia and Africa, comparable to the annexation of the Americas in the sixteenth and seventeenth centuries.

The establishment of the factory system and the growth of the proletariat created a whole new complex of economic and sociological problems to which theorists and reformers addressed themselves. The intensified study of chemistry and physics in the interests of the new industry stimulated research and revisionism in other sciences too: geology, astronomy, biology. So that there were drastic changes in man's thoughts and beliefs, as well as in his institutions and living conditions.

The two new doctrines that were most far-reaching in their effects may be conveniently labeled as Marxism and Darwinism: that is, the theory of economic determinism and the theory of evolution. Since these are matters of common knowledge, they will be discussed here only in relation to their effect upon the drama and the theatre.

The Communist Manifesto appeared in 1847, *On the Origin of Species* in 1859. The French Revolution had successfully challenged the divine right of kings; Marx went even farther and challenged the divine right of the property-owning middle class. And Darwin's hypothesis challenged belief in the divine special creation of man. Both theories were vehemently denounced as false, immoral and heretical, and enthusiastically acclaimed as enlightened doctrines that were destined to sweep away injustice and superstition. The ensuing war of opinion entailed a complete revaluation of the place of man in the universe and in society. For many, if not most, thinking individuals the findings of astronomers, geologists and biologists destroyed the concept of an anthropocentric universe and the Biblical account of the origin and age of the human species; and the economic interpretation of history threw a new light upon the structure of society and the influences that determined the status of the individual. To the ancient Greeks man was a heroic, semidivine figure, closely linked to the Olympian gods, who presided over his destiny and held him strictly accountable for even innocent violations of inexorable moral laws. To the Elizabethans he was still of heroic proportions, master of the world, proud, ambitious, unlimited in his aspirations and capabilities. These concepts are reflected in the drama of Periclean Athens and of Elizabethan England, with its larger-than-life protagonists, its cosmic sweep, its emphasis upon the majesty of man and the tragic significance of his failures and defeats.

The nineteenth century cut man down to size. In the light of the new theories and scientific discoveries he appeared to be a finite organism in the grip of forces beyond his control or even beyond his comprehension, imperfect, weak, confused, inconsistent, both the victim and the victimizer of his fellow men, but possessed at the same time of an inquisitive mind that spurred him on to a search for the truth no matter where it led. In the course of that search every aspect of human relationships and social behavior was re-examined and subjected to analysis and criticism, and this process is vividly revealed in the blossoming drama of the late nineteenth century.

Just as the new sciences are associated with the names of Marx and Darwin (and later with Freud and Einstein) the new drama is associated with that of Henrik Ibsen, and Ibsenism has become a synonym for the dramaturgic revolution that embraced subject matter, play technique and stagecraft. Today, fifty years after Ibsen's death, the drama and the theatre, for better or worse, still bear his unmistakable impress.

Though Ibsen wrote some memorable historical and poetic plays, his fame and importance rest chiefly upon his introduction of "realism" into the theatre, an approach and a method that swept away the established conventions and in the course of a few decades built up a new dramaturgy that dominated the stages of the Western world.

As we have seen, the drama of the first three-quarters of the nineteenth century was for the most part mechanical and sterile. Many of the plays were rehashes or imitations of classical drama, dealing with well-worn historical or mythological subjects, and written in bombastic prose or uninspired blank verse that was usually tedious and often ludicrous. For the rest, the theatre was given over to lurid melodramas, sugary romances and extravagant farces.

Whatever the type of play, however, the same dramaturgic

principles governed. Plots were standardized and contrived. Co-incidence, accident and fortuitous occurrences, rather than the psychology or interrelationships of the characters, shaped the course of events. Solutions were arbitrary, predetermined and usually easily predictable. Logic, consistency and plausibility were ignored. The characters were wooden lay figures drawn to familiar patterns. They behaved in accordance with abstract standards of conduct and with the exigencies of the plot rather than with any regard to human motivation. Their speech was formalized and turgid, and the dialogue was often interlarded with long expository passages, asides and soliloquies, introduced mainly for the purpose of conveying information to the audience or for affording actors opportunities for rhetorical exercises.

But by the middle of the nineteenth century a new trend in dramaturgy began to make itself felt, due largely to the influence of Eugène Scribe, the French author who wrote several hundred dramatic works and is known as the father of the "well-made" play. Though almost forgotten today, he was enormously popular in his lifetime, partly because the revolutionary political and economic changes had created a new society and new audiences, and partly because a reaction had at last set in against the romantic excesses of the stage. By the well-made play is meant simply a play in which the incidents are logically motivated, the characters reasonably lifelike, and the general impression one of plausibility. Scribe and his followers, by drawing upon the life around them, and depicting it in a manner that was recognizable, paved the way for a new and vital generation of dramatists.

It is important to bear in mind that Scribe's innovations were mainly technical. His themes were for the most part trivial, his characters feeble, his writing undistinguished. He contributed almost nothing to the literature of the drama; but his contributions to dramaturgy were of the greatest significance. It remained for Ibsen to use the new molds for the fashioning of masterworks that are unequaled in modern dramatic literature.

Ibsen was no mere journeyman playwright, no mere con-
triver of puppet shows or vehicles for popular actors. He combined an unrivaled mastery of stagecraft with poetic insight and
passionate convictions. He set out to do what Balzac, Dickens
and Tolstoi had succeeded in doing in the novel, but what had
never before been attempted in the drama—that is, to draw a
revealing portrait of contemporary society. The extent of Ibsen's
achievement may be measured by the fact that his plays, written
in Norwegian, a language known only to a few millions, and
dealing with the parochial life of a small and remote country,
were so faithful in their portrayal and so universal in their
implications that they captured the stages of Europe and America, excited the admiration and the anger of the literate world,
and inspired a whole army of disciples and imitators.

It is impossible to grasp fully today the effect Ibsen had upon
the theatre. He transformed it from an exhibition hall where un-
troubled people went for an evening's diversion, or occasionally
edification, into an arena and a forum where startled and outraged spectators were exposed to revelations of the society of
which they were a part—revelations whose relentlessness often
led to unwelcome self-recognition. For Ibsen, like Dickens, was
a keen social critic, who vehemently expressed his indignation
and scorn in his work. In his "anti-idealistic" plays (as Bernard
Shaw, one of Ibsen's earliest champions, calls them in his brilliant *Quintessence of Ibsenism*) he mercilessly attacked the new
bourgeois society that was contentedly basking in the luxurious
warmth of the new economic order. Hacking away at the façade
of complacency, self-righteousness and moral smugness, he revealed the rottenness of its foundations and the cruelty, dishonesty, hypocrisy and secret vice that it masked.

No wonder he threw the theatre into a state of uproar. His
adherents acclaimed him as an emancipator, a bringer of light, a
literary giant of the first category. His adversaries, with even
greater fervor, damned him as a sensation-monger, a meretricious journalist, a purveyor of filth. But though it was pos-

sible to denounce him, it was not possible to ignore him. The battle raged on, in private and in public, and the theatre took on a liveliness and a contemporaneity such as it had not known in a hundred years. The plays were banned by the censors or closed by the police, or else they were performed to the cheers or jeers of impassioned audiences. The Ibsen controversy has by no means abated, though today, of course, it is conducted in a much lower key. There are those who still rank his plays as undying classics. Others concede the importance of his place in the theatre, but incline to regard his plays as outdated and of historic interest only. Still others, who like to think of the theatre as a place of sheer make-believe, deplore the invasion of Ibsenism, and sigh for the gilded age of romanticism.

Ibsen lived on into the twentieth century; by the time he died there was hardly a major European country that had not made notable contributions to the drama. In fact, there is no other period in the entire history of the drama which has produced a body of dramatic literature that is so variegated in style and theme and so widespread in its origins. The Western European drama of the nineteenth century may never quite reach the heights attained by the Greeks and the Elizabethans, but it surpasses them in range and variety. The roster of playwrights is imposing indeed. It includes, in Scandinavia (besides Ibsen), Strindberg and Björnson; in Germany, Hauptmann, Sudermann and Wedekind; in Austria, Schnitzler and von Hofmannsthal; in Italy, Giacosa, Benelli, D'Annunzio and Pirandello; in France and Belgium, Becque, Rostand, Hervieu, Claudel, Brieux and Maeterlinck; in Spain, Benavente and Echegaray; in Ireland, Synge, Yeats and Dunsany; in Russia, Chekov, Gorki and Tolstoi; in England, Shaw, Wilde, Pinero, Jones, Granville-Barker, Barrie and Galsworthy.

Though all these dramatists were contemporaries of Ibsen, it would be a mistake to assume that they were all his disciples or even that they were all in sympathy with his philosophy and his methods. Many of them wrote poetical and symbolical plays in which the influence of Ibsen is not discernible at all, though they are written with a verve and a literary skill that was in refreshing contrast to the jejune tepidity of the works of the preceding era. If Ibsen had never lived it is quite probable that most of the writers I have named would have been creatively active. There are certain periods in history when the shape of society and of contemporary events seems to stimulate the production of works of art and significant artists spring up simultaneously everywhere. The Renaissance was such a time for all the arts, and so to a lesser extent was the revolutionary nineteenth century, particularly in music, literature and the drama.

But allowing for such notable exceptions as Yeats, Claudel, Rostand, von Hofmannsthal, Maeterlinck and D'Annunzio, the dramatists of the period were primarily occupied in depicting and analyzing the world they lived in and the characters that inhabited it. Realism was dominant, and the stage was given over more and more to the "problem" play—once a challenging and laudatory epithet, but used nowadays mostly in a derogatory sense. The new social order, as we have seen, brought with it many new conditions and altered many old relationships, and it was to the examination and exposure of these that the new dramatists addressed themselves. Hardly a phase of social or personal life was unexplored, and subjects that had never before been discussed in public (hardly in private even) now were openly aired upon the stage, to the accompaniment of angry cries of protest and sometimes of actual suppression. Not only Ibsen, but Shaw, Hauptmann, Brieux, Galsworthy, Schnitzler, Gorki, Wedekind, Becque, Granville-Barker and many others dealt with such matters as political and judicial corruption, prostitution, the subjection of women, the perils of adolescence, anti-Semitism, the conflict between capital and labor, commercial knavery, marital infidelity, the ruthlessness of the criminal law, venereal disease, economic injustice, the double standard of morality, the warmongering of munition makers, religious hypocrisy and intolerance, the evils of slum life, and fifty other related themes. For the first time man was shown as a social animal, and social forces, rather than gods or dynasts, as the masters of his fate. Sometimes the dramatists were prophetic. Chekov's penetrating portrayal of Russia's decadent and futile upper classes clearly foreshadowed the revolution—the felling of the cherry trees—that was to occur only a decade or so after his death; and Strindberg and others anticipated the psychological theories of Freud. It is undoubtedly true that many of these plays are outdated, partly because of ever-changing beliefs and social conditions, partly because the characters in the plays were too often subordinated to the topical theme. But most plays date quickly and the fraction that survives even one generation is small indeed. The theatre goes on, however, and the degree to which it was influenced or modified by a given play or group of plays cannot be measured by a latter-day evaluation of the merit of the plays.

The revitalization of the drama and the introduction of realism, later called naturalism, into the theatre necessitated radical changes, not only in dramatic technique, but in the purely theatrical techniques of acting, stage direction and even scene designing. The dramatic realist sought to create the illusion that the events portrayed were actually happening in the presence of the spectator, who became, in effect, an unobserved eavesdropper, looking into a room through "the invisible fourth wall," and listening to a discussion of the personal problems of its occupants. To achieve this the dramatist had to make his characters speak and conduct themselves as they credibly might have if they had been really involved in the situations they enacted. This demanded the elimination of arbitrary and mechanical behavior and rhetorical speech, and the invention of plausible motivation and a logical sequence of events, as well as of dialogue that was appropriate to the characters and relevant to the immediate happenings.

Here a note on the technique of realism seems appropriate. Many theatregoers, including a number of dramatic critics, have always taken the view that the dramatist who attempts to reproduce contemporary life upon the stage is not an artist at all, but merely a sort of journalist, who reports what he sees and hears. Some even go so far as to say that anyone who roves about with a camera and a notebook can turn out a realistic play by the simple process of casting his recordings into a dramatic mold. Nothing could be wider of the mark, and I suggest to anybody who holds this belief that he try it out. He will soon find out that a literal and faithful reproduction upon the stage of even the most hair-raising events or emotional interchanges will appear confused, formless and ineffectual. Realism at its best rejects literalism entirely and seeks to express the *essential* truth of a situation by a process of perceptive selectivity and artful arrangement. It is not reality, but the illusion of reality that the realistic dramatist attempts to depict, and the inspired use of a significant phrase may be more revealing than pages of transcribed stenographic notes. This is clearly exemplified in the plays of Chekov. The seemingly casual and rambling conversation of his characters has a cumulative effect, and in the end we are aware of a searching exploration of their minds, hearts and souls and of an understanding of their relationships to each other and to the world they live in. There can be no doubt that realism has established its hold upon the modern drama at the expense of poetry and fantasy, and that this is to be deplored. A counter-tendency may be in process and it is to be hoped that it will develop; but that does not alter the fact that the writing of a meaningful realistic play demands a high degree of dramaturgic skill.

Oddly enough, the technique of realism is sometimes strikingly similar to the dramaturgy of the Greeks, in spite of the great differences in theme and outlook. In Ibsen's *Ghosts*, for example, the single setting, the small cast of characters and the brief time span are closely in accord with Aristotle's concept of the dramatic "unities." More significant, though, is the fact that the play deals chiefly with the revelation and consequences of antecedent events rather than with immediate happenings. The same may be said of Eugene O'Neill's *Long Day's Journey into Night.*

Of course the new style in the writing of plays required new styles for their communication. Established methods for projecting romantic and artificial plays were obviously inappropriate, and new ones had to be devised. Stage scenery had to undergo radical changes in order to play its part in creating the illusion of reality. Open "wings" through which the actors made their entrances and exits almost at random, and freely painted backdrops, vaguely suggestive of the locale of the action, could not suffice as settings for scenes that were supposed to take place in a cellar, a business office, a restaurant or a courtroom. To lend a lifelike atmosphere to these interior scenes, the enclosed or "box" setting replaced the open set, which is still used in opera and musical comedy when realistic effects are not called for. This new kind of setting, consisting usually of three walls, equipped with the doors, windows, fireplaces and so on essential to the action, was well suited to the proscenium or "picture-frame" type of stage, with the proscenium outlining the invisible fourth wall. The furnishings, too, became increasingly important, for they gave clues to the status and occupations of the characters; and the rising curtain often created the atmosphere and hinted at the quality of the play before a single line was spoken. There was also a new emphasis upon stage properties, which were used only sparingly in nonrealistic plays. (In Shakespeare's plays, stage properties, except for weapons and musical instruments, were hardly used at all.) But the realists employed properties not only for atmospheric effects but for actual dramatic purposes. Ibsen attached great importance to the use of properties, a use that sometimes amounted to symbolism: the letter in *A Doll's House*, the pistols in *Hedda Gabler*, the wild duck in the play of that name.

Prevailing styles of acting had to be greatly modified too. Colloquial prose speech cannot be read in the same way as florid blank verse or forensic rhetoric. Elocutionary vocal effects and exaggerated and stylized gestures are incongruous in plays that are intended to suggest everyday human speech and behavior. The action had to suit the word, and actors had to base their performances upon observation of their fellow humans rather than upon an acquaintance with the traditions of stage performance. The increasing use of accents and local dialects, the importance that the plays often placed upon physical traits or racial characteristics or occupational and social distinctions, introduced new emphases and new concepts into the portrayal of stage personages, to which the actors had to learn to adapt themselves. In general it may be said that the play, which for so long had been an instrument for the display of the actor's talents, had now become a commentary upon life, to the exposition of which the actor lent his talents. This does not mean, of course, that the importance of the actor was diminished. On the contrary, the interpretation of the new plays often called for even greater histrionic skill.

Now that the actor could no longer come down to the footlights and deliver a long monologue, the stage director, too, had to exercise his ingenuity in finding ways that would create an impression of naturalness without impairing the effect of what the actors did and said. To accomplish this, he had to devise, particularly in ensemble scenes, a pattern of stage movement that was aesthetically pleasing and appropriate to the dramatic action, and yet at the same time kept the focus where it belonged. Here again a distinction must be made between reality and the illusion of reality. All stage movement, no matter how photographically faithful to actual behavior it may seem, is necessarily stylized and arbitrary. For one thing, in order to be visible and audible in a proscenium theatre, the actor must always stand where he can be seen from every seat in the house, and must almost invariably face the audience when he is speaking. Also he must avoid obscuring from view a fellow actor who is speaking or engaged in some important piece of stage business—avoid, in fact, doing anything that would distract attention from whoever is speaking. He must enter and leave the scene at precisely the right moment; he must not falter in his speech or make any abrupt or awkward movement unrelated to the action, and so on ad infinitum. In other words, in a well-directed play, everything that is said or done is carefully planned and rehearsed with an eye to maximum dramatic effectiveness. It is only the amateur playwright, actor or director who thinks that realism means a slavish imitation of life.

All in all, the new dramatic movement overran and almost completely revolutionized the theatre of the West in a period of less than fifty years. *The League of Youth,* Ibsen's first attempt at realism, was written in 1869. By the outbreak of World War I, Ibsen was dead, as were Chekov, Strindberg, Synge, Tolstoi and Wilde, while most of the other important dramatists of the period had either reached or passed their prime. They had their successors, of course, and many able ones, but none, I think, who ever equaled the best work of Ibsen, Shaw, Chekov and Synge.

It is now time to turn our attention to the United States, which also had its astonishing dramatic awakening. But unlike the European movement, which had passed its zenith at the beginning of the war, the American movement did not begin until the war's end.

XI THE AMERICAN DRAMA
COMES OF AGE

The brilliant dramatic renaissance in Europe coincided with the bewilderingly rapid expansion of the theatre in America and the birth and vigorous development of a native American drama. But as we have seen, the American drama in this period was, in terms of quality, far inferior to the other literary arts and likewise to the contemporary European drama. In fact, exactly half a century separates the production of Ibsen's first realistic play, *The League of Youth*, in 1869, from the production of Eugene O'Neill's *Beyond the Horizon*, in 1919.

What accounts for the long delay? Why, when all Europe was astir with the creation of mature, subtle and significant drama, was the American product still relatively adolescent, crude and trivial? Why did it take fifty years for the American drama to reach a comparable level? These questions, which cannot fail to be of interest to any serious student of the theatre, are easier to ask than to answer. Any answer must necessarily be largely hypothetical and conjectural, for it entails the consideration of social, economic, cultural and psychological factors which are hard to evaluate. All I can hope to do is offer my own interpretation for whatever it may be worth.

By the end of the nineteenth century the United States, as a result of territorial expansion and industrial development, had become rich, economically self-sustaining and increasingly important in world trade. But all sociological factors do not progress at the same rate. Politically America still played a minor role in the world order; culturally it was still to a large extent provincially linked to the countries of the Old World, particularly England. This state of affairs is of course quite typical of new, pioneer countries, where all available energies and resources must be devoted to the taming of the land and the provision of security and the means of livelihood. Political sophistication and influence and indigenous culture appear later, as concomitants of a stabilized society.

On the cultural side, it was inevitable that the early American patterns, particularly in the literary arts, should be English. In spite of its polyglot origins, the American civilization was always predominantly English in character, and from the very beginning English was the established language. In the colonial era there was no native literature worth talking about. Conditions were not favorable to its production, and with the literary riches of the mother country to draw upon there was really no demand or need for it.

With independence and the growth of national self-consciousness, an American literary movement began slowly to emerge, and though English books (often in unauthorized editions) were still widely read, a growing number of novelists, poets and essayists, whose work had a distinctively American flavor claimed the attention of the growing number of literate Americans. But for the first three-quarters of the nineteenth century there was no corresponding development in the drama, and when a vigorous native drama did begin to make its appearance it was relatively inferior in quality.

The explanation for this difference is not, I think, far to seek.

The novelist or poet worked in seclusion, hopeful that he would find a publisher, but not oppressively conscious of the exigencies of the publishing business. The dramatist, on the other hand, could never forget that he had to depend upon the theatre for the communication of his work—a theatre that was primarily a commercial enterprise. A high-minded publisher, or perhaps one who was willing to pay a certain price for added prestige, might be willing to undertake the publication of a book that offered no prospect of large sales. Melville, Thoreau or Whitman might have only a few thousand readers, but those readers constituted an intellectual elite whose influence could not be statistically measured. Besides, the favorable reception of a book is often a cumulative process, extending over a period of years.

The theatrical situation was almost wholly dissimilar. Even in the nineteenth century, the difference in cost between publishing a book and producing a play was enormous. Further, the publisher's expense after the book comes off the press is trivial, while the producer, in order to keep the play alive, must continuously incur very heavy operating expenses, as must the theatre owner. Immediate and widely popular success is essential if the play producer is to avoid disastrous losses. To recoup his investment he must count upon an audience of many thousands. Therefore, his choice of plays to be produced is determined by his judgment of their potential popularity. This state of things does not make for the choice of plays of great depth or literary value. Most readers pretend, at least, to an interest in literature; most playgoers do not.

In nineteenth-century America the theatregoer who had learned that recognition of culture is one of the attributes of a civilized man could be persuaded to pay his respects to Shakespeare, who, as everybody knew, was a famous author and therefore a source of edification if not of actual enjoyment. The same could be said for certain plays that had established themselves in the capitals of Europe. If London, Paris or Vienna applauded, New York, or even Chicago or Denver, took notice. This was particularly true when, as was so often the case, a popular actor appeared in the play. Thanks to their European reputations, augmented by the talents of such famous stars as Richard Mansfield, Alla Nazimova, Ethel Barrymore, Maude Adams and Minnie Maddern Fiske, the plays of Pinero, Jones, Barrie, Rostand, Ibsen and Shaw were often highly successful. Undoubtedly there were many in the audience who appreciated the intrinsic merit of the plays, but I suspect that they were in the minority.

The American dramatist, however, without benefit of European reputation, was strictly on his own. If he wanted his play produced he could not ignore the tastes and prejudices of the mass audience to whom the producer catered. If what he wrote troubled the waters or outraged the sensibilities and invaded the reticences of the respectable citizens who constituted the bulk of theatregoers, or placed too great a burden upon their capacity to understand, he could hardly expect anyone to run the financial risk of a production. Of course in Europe, the plays of Ibsen, Shaw, Schnitzler and other dramatists often ran afoul of these difficulties, but in a rather different ambiance. Further, the poet, the iconoclast, the man of ideas who attempts to write plays often cannot master the exacting technique of stagecraft, and he fails where the craftsman of limited insight or inferior mental stature succeeds.

In fact, on the technical side the American drama, in many respects, kept pace with the European. The principles of realism and the characteristics of the well-made play were quickly assimilated and adapted by American playwrights. Many of the plays of the period were admirably constructed and had all the outward appearances of serious realistic drama. But the resemblances were mostly superficial: clever external theatrical devices to disguise conventional plots, trite situations and thin characterizations. In the words of Pooh-Bah, they were: "corroborative details to lend an air of artistic verisimilitude to an otherwise bald and unconvincing narrative."

By the beginning of the twentieth century the cultural picture had undergone great changes indeed, brought about as usual by changes in the economic and social situation. The last frontier had vanished; steel rails spanned the continent; everywhere gushers spouted, dynamos spun and factory stacks polluted the air. The shirt-sleeves-and-overalls era was coming to an end. Coupon-clipping shears had supplanted the pick and shovel, and a mahogany desk equipped with a row of telephones and a panel of push buttons had replaced the covered wagon as a symbol of progress.

In the three hundred years that had elapsed since the landings at Jamestown and at Plymouth, the only group even faintly resembling a leisure class was the slave-owning aristocracy of the South, and it had been wiped out by the emancipation of the slaves and the casualties of the Civil War. The postwar years had been all boom, bustle and business. Now, however, people began to sit down for a minute or two; some even began to look around. Not the primary industrialists, who could not get themselves unwound and insisted upon dying with their boots on, but the second generation, which showed an increasing tendency to ease up and to harvest some of the fruits their fathers had cultivated. The members of the third generation were still farther removed from their source of sustenance and even slightly disdainful of it. Even when they continued an active participation in the vast enterprises that their forebears had erected they found that it was possible to delegate most of the legwork and most of the headwork to well-trained and well-paid subordinates.

It is not surprising that culture became fashionable. More and more students sought a degree at Oxford, Heidelberg or the Sorbonne; more and more honeymooners made the grand tour; more and more stockholders went to London, Paris and Rome on shopping, drinking and love-making expeditions. Many of these excursionists visited art galleries, opera houses and theatres and were impressed by what they saw and heard. Many came back with an altered perspective and a new sense of values. Some of them—as well as many who had stayed at home—felt promptings to devote themselves to the arts, either as a career or as an avocation. In 1913, the great Armory show made modern painting vivid for the first time to thousands of Americans; the visits a few years later of the Diaghilev Ballet and of Granville-Barker's company did the same for modern music and the theatre arts.

Greenwich Village in New York became an American Quartier Latin or Chelsea, a gathering place of painters, writers and embryo theatre workers. The whole process is neatly described in an entertaining story by Thyra Samter Winslow, called *A Cycle of Manhattan*. She tells of the arrival in New York, in the nineteenth century, of an immigrant couple from Russia. They are almost penniless, and the only lodging they can afford is a two-room apartment over a stable in MacDougal Street. But they soon begin to prosper and move to progressively better and better quarters, the East Side Ghetto, the Bronx and so on. By the time their son marries he is able to live in affluence on Riverside Drive. Wealth increases, and the son in the third generation is encouraged in his ambition to become an artist. Of course he must have a studio, and he finds a rather expensive one: the rooms his grandparents occupied when they landed in America.

The growing belief that in the mad scramble for material prosperity cultural values had been ignored, and that not only the state of the arts in America but the theretofore unquestioned standards and codes of the pioneer society were badly in need of examination and reappraisal, found explosive expression in Sinclair Lewis' novels, *Main Street*, published in 1920, and *Babbitt*, published in 1922. These attacks upon American provincialism and upon the mores of a society dominated by commercialism were widely acclaimed and have indeed become literary classics. Their very titles have been incorporated into the language as synonyms for the dull conventionality of small-town life and the semibarbarism of the American business mentality. Also in 1922 there appeared a most extraordinary book, under the editorship of Harold Stearns, entitled *Civilization in the United States*, in which some thirty leading specialists and critics (including H. L. Mencken and George Jean Nathan) examined every aspect of American culture and came to the conclusion that "the most amusing and pathetic fact in the social life of America today is its emotional and aesthetic starvation." I doubt if another example can be found in all history of a group of eminent intellectuals putting the civilization of which they were a part into the dock and bringing in a unanimous verdict of guilty.

This widespread self-criticism and dissatisfaction with the state of the national culture created a demand for works of art that not only questioned and challenged the existing order of things but that spoke a new language and employed fresh techniques. Where formerly there had been only scattered readers of heretical and avant-garde novels and unconventional verse, there was now a sizable and growing audience that was potentially receptive to theatrical innovations and to a drama that bore a closer resemblance to the facts of life. To borrow a political slogan, it was time for a change, and the change came swiftly and, if I may so, dramatically.

Two other important factors contributed to the change, one directly, the other indirectly. The first was the growing popularity of motion pictures and the consequent development of the motion-picture industry. Later I shall discuss the economic effects of this development upon the theatre, but here I want only to point out its artistic effects. The motion picture, regarded in its early days as little more than an amusing novelty, had rapidly gained favor as a form of popular entertainment. Productions became more and more elaborate, stars were developed, movie palaces began to spring up all over the country. By the second decade of the twentieth century the movies were actively competing with the drama for the public's attention and the public's dollar.

At first motion pictures were created by a process that might almost be called improvisation, the director and actors beginning with a general story idea and devising situations and actions as they went along. If a writer was employed he did little more than supply a loose outline or central narrative thread. But after a time it occurred to the producers that it might be advisable to supplement violent physical action, exaggerated histrionics and knockabout comedy with an organized dramatic structure and a plot that at least approximated plausibility. This necessitated the employment of writers, and for the first time the writer became a considerable factor in the production of motion pictures. Since the same principles of dramaturgy apply to all forms of the dramatic art, it was inevitable that Hollywood producers should turn to the writers who had demonstrated their skill in the Broadway theatre. Many of these dramatists, tempted by the monetary rewards or fascinated by what they regarded as the potentialities of the new medium, transferred their activities from the stage to the screen. With the introduction of talking pictures in 1927, the need for authors who could write dialogue was so urgent that almost every playwright was invited to work in Hollywood.

But a sharp cleavage now began to develop between stage and screen. An increasingly large section of theatregoers was developing more sophisticated tastes, and the bald melodramas, simple-minded farce-comedies and treacly romances that had occupied the stage for so long now seemed outmoded and artistically unsatisfying. However, this was exactly the sort of fare that was ideally suited to the movies, which catered to a mass audience composed largely of adolescents and children. Consequently the movies siphoned off from the theatre that part of the audience whose preference was for the trite, the obvious and the conventional, making possible the development of a more adult drama. (By the same process, the astonishing efflorescence of television drama aimed primarily at an undiscriminating mass audience has resulted in a shrinkage of the motion-picture audience and a greater willingness on the part of Hollywood producers to deal seriously with themes that have heretofore been taboo.)

The other important factor to which I referred was American participation in World War I. Here was another and even more stunning blow to American self-complacency. The old concept of a sanguine and peace-loving country minding its own business and cultivating its own garden in a wide, rich land, securely sheltered by two vast expanses of ocean, was no longer tenable. The whole world was in a state of upheaval and a startled and unprepared America suddenly had a sword thrust into its hand and found itself cast in the role of the savior of humanity—a boy sent to do a man's work! Old behavior patterns and prejudices had to be discarded; new responsibilities and attitudes had to be assumed; growing pains, headaches and heartaches had to be endured. America, suddenly conscious of its vital individuality and its high rank in the global hierarchy, swelled with justifiable pride and with a new sense of power. History affords ample evidence that at such moments in a nation's career the national genius finds expression not only in vigorous action, but in the arts. The time was already ripe for the assertion of American creativity; the war accelerated the process.

The war had another effect, too, on the theatre. For decades the stage had depended largely upon English, French, German, Austrian and Hungarian plays and operettas. Now the supply was greatly diminished as established European authors were drawn into this or that form of war work, and the younger generation was being mowed down by machine-gun fire. No one will ever know how many potentially great writers were slaughtered in Flanders fields, at Gallipoli or before Verdun. The depletion of artistic genius is by no means the least of the casualties of war. America came late into the war, and its manhood losses were relatively small. The exceptional prominence of the postwar American drama is certainly partly attributable to the decimation of European youth.

It is sometimes convenient to identify a general tendency with a single individual and the beginning of an era with a specific event. It may therefore be said that the American drama came of age in the season of 1919-20, with the production in a Broadway theatre of *Beyond the Horizon,* by Eugene O'Neill, who was to be awarded the Nobel Prize and four Pulitzer Prizes (one posthumously), and whose arresting and powerful plays, known wherever the drama is enacted or studied, have been largely instrumental in winning for the American drama a foremost place in the world theatre.

Several of O'Neill's one-act plays had been previously produced by various nonprofessional groups, and other members of the new generation of dramatists were already at work. But the production of *Beyond the Horizon* was that generation's first invasion of the commercial professional theatre. During the next two decades (and in a diminishing degree during the succeeding decades too) there was an influx of new writers and new ideas that vitalized and enlivened the American theatre and gave it a very characteristic flavor of its own.

Since I was quite active in the theatre during this period and am more or less associated with what went on, it would be highly inappropriate for me to attempt to pass judgment upon the significance or the importance of the movement or to evaluate the works of the dramatists who participated in it, particularly since I am personally acquainted with most of them and count many of them among my friends. I shall therefore confine myself to a description, based largely upon first hand knowledge, of the principal influences and tendencies.

On the technical side, the American drama had long since adopted the dramaturgical formulas of Ibsen, and the reign in the American theatre of the well-made realistic play was firmly established. But by 1920 divergences began to make themselves evident. In every art vigorous new movements, after sweeping everything before them, tend to become stabilized, and after a time are challenged by counter-movements. The very perfection of the realistic technique, with its insistence upon logic and objectivity, imposed severe limitations upon dramatists who wanted more elbow room and greater scope for the exercise of their imagination, and many of them preferred a looseness of structure and a stylization of speech that were formally more closely related to Shakespeare than to Ibsen. The greater fluidity of the motion picture had its effect too and made for a less rigid framework of time and locale. The "flashback," a device whereby a character's recollection or narration of past events is concretely enacted, was adopted by dramatists and successfully employed in many plays; it is still a very useful, though perhaps overworked, dramatic stratagem.

More penetrating was the effect of the bewildering and devastating happenings that were changing the face of the world. The ever-accelerating pace of industrialization and the holocaust of the war had, it seemed to many, dehumanized man and reduced him to the status of a replaceable cog in the industrial machine and an expendable unit in the war machine. A new word, robot, joined the English language, derived from a play called *R.U.R.*, written in 1921 by the Czech dramatist Karel Capek. This concept of man as a social mechanism helplessly caught in the toils of forces beyond his understanding was to find its way, in one form or another, into many postwar American plays.

But most revolutionary of all was the influence of the Freudian psychology, the principles of which were by now widely discussed and widely accepted. Here, indeed, was another new and startling concept of man. Psychologically, too, it seemed he was in the grip of forces beyond his control or even his knowledge. His conscious thoughts and behavior, far from being the product of his judgment and free will, were compelled by fears, desires, anxieties, guilt feelings, repressions and experiential conditioning, usually below the level of consciousness and beyond the range of memory. What he appeared to be, or believed himself to be, was something very unlike the creature that lay hidden behind the cloak of outward demeanor, and that could be revealed only by profound subjective research.

Whatever one may think of the therapeutic practices that this theory has given rise to, there can be little doubt that Freud threw a new light upon human behavior, just as Marx did upon history, Darwin upon biology and Einstein upon physics. All these theories have radically altered man's thoughts and attitudes and have found reflection in all the arts, including the art of the drama. The Freudian influence has been perhaps the most potent of all, for it deals directly with human emotions, the indispensable raw material of all effective drama. In fact, Professor W. David Sievers in his *Freud on Broadway* (subtitled *A History of Psychoanalysis and the American Drama*), a volume of some five hundred pages, attempts to demonstrate that practically every play of any importance written in the United States in the twentieth century is dominated or affected by the Freudian psychology. I think that, like most people who set out to prove something, he goes a little too far, but there can be no doubt that his approach is sound and much of his evidence very convincing.

The upheavals and dislocations of the war, together with the new concepts of the mechanized man and the unconscious man, produced a new type of drama that has come to be generally known as expressionism. It arose simultaneously, shortly after the war, in several countries, principally Germany and the United States. It is often said that American expressionists were imitators of the German, but this is not the fact. As frequently happens when social and psychological conditions are similar, comparable artistic tendencies develop spontaneously in different places. The principal German expressionists were Kaiser, Toller and Hasenclever. In the United States the movement is exemplified by O'Neill's *The Hairy Ape*, Sophie Treadwell's *Machinal*, John Howard Lawson's *Roger Bloomer* and *Processional*, and my own *The Adding Machine* and *The Subway*. All these plays, as most of the titles indicate, dealt with man in the machine age, but all of them had a strong psychological content and depicted the inner lives of their characters in the light of the new psychology.

What is expressionism? Asked this question in 1923, when *The Adding Machine* was produced, I replied: "It attempts to go beyond mere representation and to arrive at interpretation. The author attempts not so much to depict events faithfully as to convey to the spectator what seems to be their inner significance. To achieve this end, the dramatist often finds it expedient to depart entirely from objective reality and to employ symbols, condensations and a dozen devices which to the conservative must seem arbitrarily fantastic."

Obviously, expressionism is the very antithesis of Ibsenism, and these plays puzzled, bored or outraged audiences long accustomed to the well-made realistic play. As far as I know, no expressionistic play ever achieved any substantial popular success and the movement (if it can be called that) was short-lived; but some of the plays are still performed by community and university theatres, and collectively they have had an important and lasting effect upon the techniques of the drama and of stage production.

It is worth noting that although expressionism is usually regarded as a postwar phenomenon, it was anticipated by Theodore Dreiser, whose *Plays of the Natural and Supernatural*, published in 1916, contains several one-act plays that employ the expressionistic technique. However, they present production difficulties that are almost insurmountable.

The emphasis placed by Freud on the sexual motivation of behavior prompted a searching re-examination of human character and relationships. The growing conviction that things are seldom what they seem, and that every little movement has a meaning of its own, resulted in an ever-widening search for concealed motives and suppressed desires. (*Suppressed De-*

sires was the title of an amusing satiric playlet by Susan Glaspell and George Cram Cook, produced in 1917.) Dream interpretation, one of the fundamentals of the psychoanalytic technique, became the avocation of amateurs and even, in advanced circles, a sort of parlor game. "Don't tell me what you dreamed last night," sang Franklin P. Adams, in his Conning Tower, "for I've been reading Freud." Dream symbolism was a fashionable subject of study, and when the puritanical clergyman in *Rain*, a dramatization of Somerset Maugham's short story *Miss Thompson*, observed that he had been dreaming of the rounded hills of Nebraska, the knowing smiles of the sophisticates out front indicated that the connotation was not lost upon them. The enormous success of *Rain* is unquestionably attributable to its skillful popularization of Freud's theories. Amazingly enough, Maugham, a brilliant and highly successful dramatist, saw no dramatic possibilities in his story and refused to make the adaptation himself.

The impact of the new psychology dispelled the reticences that had surrounded the treatment of sexual themes in the arts and destroyed the established conventions, particularly in the theatre. A whole new approach to sexual problems became apparent: bold, frank, unromantic. In the words of William Marion Reedy, it was "striking sex o'clock in America." Old standards of morality were re-examined and questioned. Unconventional sexual behavior was condoned and sometimes even justified. Premarital chastity and postmarital fidelity were no longer the indispensable attributes of stage heroines. Subjects to which even indirect allusions had been strictly taboo were now more and more freely discussed and analyzed: illegitimacy, rape, incest, miscegenation, homosexuality. Many of the resultant plays were merely meretricious pieces written in an attempt to cash in on the craving for sensationalism; but there were also many that dealt honestly and revealingly with material that was new to the drama. O'Neill's *Strange Interlude*, Glaspell's *The Verge*, Dreiser's *The Hand of the Potter*,

Lillian Hellman's *The Children's Hour* are but a few examples.

Parent-child relationships were also subjected to a through-going re-examination, and the dominant father and posses-sive mother began to appear as the villains of the new drama. In this category Sidney Howard's *The Silver Cord* has become archetypal. The title, drawn from Ecclesiastes, presumably refers to the umbilical cord, symbol of the tie that binds the child to the mother. In the years following the production of Howard's play there has been a seemingly end-less flood of plays that deal with the problems of the younger generation, in which, almost invariably, the misfortunes or maladjustments of youth are attributed to a plethora or by analogy, a dearth of parental love. Someone has said that the twentieth century is the century of the child, and if one may judge by the preoccupation of modern drama with the im-mature, it is a true saying.

But the new drama was by no means exclusively preoc-cupied with the sexual implications of Freudianism. American dramatists, like the Europeans of the preceding generation, began turning out plays that dealt vividly with a great va-riety of themes, some universal, some peculiarly American or even regional. The war, which was partly responsible for the dramatic upsurge, itself became the subject matter for another unending series of plays. There had always been war plays, of course, but now flag waving and cloak-and-sword melo-drama had been pretty much relegated to the movies. The teachings of Freud had made even martial heroism suspect, and the mounting horrors of warfare had awakened the social conscience. The new war plays (of which *What Price Glory?* by Maxwell Anderson and Laurence Stallings was one of the first and certainly one of the best) were either serious dramas portraying the evils of war, the shortcomings of the military hierarchy, or the psychological effect of combat upon the participants; or else they were farce-comedies dealing with the lighter side of military life and based upon the sound premise that the man in the ranks is preoccupied with longings for alcohol, pretty girls and the old homestead. Some of these plays, hackneyed though they are, are enlivened by authentic characterizations, pungent dialogue and theatrically effective situations. At any rate the public appetite for them is apparently insatiable.

Many plays had social or political motifs. A recurring theme in the plays of Robert E. Sherwood (who three times won the Pulitzer Prize for drama) is man's inner conflict between his selfish desires and his sense of social responsibility. Other plays dealt more specifically with topical themes. Two of Maxwell Anderson's plays, *Gods of the Lightning* and *Winterset*, were based upon the Sacco-Vanzetti case; Martin Flavin's *The Criminal Code* was concerned with prison reform; Sidney Kingsley's *Men in White* with the inner workings of a hospital; my own *Judgment Day* and *Flight to the West* with the menace of Hitlerism; Sidney Howard's *Yellow Jack* with the extermination of yellow fever (and probably the only play ever written whose villain is a mosquito.) The depression, which came only a dozen years after the end of the war and confronted the American people with a whole new set of economic and social problems, had as one of its by-products a whole crop of dramas of protest, many of them strongly flavored with the philosophy of Marxism. Thornton Wilder depicted the life of a small community in *Our Town*, and the life of the human race in *The Skin of Our Teeth*.

Another very important and strictly indigenous group of plays concerned itself with the depiction of Negro life and character. Heretofore, the Negro in the American drama had been little more than a stereotype: a conventionally subservient menial, a grotesque comic or a shiftless ne'er-do-well. But now there were serious attempts to portray the Negro as a credible human being and to deal honestly with the whole problem of race relations, previously a forbidden subject. Many of the resultant plays were merely feeble and ineffectual tracts, but some had considerable merit. Among those worthy of notice are O'Neill's *All God's Chillun Got Wings*, Paul Green's *In Abraham's Bosom*, Marc Connelly's tender and imaginative *The Green Pastures* and DuBose and Dorothy Heyward's *Porgy* (which, in its musical version by George Gershwin, known as *Porgy and Bess*, has become a world classic).

Another new note in the American drama was the satirization or "debunking" of economic or political institutions formerly regarded as more or less sacrosanct. A series of plays written by George S. Kaufman and various collaborators poked fun at the motion-picture industry, the song-writing business, the advertising business and big business in general. In a musical extravaganza entitled *Of Thee I Sing*, which ridiculed the American political campaign, nine performers, wearing the robes of justices of the United States Supreme Court, went through a dance routine.

Mention should be made, too, of the so-called "hard-boiled" play, a topical exercise (as the title usually indicates) written primarily as entertainment but often constructed with great skill and informed with shrewd observation and colorful speech. Random examples, all great popular successes, are *Broadway* by Philip Dunning and George Abbott, *The Front Page* by Ben Hecht and Charles MacArthur, and *The Racket by* Bartlett Cormack.

Something should be said also of the literary quality of the new drama, for many of the new writers exhibited a sense of style and a command of language almost completely lacking in the work of their forerunners. There is nothing in the prewar drama comparable to the witty and perceptive dialogue of S. N. Behrman, the eloquence of Maxwell Anderson's verse and the vivid rhetoric of Edwin Justus Mayer. And there is great distinction in the writing of Sherwood, Green, Wilder, Clifford Odets, William Saroyan, Tennessee Williams, and many others.

This rapid survey does not of course adequately describe

every phase of the postwar drama in America, nor even mention every dramatist who contributed to it. And we are still too close to it to gauge its merits or its durability. Certainly a great many of the plays have dated, and many others seem far less significant than they did when they were new. Nor can it be said that America has yet produced an Ibsen, a Chekov or a Shaw. But the popularity of American plays throughout the world—in Japan and Argentina as well as in all the countries of Europe—certainly indicates that they are not lacking in vitality and in universality. There can be no doubt that the American drama, which hardly existed before the latter part of the nineteenth century, and which lagged far behind at the beginning of World War I, has at last come into its own, and that collectively it need not fear comparison with the contemporary drama of any other country in the world.

The new American drama was of course influenced by the state of the American theatre, and influenced it in turn. The interrelationship is a complicated one, and it requires detailed examination, for paradoxically enough the expansion and invigoration of the drama have been paralleled by a shrinkage and enfeeblement of the institution of the theatre.

XII THE AUXILIARY THEATRE IN AMERICA

While it is true that the American theatre has been from its very beginnings a business enterprise, and that the dramatist has always had to depend for the production of his plays upon managers and theatre owners whose primary interest was commercial rather than artistic, this is not the whole story. For although professional Broadway play production, the nation-wide chains of theatres, and the local stock companies were always in the hands of businessmen, there have been in existence since the early years of the century, mainly in New York, various producing organizations that came into being for the purpose of furthering the art of the drama rather than for achieving commercial success. Most of these organizations had only brief careers, but collectively they have performed an inestimable service in introducing new dramatists and fostering new types of drama, in developing new methods of stagecraft, and chiefly in improving the standards of taste of the theatregoing public. An understanding of the nature and functioning of these groups is essential to the student of the American theatre, and I shall try, in this chapter, to describe the principal ones—except the Federal

Theatre Project, which rates a chapter of its own.

The groups varied greatly in composition, objectives and importance, and it is hard to find a generic descriptive term for them. The best I can think of is "auxiliary theatre," which is not altogether accurate, for some of the organizations operated within the framework of the commercial theatre. But it serves to indicate a differentation from standard theatrical procedures.

Some of the groups began, and ended, their careers before World War I, that is to say before the upsurge of the new American drama. The first was the New Theatre, a magnificent, block-long, modern playhouse erected in 1909 by a group of millionaires, many of whom were supporters of the Metropolitan Opera Company, and intended for the presentation of fine plays done in repertory by a permanent company. The New Theatre opened auspiciously, under the direction of Winthrop Ames, a wealthy New Englander and ardent theatre lover, who in later years made many notable productions in the Broadway theatre. A brilliant acting company was assembled, and a series of plays was presented that included revivals of Shakespeare and Sheridan and contemporary plays by Galsworthy, Pinero and Maeterlinck. (Unfortunately there were very few American plays that measured up to the theatre's standards.) The enterprise, however, was doomed almost from its beginning. The theatre was too large to provide the intimacy that most modern plays require; operating costs were prohibitive; the rather grandiose structure and the semicircle of sponsors' boxes, reminiscent of the Metropolitan Opera House's Golden Horseshoe, created an atmosphere of snobbism more appropriate to the plushier days of the nineteenth century. After two financially disastrous seasons the sponsors decided to call it quits, for even millionaires are sometimes swayed by monetary considerations. For some years the theatre, renamed the Century, housed various spectacles and itinerant ballet and opera companies. It was then demolished to make way for a large apartment house—a shocking waste of time and creative effort and a heavy blow to those who had had visions of an enduring organization that could bear comparison with the great repertory theatres of Europe.

On a far smaller scale, but far more in keeping with the times, were three other groups: the Provincetown Players, the Washington Square Players and the Neighborhood Playhouse. They were alike in that they were nonprofessional and noncommercial and were housed in theatres that seated less than 300. This is an oddity that requires explanation. In New York there are certain licensing, building and fire regulations that apply only to theatres with a seating capacity of 300 or more. This accounts for the erection of a number of theatres seating 299: the reduced operating cost compensates for the loss of revenue. Here again we see economic forces at work.

But in spite of the similarities mentioned, the Neighborhood Playhouse resembled the New Theatre in that it was endowed by two very wealthy young women, Alice and Irene Lewisohn, nieces of the banker-philanthropist Adolph Lewisohn, donor of New York's Lewisohn Stadium. This theatre, too, was handsome, and far better equipped than almost any theatre on Broadway. Unlike the New Theatre it was built on Grand Street, in the heart of New York's swarming Ghetto, and was presumably intended—all seats were priced at fifty cents—to bring the arts of the drama and of the theatre to the slum-dwellers. (However, on the opening night the entire audience was in evening dress; an elderly lady remarked to me: "It's a beautiful theatre, and what I like is that it attracts such a nice class of people.")

Nevertheless, the Neighborhood Playhouse, which opened in 1915 and carried on for some twelve years, offered much that was fresh and stimulating. At first the performers were all amateurs and the acting left much to be desired. Further,

Alice Lewisohn was an actress and Irene a dancer, and the material for the program was sometimes selected with an eye to giving them opportunities to perform. Later, however, professional actors of great ability were employed, and in general the plays presented were unconventional and of high quality. To the best of my knowledge, the Playhouse introduced Dunsany to America and also presented some of the lesser-known works of Shaw, then still a comparative stranger in the American theatre. Two of its most memorable productions were the Hindu classic, *The Little Clay Cart*, and *The Dybbuk*, a play drawn from Hebrew folklore. Also notable were a series of topical revues known as *The Grand Street Follies*, which were far above the Broadway product in wit and sophistication and helped to create a taste for a more adult type of musical show. They also introduced talented amateurs who later achieved success in the professional theatre. The weakness of the Neighborhood Playhouse was that it was entirely dependent upon its founders for its financing and its management; with their withdrawal its existence had to end. Surviving, however, is an excellent organization for professional training, the Neighborhood Playhouse School of the Theatre.

The Provincetown Players was a very different sort of organization. It consisted of a group of young New York artists and writers who spent their summers at Provincetown, on Cape Cod. Here they founded, in 1915, an amateur company known as the Wharf Theatre. Soon after, they acquired an old stable on MacDougal Street in New York and made it over into the Provincetown Playhouse, which is still in operation as an "off-Broadway" theatre. It was a most inadequate theatre: the benches were uncomfortable, the visibility and acoustics were poor, the stage facilities meagre. The acting, too, in the first years was often quite bad. But the Provincetown Players occupy an enduring and honorable place in the annals of the American theatre, if only because they were the first to produce the plays of Eugene O'Neill. They began with the early one-act sea plays, which paved the way for the production on Broadway of *Beyond the Horizon* and *Anna Christie*. But even after these successes O'Neill continued to find a home at the Provincetown for plays that, because of their subject matter or technical innovations, were considered unsuited to the commercial theatre. Nor were its productions confined to plays by O'Neill. Its programs, in pursuance of a consistent policy to provide a forum for new American dramatists, included plays (mostly one-acters) by Susan Glaspell, Wilbur Daniel Steele, Theodore Dreiser and Edna St. Vincent Millay. After a dozen years or so the Provincetown Players, too, had run their course. O'Neill was a recognized figure, and many of the original amateurs had become successful professionals. But during their lifetime, they had done much to widen the horizons of the American theatre.

The Washington Square Players was a group very similar to the Provincetown Players, composed too of young and aspiring Greenwich Village artists and writers. It was a loosely organized group which, under the auspices of the Socialist Press Club (as some English big wig observed, we were all Socialists in those days), had been putting on occasional programs of one-act plays in a rented hall. Now they embarked upon a more ambitious venture and in 1915, almost simultaneously with the inauguration of the Neighborhood Playhouse and the Provincetown, they took over a small East Side theatre called The Bandbox and established themselves as a going concern. They caught on almost immediately, for there was an audience that was ready for anything that was new and provocative. In my program album I find a note written in 1918 which is, I think, expressive of a general feeling about the Washington Square Players: "The little theatre movement was in its infancy, and though the plays themselves were not especially noteworthy, this first bill seemed a refreshing departure from the stale and pre-digested fare of the commercial theatre."

The programs were a strange but fascinating mélange of plays written, often for shock effect, by members of the organization, of unfamiliar works by Chekov, Andreyev and Maeterlinck, and of such relatively familiar ones as Ibsen's *Ghosts* and Wilde's *Salome*. Among the youthful actors who made their early appearances with the Washington Square Players were Katharine Cornell, Glenn Hunter and Roland Young. The Bandbox soon proved too small to meet the public demand, and a move was made to one of the lesser Broadway theatres. The organization, though still thinking of itself as a noncommercial and avant-garde group, now began to assume a professional character. But with the entry of the United States into the war, the man power of the group was so heavily reduced that it was forced to disband, after only two years' activity.

Probably the Washington Square Players would seem less significant were it not for the fact that they were the precursors of an organization whose importance in the American theatre is unmatched. In 1919, shortly after the end of the war, some of the members of the old organization, and a few newcomers, utilizing their earlier experiences and counting upon a renewal of popular interest, formed the Theatre Guild, which recently celebrated its fortieth birthday. Unlike the Washington Square Players, the Theatre Guild was from its inception a professional organization and devoted itself exclusively to the production of full-length plays. Youthful bohemianism and improvisation gave way to a more disciplined and businesslike approach to play production.

However, there were three important respects in which the Theatre Guild differed from the general run of commercial producers. In the first place, it was governed by a board of directors which included actors, designers, stage directors and authors, as well as business executives, so that the predominant influence in the management of the organization was artistic rather than financial. Secondly, and as a corollary of this unique setup, the Guild adopted and long adhered to the policy of producing only plays of originality or of high literary quality. Thirdly, it undertook to organize, for the the first time in the American theatre, a body of subscribers, similar in character to that of the Metropolitan Opera Company and the larger symphony orchestras.

The establishment of this subscription system was one of the most constructive steps ever taken by an American theatrical producer. It provided for a continuity of activity and also for a certain financial security. The subscriber had the benefits of reduced prices and choice seats and the satisfaction of seeing five or six plays each season that, whatever their defects, were fresh and out of the ordinary. The Guild for its part was not only able, but obligated, to undertake a long-range production schedule. Besides, the existence of an assured audience made possible the production of plays that offered little promise of commercial success. Presumably, too, the exposure of the permanent audience to a series of plays of superior quality had the effect of raising the level of taste and appreciation.

For several years the Theatre Guild, housed in the Garrick Theatre, an antiquated playhouse on the fringe of the theatrical district, led a precarious existence, producing many unusual and interesting plays that made no great appeal to the general theatregoing public, inured to run-of-the-mill melodramas and farce-comedies. It was kept going by its subscription system and by the willingness of its directorate to forego financial rewards. At first it produced only foreign plays, some by dramatists previously unknown in the United States; but as the new generation of American dramatists began to make itself heard, the Guild turned its attention to native plays as well. It was courageous enough to undertake the production of several expressionistic plays, European and American, which no Broadway manager would have dared attempt and which, sad to relate, the Theatre Guild itself would not attempt today.

After some years of struggle, two popular successes, St. John Ervine's *John Ferguson* and Sidney Howard's *They Knew What They Wanted*, put the Guild firmly on its feet, and it soon established itself as the foremost American producer of new and vital plays. Its productions were distinguished not only for the inherent quality of the plays, but for the excellence of the acting, stage direction and scenic investiture. As the Guild's prestige increased, its subscription list grew too. It acquired a sort of monopoly in the plays of Shaw and produced also many of O'Neill's most important plays, including such monumental works as *Strange Interlude* and *Mourning Becomes Electra*. Works by the European authors Werfel, Benavente and Molnár, and by the Americans, Howard, Behrman, Anderson and Sherwood also were produced.

Some seven or eight years after its beginnings at the Garrick, the Guild undertook to build its own theatre and actually succeeded in financing it by a public bond issue. The theatre was a costly and elaborate but, as it turned out, badly planned structure. At the opening ceremonies, Alexander Woollcott, looking around at the tapestries that ornamented the walls, shook his head and said: "The Gobelins will get you, if you don't watch out." It was a quip that unfortunately had in it a germ of truth. The Guild continued for many years to produce plays of quality and to maintain a high standard of acting and production. Also, it extended its subscription system to many cities, thereby providing much-needed support to touring companies, which were having a harder and harder time of it. But the Guild was no longer a struggling art theatre that could ask for concessions from actors, authors and directors and thus keep its costs within bounds. As an established Broadway producing organization with a large staff, it had to compete commercially with other producers and, as general costs began to mount, to trim its sails more and more to the chilling wind of economic necessity. Also, its zest for the original and daring was gradually tempered by the conservatism that so often comes with success and age. Thanks largely to the pioneering of the Guild, it must be said, there were now other producers who were willing to take a chance on an unconventional or unorthodox play. So, while the Guild continues to carry on and to retain many of its subscribers, its present activities are indistinguishable from those of many other producers of, sometimes, meritorious plays. Some years ago it was saved from extinction by the production of *Oklahoma!*, a work so ill-regarded that it took extraordinary effort to raise the money for its production. Recently the survival of the Guild has depended largely upon revenue from its radio and television programs. But its over-all record is a splendid one, and its contribution to the growth of the American theatre is enormous.

At one time in its career the Guild attempted to establish a permanent acting company and a modified repertory system, but it abandoned the experiment as too costly to operate and too complicated to administer. However, in 1926, a company called the Civic Repertory Theatre was organized by Eva Le Gallienne, a well-known actress and a woman of great vision and courage. She took over an old theatre in lower Manhattan and assembled a company of fine actors, who over a period of six seasons appeared in a repertory of notable plays. Her aim was not only to offer good plays, well produced, but to make them available to theatregoers of limited means, and the admission price was far below the Broadway scale. It was so far below, in fact, that even at capacity it was impossible for the theatre to pay its way, and she had to depend upon subsidies. The repertory included plays by Shakespeare, Moliére, Ibsen, Goldoni, Chekov and

Schnitzler, though the most popular were *Peter Pan* and *Camille*. As far as I know, only one American play was produced: Susan Glaspell's *Alison's House*. The theatre developed an enthusiastic audience of its own, and its enforced closing was indeed lamentable. But it had two inherent defects, which were bound to destroy it sooner or later. One was its complete identification with the personality of Eva Le Gallienne, who was manager, play reader, stage director and leading actress. The other was the theatre's dependence upon the bounty of well-wishers, a source of support that dried up with the deepening of the depression. Many theatregoers still gratefully remember the Civic Repertory Theatre, and perhaps it was the persistence of this reputation that encouraged Miss Le Gallienne, twenty years later, to make another try at repertory, this time in association with Margaret Webster and Cheryl Crawford. They managed to raise a fund of $300,000. But the company was topheavy, the costs excessive and the choice of plays unfortunate. In a few months the money was gone and the enterprise abandoned.

Several producing organizations were more or less directly associated with the depression. By far the most important was the Federal Theatre Project, which will be described in the next chapter. Another was the Theatre Union, which took over the theatre formerly occupied by the Civic Repertory Company and devoted itself to the production of plays of—to use the fashionable term of the period—"social significance." This group was composed of a number of politically minded persons, among them the playwrights George Sklar, Michael Blankfort, Albert Maltz, and Paul Peters, who were ardent believers in the use of the theatre for agitational purposes. Whatever the nature of its partisan affiliations may have been, there is no doubt that most of its productions reflected a left-wing philosophy. Numerous plays written by the author-members, usually in collaboration, were produced, all of which presented in an unfavorable light some aspect of the capitalist system. It was the belief of the directors of the Theatre Union that its productions would attract large numbers of industrial workers, whose disillusionment with capitalism had made them eager to adopt revolutionary ideas. This expectation proved illusory. Such patronage as the theatre had was drawn largely from intellectuals of the left, while those workers who had the price of admission continued to go to the movies. The only play in which the public showed any interest was *Stevedore*, by Peters and Sklar, which dealt with racial relationships in the labor movement. Because of general unemployment in the theatre, it was possible to engage actors and other theatre workers for almost nothing, so the Theatre Union was able to scrape along for a few seasons. When this situation was altered by improved economic conditions the organization was obliged to disband. Several of the authors associated with it went to Hollywood and became very successful screenwriters.

The Theatre Union was the best known of a large number of groups that, under such names as the Theatre of Action and Theatre Collective, were trying to use the stage as a forum for political propaganda. A good many professional theatre workers of considerable talent were associated with one or another of these groups, partly because it was the only form of theatrical activity they could find (prior to the setting up of the Federal Theatre Project) and partly because they had begun to question the validity of an economic system that had deprived them not only of their livelihood but of opportunities for the continuance of their professional careers.

Mention must be made, too, of one really remarkable theatrical production. In 1937, the International Ladies' Garment Workers Union, in the course of its many cultural activities, produced a revue called *Pins and Needles* in a small theatre in the Broadway area. It was an amateur enterprise, and nearly everybody who appeared in it was a working member of the union. Though it had decidedly political overtones and voiced the philosophy of trade unionism, it also had entertainment values that caught the popular fancy and it had a run of 1,108 performances! Meanwhile a second company was touring the country.

The Group Theatre, while it can hardly be said to have been an outgrowth of the depression, coincided with it chronologically, and was related to it also in the sense that many of its prominent members were associated with the radical movements of the time, and that in its general philosophy and choice of plays it was more or less a theatre of protest. I do not mean that the plays were primarily political, as were those produced by the Theatre Union, but merely that the activities of the Group Theatre were motivated by something more than an interest in play production.

The Group was an offshoot of the Theatre Guild. The triumvirate that controlled the policies of the Group during most of its career consisted of Harold Clurman, Cheryl Crawford and Lee Strassberg, who were associated with the Guild in various capacities. The Guild, as I have pointed out, no longer found it expedient to produce plays whose commercial prospects were dubious; but, still believing in the value of the unconventional and the experimental play, it agreed to sponsor "studio" productions by members of its staff. The first production was a Soviet play called *Red Rust*. Its reception was sufficiently favorable to encourage the prime movers to break away from the Guild and establish themselves as an independent producing unit under the name of the Group Theatre.

The Group's first independent production was *The House of Connelly*, by Paul Green, a play dealing with the decaying traditions of the old South—a theme that has certainly not been neglected by Southern novelists and playwrights. In the ten years of its existence it produced meritorious plays by Anderson, Saroyan, Kingsley, Robert Ardrey and Irwin Shaw. But it is remembered chiefly as the discoverer and original producer of the plays of Clifford Odets, a member of the Group's acting company. Beginning with the extraordinarily effective *Waiting for Lefty*, Odets wrote a series of plays that vividly interpreted the lives and struggles of the newcomers to America and of their immediate descendants. It cannot be doubted that he is an important contributor to the new American drama, and that the Group, in producing his plays, performed a valuable service.

Besides its continuing interest in presenting the works of new dramatists who might otherwise have had difficulty in getting a hearing, the Group had two noteworthy policies that differentiated it from commercial producers. The first was the establishment of a permanent acting company, along the lines of the European repertory theatres, though the Group never attempted repertory. The company worked together as a cohesive unit, studying and discussing the plays to be produced, and even having a voice in certain managerial decisions. As is always the case, this teamwork and continuity gave the Group and its productions a distinctive flavor and individuality that is necessarily lacking in units that are arbitrarily assembled for the production of a single play.

Second was the group's almost religious dedication to the Stanislavski system of acting, more familiarly known as the Method. The well-known books *An Actor Prepares* and *Building a Character*, in which the famous director of the Moscow Art Theatre enunciated his theories, became for the Group the tablets of the law, and all its production activities were aimed at a realization of Stanislavski's principles. I shall have more to say about the Method when I discuss the function of the actor in play production; here I shall merely quote one of the Group's directors who said that the aim of the Method "is to enable the actor to use himself more consciously as an instrument for the attainment of truth on the stage." Much has been written about the excellence of acting in the Group's productions. It is true that the performances had a kind of unity and ensemble quality lacking in most Broadway productions; but that is characteristic of any permanent company, regardless of "method." The fact is that many of the Group's best actors were already well established when they joined the organization and only a few of the neophytes ever rose above mediocrity. Actually, the Group was far more successful in providing training for stage directors than for actors, and among its graduates are such first-rate directors as Elia Kazan, Harold Clurman and Robert Lewis.

From its very beginnings the Group led a hand-to-mouth existence. None of its plays, including those of Odets, ever attained any great monetary success. It survived as long as it did because of the willingness of its members to make financial sacrifices for an organization in which they ardently believed (and also because some of its actors took leaves of absence in Hollywood and upon their return contributed part of their earnings to the company). After ten years of struggle, the Group finally gave up the ghost, to the regret of all those who value high ideals and originality in the theatre. But it could no longer carry on with one foot in the commercial theatre and one foot out. In the words of Harold Clurman: "The basic defect in our activity was that, while we tried to maintain a true theatre artistically, we proceeded economically on a show-business basis. Our means and our ends were in fundamental contradiction." It is remarkable that it existed for so long. Today, though the Group Theatre is only a memory, the Method lingers on in the Actors' Studio, a fashionable training school that has superseded the older and more conventional institutions of histrionic instruction.

A far less significant and enduring organization that called itself the New Playwrights' Theatre was formed in the late 1920's by a group of authors that included John Dos Passos, Em Jo Basshe, John Howard Lawson and Francis Faragoh. It was decidedly leftist—Alexander Woollcott impishly referred to its members as "the revolting playwrights"—and most of its plays had a political flavor. It attracted little attention and had no discernible influence, either upon the drama or upon the theatre. After two or three abortive seasons the organization was disbanded. I mention it here only because it was an unsuccessful attempt to do what was later accomplished by the Playwrights' Company, namely the establishment by a group of dramatists of a producing company designed for the presentation of plays written by its members.

As far as I know, there is, in the entire history of the theatre, no organization that resembles the Playwrights' Company. It was organized in 1937, by Sidney Howard, Maxwell Anderson, S. N. Behrman, Robert E. Sherwood and myself. The group had a certain homogeneity, in spite of the dissimilarities in the plays of its members. We were all about the same age; all had had considerable experience and substantial success in the theatre; all were concerned about the wastefulness and the limitations of the Broadway theatre; and all were deeply interested in the maintenance of high artistic standards of production. Further, we were all old friends or acquaintances.

For some years I had been producing my own plays; the other playwrights mentioned had been variously produced, principally by the Theatre Guild. But we all wanted to be part of an organization that had form and permanence and that promised a certain amount of security. We conceived of the Playwrights' Company as a sort of artisan's guild, a fellowship of craftsmen, joining forces for mutual assistance and for the common good. We accepted from the beginning the necessity of working within the framework of the commercial theatre; but we wanted complete control of our own plays and we hoped, too, that as a group we could reduce the hazards of the unit system of production. We estimated that five established playwrights would probably turn out an average of three plays a year, and that if one of the three succeeded the organization could go on paying it own way. We had no theory, revolutionary or otherwise, and no expectation of getting rich. Each man was to be in sole charge of the production of his own plays, but at the same time was to be able to avail himself of the criticism and advice of his colleagues. We hoped, too, to be able to finance our own productions without recourse to "angels," as play backers are incongruously called. To this end each playwright contributed one-tenth of the required capital. The remaining 50 per cent was obtained through the sale of nonvoting stock in the company; that is, the outside stockholders were entitled to participate in the profits, if any, but were to have no voice in the management.

The announcement of the formation of the company was received with universal skepticism. The oracles of Broadway confidently predicted that no federation of impractical and temperamental writers could long endure and that within six months we would be not only bankrupt but no longer on speaking terms with each other. Fortunately, these dire prognostications were erroneous. The company still endures, though under altered conditions, and never in its long existence has there been the slightest disharmony among its members.

However, at the very beginning it was touch and go. Our charter provided for the production of any play submitted by a member that did not call for a budget in excess of $25,000, then an adequate figure for the average play. (How times have changed!) Somewhat to our consternation, the first plays submitted were Sherwood's *Abe Lincoln in Illinois*, a play that required an exceptionally large cast and elaborate production, and—what we had not counted on at all—a musical comedy, *Knickerbocker Holiday*, written by Anderson in collaboration with Kurt Weill. But we decided to go ahead with both, a decision that entailed the expenditure of our entire working capital. If both plays had failed, the Broadway seers would have been right. Luckily both succeeded, and the company was able to go on.

It went on smoothly for another decade, thanks to such

box-office successes as *The Eve of St. Mark, No Time for Comedy, There Shall Be No Night,* and *Dream Girl.* But the profits were absorbed by losses on plays that obviously were not destined for commercial success, and by the expense of maintaining, in a seasonal business, a year-round permanent staff, an essential part of our policy.

In later years the staggering rise in production costs made it necessary for the company to depend upon outside financing. Also the resignation of Behrman and the deaths of Howard, Sherwood, Weill (who had joined the company later) and Maxwell Anderson reduced the playwright membership to myself and a newcomer, Robert Anderson. Obviously, these changes in personnel and in economic conditions necessitated changes in policy, particularly in respect to the production of nonmember plays, which sometimes are of rather dubious quality, but commercially promising. Nevertheless, I think it can be fairly said that the Playwrights' Company has established itself as one of the foremost producing organizations in the theatre, and that its twenty-year record of productions will bear comparison with that of any other producer. The intangible benefits that its playwright members have derived from a continuity of professional association with like-minded colleagues is beyond calculation. The whole venture is a unique experiment in the theatre and in my opinion a highly successful one.

Taken altogether, the various organizations I have described, all of which owe their origin to something besides mere business enterprise, have helped in various ways to modify the form and practices of the American theatre, to broaden the dramatist's channels of communication, and to develop a more discriminating and perceptive audience. All these groups, incidentally, operated in New York. Scattered throughout the country are numerous other groups that are concerned primarily with the art of the theatre (e.g., the Pasadena Community Playhouse, the Cleveland Playhouse, the Goodman Theatre in Chicago, various university theatres and so on);

but their influence has been mainly local and they have had little effect upon the theatre as a whole.

It should be pointed out that not one of the groups discussed ever achieved economic self-sufficiency except when it adapted the business methods of the commercial theatre. The New Theatre, the Neighborhood Playhouse and the Civic Repertory Theatre were dependent upon the bounty of wealthy sponsors; the Washington Square Players, the Provincetown Players, the Theatre Union and the Group Theatre, upon the willingness of their personnel to work for nothing or to accept wages far below the prevailing, or even the subsistence, level. The Theatre Guild and the Playwrights' Company have been able to maintain themselves only by virtue of (or by vice of) their adoption of the principles of show business. These patent facts are something for the student of the drama to ponder, for they bring into focus what is perhaps the thorniest problem that everywhere confronts the dramatist and the theatre worker today: what is the relationship of commercialism to art? Before we examine that question, however, we must complete our survey of the auxiliary theatre by looking at the Federal Theatre Project.

XIII THE FEDERAL THEATRE PROJECT

A book has been written about the Federal Theatre Project by Hallie Flanagan, who was its national director. It is a fascinating volume that should be read by everyone who is interested in the living theatre, for it describes the most ambitious attempt that has ever been made anywhere in the world to provide, on a nation-wide scale, theatrical fare of high quality at prices that anybody could afford. The achievements of the Project were remarkable; its abandonment was a tragedy for those whose hopes of creating a splendid national theatre were pinned upon it. As one who helped organize and operate the Project, I shall try to outline, within the limits of this chapter, its origins, structure and accomplishments.

The stock market crash of late 1929 was followed by the worst economic depression the United States has ever known. By the time Franklin D. Roosevelt assumed the Presidency in 1933 the state of affairs was catastrophic. Tens of millions of Americans had, through no fault of their own, lost their jobs, their homes and their savings. Many were living in colonies of improvised shacks known as Hoovervilles and queueing up for handouts on municipal bread lines. The Roosevelt administration, in an attempt to remedy this situation, inaugurated a vast program of public works that provided employment for millions,

148

and by 1935 conditions had begun to improve.

However, things were still very bad, and nowhere worse than in the theatre; for theatregoing is for most people a marginal activity, and one of the first to be dispensed with when the budget must be cut. All over the country theatre attendance had shrunk, hundreds of theatres had been forced to close their doors, and thousands of theatre workers were destitute. Men and women of high professional standing were reduced to the status of vagrants, unable to find employment and forced to eat the bitter bread of public or private charity.

At this time I was attempting, in association with a group of actors, designers and directors, to organize a co-operative non-profit repertory theatre. We needed a working capital of $100,-000, but after months of effort we had succeeded in raising only $7,000 and were about ready to give up. As a last measure I went to Washington, with the faint hope of persuading the Federal Emergency Relief Administration to underwrite what was, after all, a plan for putting people to work. My request was quickly refused, but Jacob Baker, to whom I had made it, asked me to have a talk with Harry L. Hopkins, then in command of the entire relief program.

Hopkins told me that both President Roosevelt and Mrs. Roosevelt were keenly aware of the plight of workers in the arts, particularly in the theatre, and wanted very much to find a way to help them, but though numerous individuals had been consulted, no one had yet submitted a plan that seemed workable. He asked me if I had anything to suggest. I replied that I had not given the problem any thought, because I had not known of the government's interest in it, but that I was sure of one thing, namely, that if a theatre project were to be created, it could not be based entirely upon New York, as was the commercial theatre, but would have to be organized on a regional basis. Hopkins replied that that was exactly what he wanted to hear and urged me to think about it and submit a plan to him.

I did think about it, and a few days after my return to New York I wrote Hopkins a long letter, which I take the liberty of reproducing here, substantially in full, not only because it was partly responsible for the establishment of the Federal Theatre Project, but because it describes my dream of a theatrical Utopia: a dream that will never be realized, but that I shall always go on dreaming.

Dear Mr. Hopkins:

I am going to set out here the broad outlines of a scheme which I believe to be both desirable and workable. As a premise, I am taking it for granted that any such program must be designed to meet the following requirements:

1. High standards of quality;
2. Low prices of admission;
3. Security and permanence of employment for workers in the arts;
4. Decentralization; and adaptation of regional projects to local community needs.

I propose the following plan of action:

1. The creation of a Governmental agency to buy or lease existing theatres, in 100 large communities throughout the country. These buildings are now dirty, frowsy, neglected. Put your unemployed architects to work (using local talent wherever possible) to remodel and modernize these theatres. Wire them for sound, put in cooling plants and comfortable seats, overhaul the stage machinery and the lighting systems, add a pleasant refreshment room and an exhibition hall suitable for shows of painting and sculpture, scrape off the gilt and the gingerbread. Put your unemployed artists to work freshening and redecorating the auditoriums, painting murals in the lobbies and rest rooms, designing curtains. This will entail the immediate employment of masons, carpenters, house painters, electricians, technicians and construction people of all sorts. In six months or a year, every large community in the country will have a bright, modern, comfortable community theatre, suitable for plays, music, motion pictures and art exhibitions.

2. Put into each of these theatres a permanent stock or repertory company, recruited mainly from the ranks of the unemployed, but

carefully selected on the basis of talent. As far as possible, get the thousands of out-of-town actors, who are now crowding the streets of New York, to return to their home communities, emphasizing the idea of using local talent. Wherever established and worthwhile community theatres already exist, use these as the nucleus for the community project. Use local unemployed musicians to form a small orchestra to play incidental and entr'acte music. Budget all your operating costs, including salaries, on the basis of a minimum season of forty weeks. On the basis of 100 communities, permanent employment would be provided for 2500 actors, 800 musicians and 5,000 theatre employees of all other categories. To this must be added part-time work for thousands of persons employed by scenic studios, manufacturers of costumes and properties, printers, advertising agencies and the like; and a living income for numerous playwrights and composers.

3. Create a rounded program of art activities to be handled, in each community, by someone with a thorough knowledge of the professional theatre and high standards of taste, working in consultation with the leaders of local schools and cultural organizations, for the aim should be to meet the needs and requirements of the community. But there should be no compromise with quality, and whether the play is a Shakespearean tragedy or a modern farce, it should rank high in its own category, and should be excellently acted and mounted. Every effort should be made to encourage local playwrights to draw upon the life around them and the rich folk material of America. Local artists should be permitted to exhibit their work; local soloists to give recitals. Educational and scientific motion pictures should be exhibited as well as pictures which, for one reason or another, are not shown in commercial theatres. (This may well result in the production of more adult pictures.) Plays for children and adolescents should be given at low prices, in the late afternoon and on Saturday morning. There should be lectures, debates, forums and symposia, dealing with drama, literature, painting and the other arts. For all performances, seats should be available at 25¢. In no case should the top price exceed $1.50; wherever possible, it should be $1.00.

4. In the larger communities, string quartets, small orchestras, small choruses and dance ensembles should be organized, which will

augment and supplement the dramatic program. Cycles of programs consisting of the vocal and instrumental works of such composers as Beethoven, Schubert, Mozart and Bach should be given, as well as programs of folk and popular music. Wherever regional music exists, it should be fostered and encouraged. For the smaller communities, musical units should be organized to make circuits of four or more cities in a particular region.

5.   In addition to the permanent acting companies, the old, visiting-star system should be revived. Many well-known actors would be delighted to have an opportunity to appear each year, in fifteen or twenty cities, in fine plays, under dignified auspices. And audiences would flock to see, at small cost, the finest actors of the day. To put the thing concretely: imagine such a community theatre in Omaha, in which one could see, for a dollar, John Barrymore in *Hamlet*, George M. Cohan *in Seven Keys to Baldpate*, Helen Hayes in *What Every Woman Knows*, Walter Huston in *Desire Under the Elms*, Edward G. Robinson in *The Racket* and Wallace Beery in *Shore Acres*. I am not suggesting the creation of jobs for Hollywood stars, but by utilizing the eagerness of these actors to be seen on the stage, it is possible at once to ensure the livelihood of thousands of less-known players and to bring the best that the theatre has to offer to drama-hungry communities which have had to be content with third-rate road companies, shoddy stock companies or puerile amateur groups.

6.   Although each theatre should be an independent community project, the entire program should be co-ordinated, on a national basis, by some agency which can act as a clearing house and by means of which standards may be established and duplication and waste avoided.

7.   I believe that, properly organized and administered, 20% of these theatres should be self-supporting within two years, and 50% to 75% within four or five years. By pooling revenues and expenditures in a central agency, the surplus in the self-sustaining enterprises would take care of the deficit in the others.

This does not pretend to be a bill of specifications. It represents a policy and an attack. As a general approach, I believe that it is sound artistically, economically and socially. If the Government will really get behind this project, and if it is done in the right way, it will be the greatest contribution to American culture that any Government has ever made.

And so indeed it would have been! The cost would have been substantial, of course. To inaugurate the program I outlined perhaps $100,000,000 would have been needed, and perhaps as much again to underwrite it until it became self-supporting. But it would not have been too high a price to pay for the establishment of a nation-wide organization dedicated to the popularization of the arts of the theatre. Compared to the hundreds of billions spent upon weapons of destruction, most of which become obsolete before they are even completed, the amount that would have been required for the theatre program is infinitesimal.

At any rate, those of us, all over the country, who were interested in getting some relief for the artists who were victims of the depression, were summoned to Washington for a conference with Hopkins and Mrs. Roosevelt. As a result of this meeting four projects were set up: Art, Music, Writing, Theatre. Hallie Flanagan, director of the Experimental Theatre at Vassar College, was selected as national head of the Theatre Project. A better choice could hardly have been made, for she is a woman of high ideals, great capacity for work, and a wide knowledge of the drama and of the theatre. I was asked to organize and direct the New York region of the Project. After some hesitation, I accepted; had I known what was ahead, I should probably have declined.

The task of launching the Art, Music and Writing Projects was relatively simple. Artists were put to work painting murals in post offices and other public buildings. Musicians were organized into ensembles of various sorts that gave concerts, usually free, in school buildings or outdoors when weather permitted. Writers were set to work on the composition of guidebooks, a job that really needed doing; eventually they turned out a series of informative and readable volumes, covering practically every state in the Union; some were subsequently issued by commercial publishing houses. All these activities could be undertaken with a minimum of organizational work, a small executive staff, and little expenditure for the materials or overhead.

The Theatre Project was in an entirely different category, as must be evident to any reader of the preceding chapters. To begin with, physical plants had to be made available: halls in which to rehearse plays and theatres in which to perform them; workshops for the manufacture and assemblage of scenery, costumes, properties and electrical equipment. Space also had to be provided for casting directors, play readers, designers, typists and publicists. And, of course, finding qualified specialists required an enormous expenditure of time and energy.

These organizational problems were aggravated by the financial limitations within which the Project had to work. The Projects came into existence primarily as a means of taking unemployed workers in the arts off the relief rolls and putting them to work. Consequently the amount allocated for executive personnel, and especially for materials, was only a small fraction of the total cost of the Project. Even when established theatre workers could be found, capable of handling the directorial and managerial jobs and willing to accept the nominal compensation provided, it was not easy to fit them into the rigid framework. And of course even the simplest theatrical production calls for a substantial expenditure for equipment and accessories. It took condiderable ingenuity to find ways of cutting costs and of doing without.

Even with the good will and co-operation of the ruling powers, it would have been hard enough to cope with these conditions; but the hostility and obstructionism of influential elements, both inside and outside the government, made the difficulties almost insurmountable. In the first place, in Congress, which was the source of appropriations, there were from the beginning many vociferous and persistent opponents of all the art projects. Some of these dissenters were motivated by considerations of economy; some by a suspicion that all the arts, but particularly the theatre, were allied to the machinations of Satan (or Stalin); but mostly they belonged to the anti-Roosevelt faction, to whom all manifestations of the New Deal or the "welfare state" were anathema. So the Projects, regardless of their purpose or achievements, were always used as a horrible example of the workings of the Rooseveltian philosophy. (As Philip Guedalla once said: "Any stigma to beat a dogma.")

Further, the Projects were set up under the authority of the Works Progress Administration and all organizational activities were governed by its regulations. Every expenditure had to be approved, which meant that every roll of canvas, electric lamp or false mustache had to be separately "requisitioned" by the directors of the Project and steered through the not always clear "channels" of the regional WPA office. Attempts to expedite procedures were not always successful, for a good many of the Works Progress Administrators (mostly businessmen who had been reluctantly drafted into the public service) were hostile to the principle underlying the Project or annoyed at having another burden added to their already heavy load.

Outside governmental circles the opposition was equally formidable. Wealthy and influential taxpayers did not attempt to conceal their dissatisfaction with the large-scale expenditure of public moneys for the support of vagabond players, most of whom were presumably Communists or they would not have been unemployed. Nor were they hard put to find space for expression of their complaints in the columns of the powerful anti-Roosevelt press, which lost no opportunity to denounce wastefulness, vote buying and what was quaintly called "boondoggling." But most painful of all, at least to me, was the opposition of many leaders of the professional theatre, who argued that the Project's performances at nominal prices were taking business away from them, shortsightedly refusing to see that the Project was making it possible for millions of young people to become interested in the theatre and thereby creating a vast audience for the coming decades.

Within the Project itself all sorts of political and emotional cross-currents were constantly in action. At various times, often simultaneously, I was charged with running a nonunion shop and with being dominated by the unions; with favoring Communists and with excluding them; with discrimination against Jews and Negroes. My devotion to the cause of civil liberties was quite generally known, but people with political axes to grind seldom bother about facts.

From the foregoing it might well be inferred that the Theatre Project was doomed to disastrous failure. But surprisingly enough, from an over-all point of view, it turned out to be a brilliant success, thanks to the soundness of its underlying principles and to the skill and devotion of hundreds of its workers. It was clear from the beginning that many of the things hoped for by its inaugurators could never be realized. No money was available and no authority existed for governmental acquisition and renovation of theatres—it took the utmost ingenuity on the part of the New York staff to get the use of any theatre whatever. Nor was it possible to break up the log-jam in New York and send people back to their own communities, where many of them had homes and friends, and where they could have participated in local activities of the Project. There was no money available for transportation; and had there been, the WPA regulations would have made it impossible to transfer relief "clients" from one jurisdiction to another. And so it went, right down the line, with this or that item in the theoretical program eliminated or curtailed by fiscal policies, governmental routines, and the usual administrative reluctance to break with tradition.

However, many of the objectives were attained. Foremost, from a humanitarian or social point of view, was the provision for some 10,000 unemployed theatre workers of opportunities for engaging in their professional activities and advancing their careers. In the New York region alone, in the course of three or four months, some 4,500 persons were put on the Project's payroll: about 60 per cent were actors, about 15 per cent technicians of various sorts, the rest playwrights, box-office employees, ushers, cleaners and so on. The effect upon the morale of most of these individuals, many of whom were rapidly succumbing to despair, cannot be overestimated. While the pay they received (the maximum was about twenty-four dollars per week) was barely above subsistence level, the restoration of their self-respect was beyond monetary appraisal. Many, many workers in the theatre today, some of the highest rank, remember with gratitude the help they received from the Federal Theatre Project when they most needed it.

But it is the theatrical record that concerns us here, and that is really extraordinary. In the first place, the regional scheme was strictly adhered to and by the time the Project was in full operation theatre units were performing in forty states. The able leaders of existing community theatres, from the North Carolina Playmakers to the Pasadena Community Theatre, were called upon to lend their experience and influence to the organization of regional units. Resident companies were established in large cities, touring companies in rural areas. A second main item in the program that was fully achieved was the presentation of good theatre at nominal prices (or without charge) to millions of Americans who either were unfamiliar with the theatre or could not afford to patronize commercial playhouses. According to Mrs. Flanagan, something like 63,000 performances were given by the Project in the three and one-half years of its active existence, and the total attendance was over 30,000,000. When admission was charged, prices ranged from twenty-five cents to one dollar; yet the total receipts were in excess of two million dollars.

It takes some fifty pages of Mrs. Flanagan's book to list the productions made by the Project. All I can hope to do here is to give some indication of the scope of its activities and to mention a few of its especially noteworthy enterprises. It organized companies that presented cycles of plays by Shakespeare, O'Neill, Shaw (including the première of *On the Rocks*), and a classical repertory that ranged from the Greeks to Molière and Sheridan. There were units that performed in German, Spanish and Yiddish. There were an Experimental Theatre; a unit for the production of new plays; a Gilbert and Sullivan unit (and a production called *The Swing Mikado*); companies offering contemporary American and European plays, including many old-time favorites; presentations of Paul Green's pageants dealing with colonial history which are still being successfully done every summer; plays and puppet shows for children; and a production of Christopher Marlowe's *Doctor Faustus* by Orson Welles, which resulted in the post-Project organization of the Mercury Theatre. (In the course of the many inquiries into the Project's "subversive" tendencies, one member of Congress asked suspiciously whether Marlowe was a Communist!)

Perhaps the most spectacular feat of the Project was the simultaneous opening in twenty-one theatres, in seventeen different states, of a dramatized version of Sinclair Lewis's anti-Fascist novel *It Can't Happen Here*. Eventually the nation-wide performances of this play totaled 260 weeks, the equivalent of a consecutive run of five years.

A few of the activities in the New York region deserve notice. Outstanding was a production of T. S. Eliot's *Murder in the Cathedral*, which I insisted upon doing against the advice of some of my associates who saw no appeal in the play. Brilliantly staged and acted, it filled a large Broadway theatre to capacity during the limited period for which I was able to obtain the rights. Another splendid production was *Macbeth*, acted by an all-Negro cast under the direction of Orson Welles and John Houseman. The setting was Martinique at the beginning of the nineteenth century, and among the interesting features of the presentation were the vivid costumes (homemade affairs that cost practically nothing) and the performance of voodoo rituals by the witches. There was also a charming puppet interpretation of *Pinocchio*, which originated in New York but eventually delighted large audiences of children throughout the country.

Finally, there was *The Living Newspaper*, an original and fascinating type of drama that arose out of the Project's interest in finding employment for jobless newspapermen. At first it was planned to present dramatizations of current news events, but it soon became evident that the news would be stale by the time the shows could be written and staged. It was then decided to use background material of a more or less topical nature, and scripts were prepared by news writers dealing with the Ethiopian crisis, the agricultural situation brought about by the depression, and the slum problem. The last-named was called *One-Third of a Nation*, a phrase borrowed from President Roosevelt's statement to the effect that one-third of the nation was ill-fed, ill-clothed and ill-housed. These productions employed a fluid, cinematographic technique and were lively and exciting. They were enthusiastically received; taken altogether they constituted a valuable contribution both to the drama and to the theatre.

Everything the Project did was not first rate, nor could it have been under the existing conditions. It was impossible to find enough trained executives and there was no time to train new ones, though many received training in the course of the Project that enabled them to make great progress later on. Further, there was no workable way of applying aptitude tests, and consequently many of the unemployed who were put on the payroll were actually unemployable. Then there was the usual number of malingerers, troublemakers and opportunists. Many of the planned productions were therefore never realized and many others turned out to be dull, ineffective or worse. That was inevitable, considering the magnitude of the enterprise, the haste with which it had to be organized, and all the restrictions that hemmed it in.

On balance, the experiment (for it was an experiment) was

notably successful, both socially and artistically. If it had been allowed to develop, with more emphasis, as economic conditions improved, upon the art of the theatre than upon the relief of unemployment, it could have become an integrated nation-wide organization, offering fine theatrical entertainment to tens of millions of Americans. The cost of maintenance, measured in terms of cultural gains, would have been trivial. The net cost of the Project over a period of more than three years was less than fifty million dollars, an amazingly low figure when one remembers that the average number of persons on the payroll was about ten thousand.

The Project was killed by the cutting off of Congressional appropriations—a deliberate act of political sabotage, of which the perpetrators should be everlastingly ashamed. The notable achievements and great potentialities of the Project were never taken into account by its enemies. In fact, most of them never even saw a single production. They chose instead to use it as a pawn in their private political game, and as a means of discrediting the Roosevelt administration.

Whether or not anything resembling the Federal Theatre Project could ever again be attempted is, of course, entirely a matter of conjecture. Those who remember the obstacles it encountered and the nature and swiftness of its demise are likely to feel that no worth-while theatre can flourish under governmental auspices, particularly when its existence depends upon the political calculations of partisan and semiliterate legislators. On the other hand, there are incorrigible optimists who believe that, given an enlightened administration and a sufficient amount of influential pressure, both from theatre workers and theatregoers, it might be possible to devise a plan that would provide governmental support for the theatre and at the same time keep political interference at a minimum. Admittedly it is a faint hope; but it will persist as long as there are people who cherish the theatre as an instrument for enlightenment and for emotional and spiritual satisfaction.

XIV COMMERCIALISM VERSUS ART

In our examination of the American theatre we have seen that it has always been primarily a business enterprise. The various noncommercial organizations that have been described have undoubtedly played an important part in developing the theatre and in furthering the drama, but it must be borne in mind that, almost without exception, these organizations either have been forced to disband for lack of funds or have adopted the practices of the commercial theatre. The persistent pattern, then, of the professional theatre in America is that of a privately financed institution whose investors and managers are preponderantly motivated by the hope of monetary profit. It is inevitable, therefore, that in the selection of plays for production in the professional theatre the producer's estimate of the prospects of commercial success is a determining factor.

Clearly this is a consideration of the utmost importance, not only to the dramatist but to that portion of the public that is interested in fine drama and fine theatre. If we accept the premises that the artist is as much concerned about communication as he is about expression, and that the dramatist, more than any other artist, is dependent for communication upon interpretative and technological adjuncts, then it is evident that he must be influenced, consciously or unconsciously, by the state of the theatre in which he hopes to have his plays produced. It is hard to conceive of anyone sitting down to write a play without the intention of having it performed upon the stage.

But to what extent is he influenced, and what is the ultimate effect upon the arts of the drama and of the theatre? These questions are frequently discussed by those who take the theatre seriously, and the consensus apparently is that the emphasis of the American theatre is on commercial success rather than on art, and that the dominance of the businessman in the theatre is a deterrent to the production and hence to the creation of drama of high quality. In fact, "commercial," as applied to the theatre, is nearly always a term of derogation.

I found that this opinion was vehemently and almost universally held by the members of my class at New York University, and in an effort to appraise its validity, I inaugurated a discussion of the question which went on animatedly for weeks. As we moved on from generalities to a more detailed examination of the contemporary American theatre, it developed that what had seemed at first to be certainties had to be considerably qualified and even regarded with doubt. The picture of a noble art debased and aborted by greed became less and less clear cut. For, taking the theatre as a whole, over a period of years, it becomes evident that along with the crude melodramas and cheap farces, empty spectacles and all the other contrivances designed to catch the pennies of the witless and the tasteless, there have been presented an extraordinary number of fine plays by the foremost American dramatists as well as the established works of foreign masters. O'Neill, Sherwood, Wilder, Anderson, Behrman, Hellman, Odets, Williams and Miller are among those who owe their fame (and fortune!) almost entirely to the commercial theatre. True, O'Neill was first produced by the Provincetown Players and Odets by the Group Theatre, but there can be little doubt that they would have been commercially produced anyhow, as were the others I have named, without benefit of apprenticeship. Apparently, then, there are contradictions and cross-tendencies that complicate and confuse the question and make it difficult, if not impossible, to give an authoritative answer. In an effort to present the issue objectively, I formulated a series of axioms or propositions, which I offer here, not as the last word on the subject, but merely as the empirical conclusions of one who has long worked in the theatre:

1. When we speak of the art of the theatre, we are referring to aesthetic values, or, let us say, creativity.

2. By commercialism we mean the economic exploitation of plays, or, let us say, merchandising.

3. Plays are written to be presented to audiences, and to achieve this objective in a nonsubsidized theatre merchandising is essential.

4. Almost without exception, everyone professionally engaged in the theatre, however mercenary, would rather be associated with a good production (that is to say an artistic one) then with a bad (or inartistic) one.

5. Without exception, everyone professionally engaged in the theatre, however artistic or idealistic he may be, would prefer commercial success to commercial failure.

6. However, it is frequently asserted that in our theatre artistic excellence often precludes commercial success, and on the other hand that commercial exploitation often debases artistic quality. In testing the validity of this assumption the following facts must be considered.

7. There are no generally accepted objective criteria for determining whether a given play is artistic (that is, good) or inartistic (that is, bad). Such evaluations are mainly subjective.

8. There is no method for determining in advance whether or not the production of a given play will be commercially successful.

9. It is almost impossible to determine to what extent the success or failure of a production is affected by such contributing factors as managerial editing, direction, acting, critical opinion and salesmanship.

10. A play that is prompted by the highest ideals and artistic intentions is not necessarily a better play than one written with a weather eye to the box office. In fact the contrary is often true.

11.   Of all plays written, most good ones get produced in the commercial theatre, whereas most bad ones do not.

12.   A good play is more likely to succeed in the theatre than a bad one.

13.   However, good plays often fail, and bad plays often succeed. It becomes impossible, therefore, to establish any clear correspondence between artistic excellence and commercial success.

14.   Nevertheless, it must be recognized that in our civilization success is only too often equated with exellence, and failure with lack of it.

15.   Hence there can be no doubt that the eventual evaluation of a play may be greatly influenced by economic factors unrelated to its inherent quality, for it is only rarely that a play that fails when it is first produced is subsequently revived and reappraised.

16.   It seems to follow that no generalization about the evil effects of commercialism upon the art of the drama will survive an objective examination; and that in so far as the evil does exist it is an integral part of our society, and could be eradicated only by drastic alteration of our psychology, cultural habits and economic institutions.

It is the old story of the optimist seeing the doughnut and the pessimist the hole. You can begin with any theory about the merits or the defects of the American theatrical system and have no trouble in finding facts to support it. The range of a typical Broadway season will include tawdry and inane pieces of stage carpentry that run for a week (or two years!) and a tragic (and outstandingly successful) masterpiece like *A Long Day's Journey into Night*, which a dozen commercial managements were eager to produce, or an esoteric work like *Waiting for Godot*, with an appeal limited to the highly sophisticated few. A bad feature of the system is that it militates against the meritorious play that cannot, for economic reasons, be kept running long enough to find its audience. A good feature is that the theatrical business, unlike the mass-production monopolistic motion-picture and broadcasting businesses, is largely in the hands of individuals, who are also individualists. This makes for a healthy diversity in taste and judgment, which, even in strictly commercial terms, makes the play that to A seems utterly hopeless look like a potential hit to B. Woe to the dramatist (and to the theatre) if play production ever becomes syndicated and controlled by a handful of autocrats!

Certainly the contemporary dramatist in America—or in England, Germany or France, for that matter—is entirely free to write as he pleases, knowing, too, that the means of communicating what he writes is potentially available to him. But no artist or anybody else is ever entirely free. He is always subject to the limitations of his environment. If he lives under a non-democratic regime he must abide by its proscriptions, whether they be political or ecclesiastical. If there is a state theatre, even in a democracy, it is likely to be bureaucratically controlled. If the theatre is in the hands of businessmen, he is subject to business considerations.

He must know, for example, that if he writes a play that calls for twenty sets of scenery and a cast of a hundred, the chances of its production are slight and of its success even slighter. There are sound economic reasons why so many modern plays have only one set and a cast of ten or less. Does this cramp the dramatist's style, or does the tax upon his ingenuity and inventiveness result in sounder, better-constructed plays? It probably works both ways. Again, every experienced dramatist is well aware that plays of excessive length, plays written in verse, plays dealing with abstract ideas or with "depressing" subjects are not very good box-office prospects. Yet this knowledge did not prevent the writing of *Strange Interlude, Winterset, The Skin of Our Teeth,* or *Death of a Salesman,* all of which were first produced in the commercial theatre and were substantial commercial successes. On the other hand, there is no way of knowing how many masterpieces have gone unwritten because their potential authors saw no hope of ever finding an audience for them. (However, I should say that usually, if an author is sufficiently fired by an idea, he is likely to plunge ahead, persuading himself that somehow, somewhere, he will find his means of communication.)

So far we have used commercialism as a sort of blanket term to indicate that in the American theatre the profit motive takes precedence over the artistic motive. But the commercial structure of the theatre is a complex one that includes diverse factors that often work against each other. To understand how the theatre works and how its economy affects not only the dramatist and his interpreters, but the theatregoing public and the cultural state of the dramatic art, we must consider in great detail such matters as the ownership and operation of theatres, the craft organizations of theatreworkers, the financing of plays, and the high cost of everything.

XV REAL ESTATE

For the presentation of any play anywhere some sort of show-place is indispensable. The minimum requirement is an area in which the actors can perform and another in which spectators can be accommodated. This of course allows for wide variety, both indoors and out; indeed, plays are performed in all sorts of places and under all sorts of conditions.

However, when plays are professionally produced for paying audiences, a very highly specialized type of structure containing a stage equipped for lighting and the handling of scenery, and an auditorium seating some hundreds of persons is required. This is the concrete physical entity known as a theatre, as distinguished from the over-all apparatus or institution which we call *the* theatre, and its characteristics and method of operation are of primary importance in the process of dramatic communication.

Since most professional dramatic activity in the United States originates in New York, and the success or failure of a new play is almost invariably determined by its New York reception, we can best understand the relationship between play and playhouse by concentrating on a study of New York's theatres. The theatre situation in other large cities, particularly Boston, Chicago and Philadelphia, is substantially the same as New York's.

167

In New York the buildings devoted to the presentation of professional, or "legitimate," drama (which includes musical comedy) are almost all to be found within a small area, generally known as the theatre district (but also known as the Rialto, the Gay White Way, the Main Stem, or simply Broadway), about a half-mile long and a quarter-mile wide. Because this area is located in the very heart of Manhattan, land valuations are abnormally high and are reckoned in terms of front footage, a fact that has a most important bearing upon the construction and operation of theatres.

The high price of land, together with the ever-mounting costs of building construction, have made it impracticable for anyone to build a new theatre in New York since 1926, though it is generally recognized that new theatres are sorely needed. The only exception I know is the Center Theatre, erected as part of the Rockefeller Center complex in 1932, an opulent playhouse that seated 3,700. But it was too large for the presentation of plays, and after being used for two decades or so for ice shows, ballets and what not, it was torn down, like the New Theatre a generation earlier—another example of a lavish wastefulness that is peculiar to America.

The theatre owner then, whether he likes it or not, is primarily a real-estate operator, whose first concern is with protecting his heavy investment and meeting his carrying and operating costs. This is true even when he is also the producer of the plays his theatre houses, as was often the case in the first decades of the century, when well-known producers like David Belasco, Winthrop Ames, William A. Brady, A. H. Woods, Charles Frohman, Florenz Ziegfeld, and Cohan & Harris found it advantageous to control the playhouses in which their productions were presented. (Many of these theatres—e.g., the Empire, the New Amsterdam, the Globe—had a distinctively individualistic flavor and were identified by many theatregoers with a particular kind of production.) For if a theatre is operating at a substantial loss the owner is more likely than not to evict the play, even though it is paying its way. The duality of interest becomes sharper, as is usually the case today, when the theatre owner and the play producer are different persons. This economic conflict is a factor in almost every production and its outcome often determines the length of the play's run. Sometimes one has the upper hand, sometimes the other. It depends not only upon the resources and astuteness of the respective parties, but upon general economic conditions. If the theatre as a whole is prospering and there is a shortage of playhouses, the real-estate owner can be as arbitrary as he chooses. But in times of stress, when theatre attendance shrinks and theatres are going begging, it is the producer who can write his own terms. In a sense, therefore, the ups and downs of dramatists and actors correspond to the ups and downs of the real-estate business.

And surely there is no branch of the real-estate business that is more hazardous than theatre ownership. It would be hard to think of any type of building that is as limited in its economic possibilities as a New York theatre. The very nature of its construction and equipment makes it unsuited to any use other than the presentation of plays, so that on the standard basis of eight performances per week the theatre is being gainfully used about twenty-four hours per week, or in the aggregate one full day out of seven. Further, the theatrical business is seasonal: attendance begins to diminish in the late spring, falls off sharply in the summer, and does not pick up again until mid-September. Unlike London's theatres, which remain open throughout the year, more than half of New York's are entirely closed for three months. At other times the sudden closing of a play may leave a theatre unoccupied until another booking is found—a hiatus that might extend over several weeks. So that most theatres are not likely to be in operation more than eight months in the year on the average; and when they are in operation the plays they accommodate are more likely to be financial failures then successes.

Meanwhile the overhead goes on. During the depression I

owned the Belasco Theatre for a short period. The annual expenditure for taxes, insurance and interest on the mortgage came to something like $36,000. This was without utilities or services of any kind. In other words, it cost $700 per week to keep the theatre dark, without light, heat, cleaning, a doorman or a telephone operator. Today, of course, the cost would be much greater.

Obviously, it is incumbent upon the theatre owner to seek a production that will keep the house filled and perhaps even prove sufficiently popular to attract audiences during the slack summer months. The New York City building code has a provision —enacted immediately after the disastrous Iroquois Theatre fire in Chicago in the early years of the century—which prohibits the use of any construction over the auditorium of a theatre, so that it is impossible to supplement the theatre revenue by the construction of offices or apartments. The law does not apply to motion-picture theatres, for the simple reason that at the time it was passed there were almost none in existence; consequently many movie palaces are housed in large office buildings. Also, there are technical restrictions upon the establishment of bars in New York theatres. In London every theatre has a bar, which does a lively business; the bar receipts are often more than enough to offset a deficit in the play-booking operations.

The theatre owner, therefore, can hardly be blamed if he surveys forthcoming attractions with an eye to commerce rather than to art. It is the smash hit he is after, not the dramatic masterpiece. Sometimes a play happens to be both, and if so, why of course so much the better. Yet how can he know what will succeed and what will not? The answer is that he cannot, any more than the producer, the director, the actors or the author can. So he must rely upon his judgment, for what it is worth. He may read the script and form his own opinion of it, or he may be influenced by the opinion of his wife, secretary or inamorata. (We are told that Molière gauged the laugh value of his plays by reading them to his cook. There is a street named for her, near the Comédie-Française: rue Thérèse.) He may go to New Haven or Washington to see a tryout. Here he has at least the benefit of observing the response of an audience to the play, but that too is a criterion that is far, far from infallible. His inclination is to play it safe; to avoid the unconventional, the arty, the highbrow; to stick to established values, the tried and true. A producer or a director with a good record of successes, preferably one last year, is in a favored position; so sometimes is the author of a recent hit. But best of all is the popular star whose mere presence in the play will create a demand for tickets the moment his or her name is announced, so that by the time the play opens there is an advance sale sufficiently large to keep the play running for months, regardless of its merits or of what the critics and the audiences think of it. (Numerous examples will suggest themselves to anyone familiar with the New York stage.) However, there are only a few plays in this category, and on average the odds are all against box-office success. In a typical recent season, some sixty new productions appeared on Broadway. About one-third of these ran for less than three weeks; hardly one-quarter ran for twelve weeks or more; and it should be noted that many of the long-run plays were musicals, which can be profitably presented only in the few theatres of large seating capacity, so that they are not available to the owners of the smaller theatres.

The fact that no new theatre has been built in New York since 1926, though the population has grown and office buildings and apartment houses have sprung up everywhere, is sufficient proof that theatre ownership is not regarded as a lucrative business. But even more convincing is the fact that in the thirty-year period the number of so-called first-class theatres in operation has dwindled from seventy to thirty!

What has become of the other forty is a question that may well be asked. Some were so dilapidated and outmoded that they simply died of old age. Others were demolished so that the valuable sites they occupied could be put to more profitable use.

Still others became movie theatres. On Forty-second Street, between Seventh and Eighth Avenues, there are half-a-dozen or more theatres that were once considered among the most desirable in New York. Since the advent of talking pictures they have been converted into "grind" houses, given over to continuous performances of old movies at low prices. Finally, the mushroom growth of television has resulted in the acquisition by broadcasting companies of numerous theatres as rehearsal and production stages.

But the theatre owner's troubles are largely of his own making. The desire of the real-estate operator who engages in the hazardous business of theatre management to cash in on his investment is understandable enough, but like many another presumably astute businessman, he has shortsightedly allowed his eagerness for the immediate dollar to divert him from the long-range policy of keeping up with the times, and above all of providing for the comfort and fostering the good will of his clientele.

The high cost of Manhattan real estate and of building construction has led the theatre owner to crowd his playhouse into the smallest possible space and to make most of that space productive of revenue. In other words, the emphasis is put upon seating capacity at the expense of play-producing facilities and of the public convenience. Compared to the best theatres in Japan, Germany and the Soviet Union, every theatre in New York is hopelessly outmoded, without facilities for utilizing modern techniques of stagecraft or for catering to the needs and pleasure of its audience.

If we compare the average Broadway theatre with Radio City Music Hall the distinction becomes painfully apparent. The Music Hall has comfortable seats; loges where smoking is permitted; a flexible and restful lighting system; a vast stage equipped with splendid stage machinery; excellent acoustics; air conditioning; spacious and tastefully decorated lounges and lavatories; fleets of elevators; a staff of courteous attendants.

The Broadway theatre presents a very different picture. The seats are too narrow, the rows too close together, for the comfort of anyone over average size. There are always many side seats, too, from which a full view of the stage cannot be had—a situation which compels the stage director to play every important scene as near the center of the stage as possible. Frequently there are stage boxes, relics of a plushier era, which are so undesirable that they can be sold only when the play is a great hit. Many of the older theatres have second balconies, accessible only by steep staircases and equipped with torturesome wooden seats from which one gets an excellent view of the tops of the actors' heads. In spite of theatregoers' justifiable complaints about the high price of theatre tickets, it is often easier to sell the orchestra seats than the far cheaper second-balcony seats. Often, too, there are "dead spots," where one must strain to hear.

Most theatres have antiquated cooling systems or none at all, one reason why so many of them are forced to close during the summer months. As I have said, there are no bars or pleasant refreshment rooms such as one finds in many foreign theatres. Smoking is not permitted, except in the lobbies and lounges. Most lobbies are tiny, and the hundreds who crowd out for a smoke during the intermissions stand elbow to elbow in the dense air. Only a few theatres have comfortable lounges; lavatories are ill kept and inadequate. Checkroom facilities are even worse, and one has the choice of holding a heavy overcoat on one's lap for two hours or of queueing up for ten minutes to reclaim it.

To all these discomforts must be added the difficulties of getting to and from the theatres. The concentration of practically all theatres in a narrow area which also contains many movie palaces, large hotels and restaurants results in a convergence of cars at curtain time that makes progress exasperatingly slow, and is hardly conducive to a mood of enjoyment. Curb parking is prohibited, and off-street parking space is insufficient and expensive. At the end of the evening the situation is even worse, as all the theatres simultaneously pour forth their occupants.

One either engages in a competitive scramble for the scarce taxis or shuffles along in the crowds to the nearest bus or subway station, sometimes several blocks away. When the weather is bad, experienced theatregoers remain at home rather than face the discomforts of the traffic situation. A heavy rainfall or snowstorm can easily cost a theatre a thousand dollars in a single night.

Of course nobody can do anything about the weather; nor can anybody afford to erect theatres comparable to the Music Hall, which was built with Rockefeller money, has a seating capacity of 6,500 and can give continuous performances from early morning until late at night. But that is not the point. There are many thousands who will always prefer grandiose films and banal spectacles to any allurement that the theatre can offer. But there are many other thousands who could be won back to the theatre if theatregoing were made more convenient and pleasant. It is safe to say that even the greatest success never reaches one-half of its potential audience. The communication of the dramatist's creative output is therefore seriously impeded by the imperfect functioning of a most essential part of the communicative machinery.

Bad as physical conditions are out front, for the accommodation of audiences, they are even worse backstage, for the production of plays. Again because of spatial limitations, all stages are far too small to give full scope to the director, actors and scenic designer. There is almost no room for storage, or even the stacking of scenery and properties not in immediate use. Off-stage space is insufficient for the use of wagon stages, for example; and sometimes it is so obstructed by light bridges or other impediments that it cannot be used at all. Switchboards are old-fashioned and incomplete and must almost invariably be supplemented with auxiliary boards, sound-projecting apparatus and the like. Elevator stages are practically nonexistent, as are permanent turntables.

Little or no provision is made for the comfort or health of

the theatre workers. There is no proper regulation of temperature, and the stage is usually either overheated or swept by drafts, sometimes both at the same time, so that the actors are forever fighting lethargy or coming down with colds. If the cast is sizable, dressing-room facilities are always insufficient, and the minor actors must share a room with five or six of their fellows, or sometimes must use improvised booths beneath the stage. Even the star dressing rooms are, with few exceptions, small, bleak and ill equipped. Often the rooms are up three or four flights, so that the actors are forever running up and down stairs—not to the benefit of their performances, one may be sure. There is one theatre in Philadelphia in which the architect failed to make any provision at all for dressing rooms. The mistake was discovered too late to be remedied, so dressing rooms were constructed in a building across the street, to which the actors have access by way of a tunnel. (I know of no theatre in which the architect failed to include a box office.)

In justification of the theatre owner it must be remembered that every Broadway theatre is at least thirty years old, and that some were built in the nineteenth century. Modernization would be not only costly but very difficult, for most of the worst defects are structural. If new theatres were built, they would undoubtedly incorporate many improvements in engineering and in audience accommodation. But the cost of building theatres is prohibitive, particularly in view of the risks attendant upon operation. It seems unlikely, therefore, that the theatre situation will change for the better in the immediate future, and the dramatist and his co-workers will have to go on struggling with what is available.

XVI LABOR

The economic and technological problems that pertain to theatres are exceeded in complexity and gravity by those that pertain to employment practices and contractual relationships
between theatre operators and play producers on the one hand,
and theatre workers, whose various skills and services are essential to the professional presentation of plays, on the other. From
any point of view the theatre is not big business, but it is doubtful if any other business or industry presents a tighter and more
complicated pattern of labor organization. It is so complicated
that all that one can attempt to do in a chapter is describe the
various unions and associations and the nature of their regulations, deferring the discussion of the dollars-and-cents implications and the economic consequences thereof.

Since most theatrical activity centers about the production of
plays, the logical person to begin with is the dramatist. The
exclusive right of the writer to the use of the literary material
he creates, known as copyright, has long been recognized both
by common law and by statute. No publication or, where plays
are concerned, no production, may be made without the formal
consent of the author, which ordinarily is granted only in consideration of some form of monetary compensation. The dramatist may sell his copyright outright to the producer, and this

was long the usual practice. But in the theatre of today outright sale has been almost universally superseded by the licensing system: that is to say, the dramatist does not surrender his copyright, but merely licenses the performing rights in his play to the producer, who agrees to pay for its use. Payment almost invariably takes the form of a royalty: a specified percentage of the revenue derived from performances of plays.

The rate and manner of payment have always been a matter of negotiation between dramatist and producer, but by the late nineteenth century, when the theatre developed into a widespread and lucrative business enterprise, the terms and conditions governing the licensing of plays had become fairly well stabilized. In general, royalties were paid on total box-office receipts, and usually, for established dramatists, on a sliding scale, ranging from 5 to 10 per cent. Income from "subsidiary" rights—productions by stock and amateur companies, foreign productions, and the like—was divided equally between dramatist and producer, and the producer's participation continued for the life of the copyright, fifty-six years, even though his license to produce had long expired. When the dramatist's plays were in demand and the producer was honest, the dramatist's rewards were huge; the earnings of Avery Hopwood, Owen Davis, Winchell Smith and others ran into the millions. But when the dramatist was inexperienced or in financial straits, even an honest producer might be inclined to use his bargaining power, while a dishonest one could negotiate a contract that brought the author almost nothing. Further, it was not unusual for producers of unsuccessful plays to go into bankruptcy, listing among their liabilities thousands of dollars of unpaid and uncollectible royalties; crooked producers would simply find devices for swindling dramatists out of what was coming to them. On the production side, too, the young or timid dramatist suffered serious disadvantages. He had little or nothing to say about the choice of actors and director; changes in his script were made arbitrarily by the producer or by a "play doctor" who demanded a substantial share of the royalties. Sometimes he was even barred from attending rehearsals. Redress could be obtained, if at all, only by costly and protracted legal proceedings, so usually the dramatist had the choice of submitting or having his play withdrawn. How many promising plays were ruined, it is impossible to say (perhaps some were improved); but that many dramatists were deprived of their inherent right to control their literary creations there can be no doubt.

In 1912, the Authors League of America was organized, along the lines of the authors' societies of Europe. Membership was voluntary and consisted at first of a relatively small number of well-known authors, only a few of whom were dramatists. The purpose of the League was to protect the rights of the creators of "copyrightable" material. It occupied itself chiefly with the correction of abuses in the book- and periodical-publishing field, and its approach was necessarily persuasive rather than mandatory. However, its achievements were considerable, and as its power and prestige developed and its membership grew, it prepared a standard form of contract for the production of plays, embodying most of the practices in general use. This contract was accepted by many producers, though often with important modifications, and by the mid-1920's it was being used more and more.

By this time the motion-picture industry had undergone an enormous expansion. The demand for story material had increased greatly and so had the prices paid for it. The movie rights to a play had now become its principal by-product, and it was clear that with talking pictures in the offing, payments would keep on getting larger and larger. These rights were of course one of the subsidiary rights in which dramatist and producer shared equally. Since it was generally agreed that the dramatist was an impractical artist and the producer a hard-headed businessman (a dual fallacy, if ever there was one!), negotiations for the sale of subsidiary rights were customarily left in the hands of the producer. Now a new and troublesome practice began to develop. The impecunious or cautious producer would take an unproduced play on which he had an option to a motion-picture company and arrange for backing in return for pre-emption of the motion-picture rights. Sometimes he would receive substantially more than was needed for production costs, so that he pocketed a bonus, besides being indemnified against loss. The motion-picture company, on the other hand, acquired a desirable dramatic property at a price far below what it would have had to pay for a successful play. Both parties profited at the expense of the dramatist, who, often unaware of the secret deal, allowed himself to be persuaded that it was better to accept an immediate offer than to await the dubious outcome of a production. Some of these transactions were within the wide ambit of business ethics, but others were downright fraudulent.

As we have seen, the dramatists of the postwar generation were no longer knocking at the door; they had moved in and were taking over. In the spring of 1926 they decided that it was time to take action to safeguard their property rights. Accordingly, more than one hundred dramatists, including most of the best-known, organized themselves, under the leadership of George Middleton, as the Dramatists Guild of the Authors League of America, and pledged themselves not to offer any play for production until the producers had recognized the Guild as the collective bargaining agent for all dramatists, and had agreed to accept a standard contract that protected the dramatist's rights. In short, the dramatists went on strike, with the orthodox objectives of recognition and better pay. It was probably one of the briefest and most effective strikes in the entire history of labor relations. The producers, many of them theatre owners, were thrown into a state of panic. They had been beginning to make plans for the coming season, plans that depended largely upon the creations of the insurgent dramatists. Now suddenly the source of supply had dried up, and the producers were faced with the bleak prospect of shutting down their production activities and maintaining their expensive real property in idleness. Meetings between the dramatists and the producers were quickly called, and it did not take long for the dramatists to win acceptance of almost all their demands.

Unlike most strikes, what counted most in this one was the qualitative, rather than the quantitative, element. If a dozen or twenty of the dramatists whose plays were most in demand had abstained from participation and put their plays on the market, the producers would have told the rest to go hang. Secondly— and this has a significant bearing not only in this connection but upon the whole labor situation in the theatre—the producers were unorganized: they still are! They had a loose voluntary organization, it is true, but it had no control over its members and no way of enforcing adherence to a policy of resistance. Any individual producer who chose to act independently in dealing with the dramatists could have had the pick of the crop of new plays. So there was no alternative to capitulation. But it must be added that some of the producers were fair-minded enough to recognize that the grievances of the dramatists had ample foundation.

It is impossible to deal here with all the details and implications of this revolutionary change in the position of the dramatist. But the major ones must be stressed, for they have radically altered both the economics and the methods of play production. The agreements reached at the joint meetings were embodied in what is known as the Minimum Basic Agreement. It is a curious document, in that it is entered into by the Dramatists Guild on the one hand and the individual producer on the other. Though it is negotiated by the producers' organization, now known as the League of New York Theatres, that organization lacks the power to make a binding collective agreement. Under the terms of the M.B.A. the signatory producer agrees to deal only with members of the Dramatists Guild, and Guild members may not offer their plays to any producer who is not signatory to the agreement. Of course a nonsignatory may produce a play by a non-Guild member, but I do not know of any such production. In effect then, no dramatist can have a play produced in the professional theatre unless he is a member of the Guild, and no producer can present a play unless he is signatory to the M.B.A. In trade-union terminology this constitutes a closed shop, though not a closed union; for anyone who has a play optioned for production may become a member of the Guild merely by applying. Whether or not the Dramatists Guild is in fact a trade union is a question that has produced a great variety of legal opinion and has troubled even the courts.

The M.B.A. set up regulations for the sale of motion-picture rights, first by requiring the manager to run the play in New York for at least three weeks in order to be entitled to a share in these rights as well as in all other subsidiary rights; secondly, by setting up an impartial functionary known as the Motion-Picture Arbiter (later called the Negotiator) to whom all bids for motion-picture rights had to be submitted, and whose decision as to which to accept was binding upon both the dramatist and the producer. These provisions eliminated the possibility of any collusive preproduction sale and gave assurance that an eventual sale was based upon competitive bidding.

In the course of the decades that have elapsed since its adoption in 1926, the M.B.A. has been renegotiated many times and has undergone many changes. As one who has participated in all the negotiations, I can testify that they have been protracted and often bitter. The effect, on the whole, has been to improve the status of the dramatist, thanks to the solidarity of the Guild and to its power to discipline both dramatists and producers who violate terms of the agreement. Almost every phase of play production and of the disposition of rights is covered by the M.B.A., which has steadily grown in length until it is now a bound document of thirty-four closely printed pages of a size somewhat larger than those of this book. It safeguards the dramatist by prescribing that royalties must be paid promptly each week to the Guild, as the dramatist's representative, and that the Guild may also require the posting of a bond to ensure payment. Minimum rates of royalty are established, though the dramatist may get more if he can; the producer's share of subsidiary rights has been reduced from 50 per cent to 40 per cent and the period of his participation limited to eighteen years. The option period is strictly limited too, and a schedule of minimum advance payments is provided. All contracts must have the approval of the Guild; so must all modifications, even though both parties request them.

All these regulations have to do with the dramatist's economic interests. But equal emphasis is placed by the M.B.A. upon his rights as a creative artist who is primarily concerned about having his play effectively presented. The contract gives him the right of approval of cast and director, the unqualified right to attend rehearsals, as well as tryout performances at the producer's expense, and the right to refuse to make any change whatever in his play. There can be little doubt that contractually the American dramatist is in a more favorable position than any other creative artist anywhere in the world. Of course, artists whose works are known and who are commercially successful can always more or less make their own terms and conditions. But the Dramatists Guild makes no distinction among its members. The M.B.A. affords the same protection and privileges for the young author of a first play as it does for a world-famous veteran. Not the least extraordinary thing about the Dramatists Guild is that its governing council, which rigidly polices the M.B.A., is composed almost entirely of successful dramatists who no longer need the protection of the Guild, and many of whom indeed are more or less involved both actively and financially in the business of producing plays.

The dramatists were not the first important group in the theatre to organize and to employ militant tactics to win recognition. In fact, their decision to strike was probably influenced by the successful action taken by the actors seven years earlier. For bad as the status of the dramatist was, that of the actor was probably even worse. Here again the stars and the handful of actors whose services were in great demand could more or less dictate the terms of their employment, but for the rank and file conditions were bad indeed. To mention only a few of the abuses, there was no minimum salary, no rehearsal pay, no time limit for rehearsals, no guaranteed period of employment, and no assurance that the actor would ever be paid at all. An actor could be kept in rehearsal for six or eight weeks and then be dismissed without notice; or the play might close after a few performances and all he would receive would be a week's pay for perhaps two months of his time. Frequently plays would close on tour because of bad business, and the actor would not only be unable to collect his back salary from the bankrupt or crooked manager, but would have to make his way back to New York as best he could. (Eddie Foy, a great vaudeville favorite, had a song that began: "I'm the ghost of a troupe that was stranded in Peoria." The allusion was familiar enough to be recognized by a lay audience.)

In an effort to remedy these conditions, the actors, in 1913— just about the time the Authors League was organized—formed a trade union called the Actors' Equity Association, more generally known as Equity. For six years Equity tried unsuccessfully to get the Producing Managers' Association (as the inchoate producers' organization was then called) to agree to a standardized contract that offered some protection to the actor. Finally, in 1919, finding that persuasion was bringing no results, Equity called a strike. The actors walked out, and every theatre on Broadway was dark. This unheard-of action threw the managers into a state of panic. Faced with closing successful plays and ruinous overhead expenses of empty theatres, they capitulated in less than a month. Equity was recognized as the collective bargaining agency for the actors, and a standard contract was adopted. Again, in the absence of a producers' organization authorized to act collectively, each producer had to enter into a separate arrangement with Equity, though of course the

terms were the same for all. A few of the stars indignantly refused to join Equity, declaring that it was infra dig for an artist
to belong to an organization that was associated with the American Federation of Labor—a feeling that the lower orders, who
had bread-and-butter problems, did not share. But Equity, having won a great victory, could afford to be magnanimous, and it
very sensibly allowed the dissenters to form their own unaffili-
ated organization, known as the Actors' Fidelity Association
(and to Equity members as the Fidos). It was limited to actors
already well established. Eventually, of course, the Fidos disappeared from the scene and Equity became the sole possessor of
the field.

From its inception Equity has been a straight trade union,
operating along regular trade-union lines. It functions as a
strictly closed shop, and only Equity members may appear in
professional productions; but it is an open union, which anybody
who is offered a job in the professional theatre may join, upon
payment of an initiation fee and moderate dues. The system has
both merits and defects. Since it confines its activities to the
"legitimate" theatre, many of its members also belong to the
actors' unions that deal with motion pictures, broadcasting, night
clubs, vaudeville and grand opera. Sometimes these fields of
theatrical activity overlap, and jurisdictional disputes among the
unions are not uncommon.

In the course of forty years, the Equity contract has been repeatedly renegotiated, almost invariably in favor of the actor.
Again it is impossible to describe all the provisions of the contract, and all the changes that have been made. At present the
actor's individual contract consists only of two long pages, in
type that is familiar to holders of insurance policies; but this
contract is subject to the Equity Rules Governing Employment,
a sixty-two-page booklet containing seventy-five sections and
many subsections. The five-page alphabetical index runs from
Abandonment of Play to Welfare Fund, and includes such items
as Baggage; Blue Cross; Cleaning of Costumes; Color of Hair;

Day of Rest; Extraordinary Risks (defined as "performing acrobatic feats, suspension from trapezes or wires, the use of or exposure to weapons, or the taking of dangerous leaps or falls"); Legal Tender; Plays Alleged to be Salacious; Rocky Mountain Rule; Safe and Sanitary; Social Security; Souvenir Programme; Triplicate Contract; and Voluntary Classes. It is a far cry from the days of Mr. Vincent Crummles, to say nothing of Richard Burbage!

The main provisions of the Equity contract establish minimum salaries, both in New York and on tour; rehearsal pay (which is the same for everybody); strict limitations upon rehearsal time; a guarantee of two weeks' pay whether the play runs or not (or even whether it opens or not); the posting of a bond by the producer to ensure payment; and numerous regulations governing costumes, transportation and publicity. Grievances of either the actor or the producer are referred to the Equity Council, which is composed of well-known actors, and if the difficulty cannot be resolved recourse may be had to arbitration. This procedure is the same for all the theatrical unions as well as for the Dramatists Guild.

With minor variations, the Equity pattern of union organization and control prevails throughout the theatre. Each specialized group of theatre workers has its own union and its own standardized contract, which sets up a closed shop, minimum rates of pay and regulations governing duties and working conditions. Besides the dramatists and the actors, the two most important groups are the scenic designers and the stagehands. Recently the stage directors, about the only group not previously organized, have formed a collective bargaining agency under the name of the Society of Stage Directors and Choreographers. The scenic designers and costume designers belong to the United Scenic Artists, which is not only a closed shop, but a closed union, admission to which is very difficult; applicants are required to pass a stiff examination and also to pay a high initiation fee. The stagehands—carpenters, electricians, property men, flymen, sound-machine men—are members of the Theatrical Protective Union, known in New York as Local Number One, its former designation as part of the powerful International Alliance of Theatrical Stage Employees, which covers the whole entertainment field.

It will suffice merely to enumerate the other craft organizations. Theatre musicians, whether onstage or in the pit, are members of the American Federation of Musicians; advance agents, company managers, house managers, and press agents, of the Association of Theatrical Press Agents and Managers. Porters, cleaners and lavatory attendants belong to the Theatre and Amusement Service Employees Union, wardrobe women and dressers to the Theatrical Wardrobe Attendants Union, building employees to the International Union of Operating Engineers. Finally, box-office treasurers are affiliated with the Teamsters Union. It should be noted, too, that all scenery and costumes must be manufactured in union shops, and all hauling must be done by members of the Teamsters Union.

Since all the principal unions, except the Dramatists Guild, are affiliated with the AFL-CIO, their respective members are more or less pledged to support each other if a strike situation should arise, even though the several groups are sometimes openly hostile to each other. Presumably the members of one union would not cross a picket line organized by other unions, and a walkout by any one group would result in an immediate closing of the theatres. This state of affairs gives all the unions a powerful weapon in bargaining with the producers, for the latter prefer to accede to whatever demands are made rather than risk a strike that would jeopardize their heavy investments in real estate and in productions.

The effects of the ever-growing power of the unions in the theatre are far-reaching indeed, both economically and artistically; and any discussion of the relationship between the theatrical business and the communication of drama must take those effects into account.

XVII DOLLARS AND CENTS

Economics may be, as someone has said, the dreary science; but dreary or not, it is a subject that cannot be ignored by anyone who is professionally engaged in any form of theatrical activity, not only because the operation of its laws vitally affect his livelihood, but because they determine the conditions under which he must work and the degree to which he can practice his profession at all. There can be not the slightest doubt that the strong unions which dominate the theatre have vastly improved the economic condition of such of their members as are employed. But neither can there be any doubt that the shrinkage in professional theatrical activity, not only in New York but throughout the United States, has greatly reduced employment opportunities; and the increased cost of operation has forced the closing of many plays, particularly on tour, that in earlier days might have had long runs.

It must be borne in mind that although theatrical workers are economically organized along standard trade-union lines, there is an enormous difference between the status of individuals employed in the theatre and those employed in industry. One bricklayer, steel worker or miner is pretty much like another in technical skills and in relation to the demand for his services; but in these respects one dramatist, actor, director or scenic designer is certainly not very much like another. The range of opportunity and of income is vast indeed. Even if there were always a clear correlation between financial success and artistic merit, the situation would still be complicated by the fact that collective agreements suggest an equality which is actually nonexistent. But since no one can seriously contend that economic rewards are strictly consonant with artistic talents and achievements, it is obvious that there are serious handicaps for the artist and serious losses to the general cultural fund. Some of the most successful artists are also among the most gifted; but some of those who strike it rich do so, indirectly, at the expense of their worthier but less fortunate fellows. How much wastage this entails it is impossible to estimate, but it is certainly considerable.

The popular dramatist today is in a very favorable economic position. Due to increased admission prices, longer runs for smash hits, higher prices for motion-picture rights, and a greater demand for foreign and amateur rights (as well as a greater percentage of participation in these rights), it is quite possible for the author of a sensationally successful play to make a million dollars. In terms of the probable earnings of Euripides, Shakespeare, Molière and Congreve, that is a substantial sum. Actually, when one takes into account the diminished value of the dollar and income-tax rates that are almost confiscatory, the dramatist who makes a million today is probably no better off than his predecessor of fifty years ago who made two hundred thousand. But he is still doing well! However, such bonanzas are of very infrequent occurrence. Numerous dramatists have fared well with lesser successes, but I doubt if there are more than twenty active members of the Dramatists Guild who, in the course of a career of, let us say, thirty years, have had more than three successes; or if there are as many as fifty who have had more than one. Whatever the actual figures, it is certain that well over 90 per cent of the Guild members cannot, over the years, make a living by writing plays, and must depend for their subsistence upon other forms of writing or on some employment unrelated to writing. Besides, even successful dramatists often find it necessary to supplement their income from their plays by writing for motion pictures or for television. Some find this work enjoyable; but for most of those who engage in it it is hackwork that consumes time and creative energy, and that sometimes debases standards of excellence. Again it is impossible to determine what the loss is to the art of the drama, but it is safe to say that almost no dramatist is entirely free from preoccupation with monetary considerations.

The actor's plight is similar. A few stars and featured players derive handsome incomes from their theatrical activities, though almost invariably they can make even more in Hollywood or in television. The rest have a hard time of it, and it is easy to see why. There are about sixty Broadway productions each season, including musical comedies, with casts ranging up to fifty. If we assume that these productions employ, in the aggregate, fifteen hundred actors and another fifteen hundred for touring companies, stock companies, summer theatres and off-Broadway productions, we arrive at an approximate total of three thousand job opportunities. However, this is by no means the actual employment at any one time. The summer theatres operate only for about two months, tours are seldom longer than four or five months, and most of the plays that open in New York run less than twelve weeks, many only for a week or two. I should say that the actor who works in the theatre for more than fifteen weeks a year is exceptional. Certainly the overwhelming majority of Equity's ten thousand members are unable to make a living in the theatre or even to find employment. It has been estimated that the average theatrical income of Equity members is under two thousand dollars per year.

How do they manage to live? In all sorts of ways. A good many find occasional work in movies or in radio and television, including dramatized advertisements. Others have private means or are supported by a husband or wife. Many are engaged in occupations that have nothing to do with acting. I have known unemployed actors who worked as secretaries, receptionists, truckdrivers, ushers, department-store employees, laboratory technicians, models, night-club hostesses, photographers and teachers. Most of their free time is spent in theatrical job-hunting: hanging about the offices of casting agents; writing appealing or petulant letters that are never answered; trying to get to see a producer or a director, and mostly meeting with a quick dismissal if they succeed. It cannot be said that these conditions are beneficial to the morale of the actor or conducive to his development as an artist.

All the other groups of theatre workers are in more or less the same situation as the actors. Employment is not only seasonal, but is without continuity or security, since each production is an independent enterprise, and more often than not an unsuccessful one. In business and in industry, year-round employment is the norm; in the theatre it is the exception rather than the rule. The theatre worker who averages twenty-five weeks of work, year in and year out, is lucky indeed. Therefore wage scales must be adjusted to the uncertainties of employment. And since wages are fixed by contract, before the fate of the production can be ascertained, the worker who is fortunate enough to be associated with a hit continues throughout its duration to receive compensation that is often far in excess of what would have been acceptable to him for a guaranteed period of employment. The effect of this is to increase operating costs so greatly that almost every play is forced to close sooner than it would in a sounder economic setup.

Again, because of the fact that a large percentage of their membership is always unemployed, the unions have systematically undertaken to provide more jobs by the increasing use of what is known as "featherbedding." This practice, which is by no means peculiar to the theatrical business, involves the compulsory employment of union members whose services are not essential. For instance, a producer who had two or three plays running simultaneously used to employ one press agent and one company manager, who, with a little extra clerical assistance, could easily perform the required duties. Under present regulations, there must be a press agent and a company manager for each production. Formerly stage managers almost invariably understudied and frequently played small or important parts as well. This is no longer permissible under Equity rules, and so additional actors must be engaged to understudy and to play the bit parts.

In other departments the requirements are even more exacting. If recorded music is used in a play the American Federation of Musicians demands that a certain number of its members be put upon the payroll, whether or not there is anything for them to do. For example, in my play *Dream Girl*, bits and snatches of incidental music of various sorts were used throughout, all of it on records, played on a machine operated by a stagehand known as a sound man. The union insisted upon the employment of four musicians. There was no orchestra pit in the theatre so that they could not be used even to play entr'acte music. The added cost to the weekly payroll was $400. The play ran for about fifty weeks, so the total cost to the producer for maintaining four men in employed idleness was $20,000.

The regulations governing the employment of stagehands are perhaps the most arbitrary and exacting of all. Working hours are strictly limited and enforced to the split second, and overtime and Sunday rates add heavily to the cost of production and operation, particularly during dress rehearsals, which sometimes go on through the day and through the night. The union delegate decides how many men are required and his decision is usually irrevocable. The work is strictly departmentalized: a carpenter or electrician cannot touch a piece of furniture, nor can a property man handle scenery or pull a light-switch. Every show must have a "house" crew and a "company" crew, each consisting of at least three "heads" of departments (lights, scenery and props) even though there is only one set and nothing is moved in the course of the play. If sound effects or portable switchboards are used, extra men must be employed, and if there are changes of scenery the number is greatly increased. A recent play, *Two for the Seesaw,* had only two actors in the cast—though the understudies and stage managers brought the number up to six. This would appear to be economically ideal for the producer—until one discovers that he had to employ nineteen stagehands!

Many more examples of union practices could be cited. Taken together they entail an enormous expenditure for services that are technologically dispensable. Whether or not the union requirements are justified by the instability of theatrical employment, and to what extent the inefficiency and lack of organization of the producers are responsible for the conditions of which they complain, are highly debatable questions which need not be discussed here, for we are concerned not with the ethics or with the logic of the situation, but with its relation to the mechanics of communicating a play to its potential audience. On this score there can be no doubt that both the presentation of a play and the continuance of its run are vitally affected by the costs of production and of operation. The whole subject of costs is therefore of utmost importance, not only to the dramatist, but to those who are interested in seeing his plays.

In every business and industry, all costs, particularly labor costs, have risen at an ever-accelerating rate over the past fifty years, but nowhere, I believe, to the degree that they have risen in the theatre. In the early years of the century, it was quite possible to make an adequate production of a play for as little as $5,000. For the producer with a warehouseful of furniture and old scenery that could be repainted, the cost was even less. (Today warehouse costs are prohibitive and it has been found cheaper to pay to have scenery hauled away and burned, even though it has been used only for a week, than to pay storage charges.) The theatre workers were not yet organized, and hard-bargaining producers did not fail to take advantage of the needs and defenselessness of actors and other employees. With the advent of the unions wage scales began to go up, and when talking pictures came in, in 1927, the producers found that they had to compete with Hollywood for the services of the actors they wanted. But even as late as 1931 I was able to produce my play *Counsellor-at-Law*, with two sets of scenery, a large cast (including Paul Muni as star) and a sizable stage crew, for $11,000. The play was an immediate success and the production cost was recouped in three weeks. This cost was abnormally low, for I produced and directed the play myself and opened "cold" in New York: that is, without a tryout. But the most it could have cost anybody would have been $20,000. Today a comparable production would cost $100,000; and even if it were an instantaneous sellout it would have to run at least twenty weeks before the cost could be written off. The organization of the Playwrights' Company in 1938 was predicated upon an estimated production of $25,000 per play. Today a Broadway production can hardly be budgeted for less than $60,000; the usual figure is $75,000 to $100,000.

The situation can perhaps be made clearer by the use of concrete illustrations. I have the actual figures for comparable productions made by the Playwrights' Company in 1939 and in 1955. In the former year, the company produced *No Time for Comedy*, by S. N. Behrman, a one-set play with a small cast that included Katharine Cornell, Laurence Olivier and Margalo Gillmore. The 1955 play was *Cat on a Hot Tin Roof*, by Tennessee Williams, also a one-set play, with Barbara Bel Geddes, Burl Ives and Mildred Dunnock in the cast. The first cost something over $20,000, the second—only sixteen years later—something over $75,000—almost four times as much. On the following page is a breakdown of the respective figures.

Of course, along with mounting costs there had been a substantial increase in the price of theatre tickets and a consequent augmentation of income; but whereas production cost quadrupled and operation costs doubled, the cost of tickets went up

	No Time for Comedy	Cat on a Hot Tin Roof
Scenery (designing, painting and building)	$ 5,177.13	$18,389.94
Properties, costumes and electrical equipment	6,048.59	23,137.44
Stage director's fee	5,000.00	5,861.90
Rehearsal expenses	2,307.65	14,205.81
Preliminary advertising and publicity	1,534.26	5,034.69
Miscellaneous (carting, office expense, auditing, taxes, etc.)	905.44	8,631.96
	$20,973.07	$75,261.74

And here are the comparative operating costs for a typical week:

	No Time for Comedy	Cat on a Hot Tin Roof
Salaries	$5,734.72	$11,376.06
Royalties (author, director and designer)	2,252.20	4,147.75
Publicity and advertising	336.03	1,062.16
Miscellaneous (office expense, taxes, auditing, etc.)	919.13	1,535.72
	$9,242.08	$18,121.69

only about 75 per cent. Both plays were solid hits and it is interesting to note that in the typical weeks cited, each made a profit before taxes of about $4,000. The rate of shrinkage is immediately apparent. In the first instance the profit represents about 22 per cent of the gross box-office receipts; in the second, about 12 per cent. Or to put it in terms of investment risk and return: *No Time for Comedy* was able to pay off its production cost in five weeks, while twenty weeks were required for *Cat on a Hot Tin Roof*. The weekly profit of $4,000 is a gross return of about 20 per cent on a investment of $20,000, and of about 5 per cent on $75,000. When the increase in taxes and the diminished value of the dollar are taken into account, the contrast is even more marked.

Without going into details, I offer one more example of a pair of comparable productions, made by the Playwrights' Company: *Abe Lincoln in Illinois,* produced in 1938, and *Time Remembered,* produced in 1958, both multi-set plays with relatively large casts. The first cost about $39,000 to produce, and made substantial profits for the producer and the investors; the second cost about $160,000, which was never fully recouped.

It must be kept in mind that all the plays I have mentioned were outstanding hits, and that not one Broadway production in ten achieves a similar measure of success. In fact, most productions wind up in the red. Is it any wonder then that dollars and cents must be uppermost in the producer's mind, and that one of his chief determinants in the selection of plays must be the financial risk involved? Unless he happens to be a man of unlimited means who can afford to indulge his whims and produce any play he takes a fancy to, he must weigh, as best he can, the monetary potentialities of the scripts he reads. And since the high costs of production have made almost every producer dependent upon outside backing, he must take into account not only his own judgments but those of his investors. Even if they do accept his opinion, a series of wrong guesses is certain to weaken their confidence, and eventually he finds that his source of supply has dried up and that he is out of business. Thus, play producing is not only a gambling game but a guessing game, and while there are certain well-defined laws of probability applicable to roulette, dice games and poker, there appear to be none that have any practical bearing upon the choice of plays.

Also to be noted here is the effect that these financial considerations may have upon the quality of a production. The time limitation upon rehearsals imposed by Equity, and the stagehands' union's restrictions upon the use of scenery and properties (except at prohibitive cost) during the rehearsal period, often result in the opening of a play before the actors are adequately prepared or the mechanical problems of the production satisfactorily resolved. Since so much depends upon the first-night reception of a play, a ragged opening can actually kill its chances of success. Again, budgetary considerations may lead the producer to engage a second-rate director, or to keep his operating costs down by settling for a mediocre actor when a brilliant one might save the play and the day. Sometimes the inexperienced producer errs in the other direction and so overloads his payroll with expensive "name" players that he cannot come out ahead even if the play is a great success.

Whether the producer is to be condemned for his preoccupation with the dollar, pitied for his subjection to economic pressures or derided for his inability to conduct his business efficiently and intelligently, the fact remains that the art of the theatre must function as best it can inside the existing economic framework; and the dramatist, the actor, the director, the designer, no matter how gifted and how idealistic he may be, must find a way of expressing himself within its limitations.

XVIII WHAT DOES THE PUBLIC WANT?

That is the central question in the guessing game which the producer and the theatre owner are forced to play. It is a question to which no one has ever found a satisfactory answer. Anyone who should happen to discover even a moderately reliable formula for determining the box-office values of a playscript would become a multimillionaire in a very short time. If proof of this incontrovertible truth is needed, it is only necessary to point out that of all the plays produced perhaps one in seven or eight earns back its production cost (the percentage for musical comedies is somewhat higher).

This high incidence of failure is very hard for the layman to understand. A thousand times I have been asked how it is possible for men who have spent a lifetime in the theatre, and have presumably had ample opportunity to familiarize themselves with public taste, to go so wrong in their choice of plays. In any other business, they point out, the manufacturer or producer has devised means of gauging the public demand and of adapting his product to it. In fact, many a successful businessman, scornful of the lack of acumen displayed by theatrical producers, has backed his own judgment of a play with disastrous results; or perhaps, striking it rich with his first endeavor, has plunged triumphantly ahead, only to wind up in bankruptcy. (It should be noted that the backers of unsuccessful plays are for the most part businessmen, many of whom have insisted upon reading the play before putting their money into it.)

When one begins to examine the circumstances, the reasons for the theatrical producer's apparent ineptitude become a little clearer. In the first place, nearly all industrial products are standardized and strictly utilitarian. One automobile, toothpaste, cigarette, canned soup or brassière is, in spite of the TV commercials, very like another; and the public demand for these articles is constant and quite predictable. But the demand for cultural products is variable and is determined by taste rather than by necessity or the fulfillment of a specific purpose. It is easy to see that a marketable bicycle must have certain characteristics and meet certain requirements, but who can say the same for a marketable play?

Another difference between an automobile and a play is that a car rolling off the assembly line is an exact realization of the designer's specifications and blueprints; but no two productions of a play—or for that matter no two performances —are exactly alike, and the finished article, as realized by the director, the scenic artist and the actors, may be quite unlike what is indicated in the dramatist's script. And as we have seen, a listless first-night performance or an unforseeable technical mishap may have disastrous results. On the opening night of a play I attended somebody backstage miscued, and the curtain came down in the middle of the climactic scene at the end of the second act. The author, attired in tails, hastily appeared before the curtain, and told the audience in great detail what it would have seen had the accident not occurred; but the mood had vanished and with it the play's chance of success. This is not a usual happening, but it is indicative of the sort of thing that even at the very last moment can determine a play's fate.

Again, just what does one mean when he speaks of the "public taste"? Is it valid to assume that there is only one public and that it has fixed and ascertainable tastes? I think not. Surely there is one public for *The Iceman Cometh* and another for *Hellzapoppin*; nor do I believe that the audience that reveled in the Old Vic's esoteric (to put it gently) production of *Troilus and Cressida* is the same audience that was delighted by the antics of Menasha Skulnik in *Uncle Willie*, which one commentator said had a story "that made *Abie's Irish Rose* seem downright avant-garde." For many plays these disparate audiences seem to overlap, and some plays—*My Fair Lady* and *The Voice of the Turtle*—seem to have an appeal that is universal. To which audience is the producer to address himself and what principles, if any, can he use for his guidance?

It is often falsely assumed that what has succeeded once will succeed again, and there are certain well-tried formulas that seem to have a recurrent appeal—witness the dreary succession of plays dealing with the adventures and peculiarities of the enlisted man. But there is no certainty that the standardized product will invariably succeed. George Abbott, an astute and skillful showman, who aims at the public that goes to the theatre primarily for an evening's fun, once had an unbroken series of sixteen failures. An outstanding success is frequently followed by numerous plays of the same genre, yet these imitations are seldom well received. Indeed, it is often the play that is unusual in theme or in treatment that catches the public fancy: *The Skin of Our Teeth; Harvey; The Glass Menagerie; Strange Interlude; Street Scene.* But other meritorious plays of great originality have been ignored: *Billy Budd; Madam, Will You Walk; The Potting Shed; Barefoot in Athens; Thunder Rock.* Of course I am offering my own opinion of individual plays in support of a general observation. But apart from the soundness of my judgment of this or that play, the observation itself is, I think, indisputable.

A few notorious examples may be helpful in emphasizing the utter impossibility of predicting the fate of a play. As I pointed out earlier, Somerset Maugham, a very successful dramatist, was convinced that there was no play in his short story, *Miss Thompson*, and refused to make the dramatization himself. When the play, entitled *Rain*, opened in Philadelphia, its reception was so poor that the producer's friends advised him not to bring it into New York. But he decided to chance it, and the play of course became a sensational success. Substantially the same thing happened with *Our Town*, which was a failure in Boston, and hesitantly brought to New York by its producer, Jed Harris, after scrapping the scenery and presenting it on a bare stage with kitchen chairs and stepladders—a novelty that may have had something to do with the play's success. An even more striking example is *Journey's End*, by the English dramatist R. C. Sherriff. This play, written in the 1920's, made the rounds of the London managers, all of whom turned it down. It was the consensus that nobody wanted to see a war play with an all-male cast, a complete absence of love interest and a tragic ending. Eventually, the play was given a single performance by the London Stage Society, a noncommercial organization that makes Sunday-night productions of presumably noncommercial plays. The managers came to see it but did not alter their opinion. However, Maurice Browne, an actor-director theretofore associated mainly with Shakespearean productions in community theatres, acquired the rights to the play and subsequently produced it in a West End theatre. It was an instantaneous hit, and its success was duplicated in New York —in fact throughout the world. Browne made a million or more out of it, and, flushed with success, proceeded to lose it all in a few years, by buying a theatre and producing a string of failures.

But if there are no "sure-fire" formulas, are there perhaps certain themes that the sagacious producer will carefully eschew? Well, let us see. The average theatregoer is usually depicted as a harassed individual who goes to the theatre in search of "amusement" and "entertainment" that will help him "forget his troubles." Tragedy, it would appear then, is not his cup of tea. Yet Clyde Fitch's *The Climbers*, which everyone thought destined for failure because "it began with a funeral and ended with a suicide," was a great success. So were such tragic plays as *Long Day's Journey into Night*, *The Diary of Anne Frank* and *Death of a Salesman*. Again, in theatrical circles, religious and political themes are generally recognized to be "death at the box office." How does this theory square with the reception of *The Green Pastures* and *State of the Union?* George S. Kaufman, as shrewd a judge of public taste as can be found in the theatre, once defined satire as "what closes Saturday night." But some of his greatest successes lean heavily upon satire: *Once in a Lifetime, June Moon, Of Thee I Sing.* Fantasy is often said to be lacking in popular appeal, yet *Peter Pan* is a perennial favorite, and *Harvey, Beggar on Horseback* and *Death Takes a Holiday* have played to packed houses. It becomes apparent, I think, that as Shaw once put it, though not in this context, "the Golden Rule is that there is no Golden Rule."

In my lecture course at New York University I conducted an experiment, the results of which I found very illuminating. I asked each member of the class to imagine himself the director of a repertory theatre in a good-sized city other than New York. Funds were available to operate the theatre for three years, so that the financial factor was not involved; and in the course of the operation ten plays were to be presented. The student was required to give three criteria that he would employ in the selection of plays, and also list the ten plays of his choice. The purpose of the test was to find out how a good-sized group of exceptionally intelligent and well-informed drama students and theatregoers, unimpeded by monetary considerations, would go about selecting plays, and what plays they would select.

Fifty-one papers were turned in and carefully analyzed. The following is a summary of the criteria listed, arranged in the order of frequency of choice:

Audience appeal	21
Artistic merit	20
Entertainment value	16
Educational value	16
Historical or geographical variety	16
Variety of dramatic type	16
Similarity of dramatic type	13
Adaptation to capacities of performers	12
Classics	8
Demonstrated previous success	6
Encouragement of the experimental	5
Avoidance of the experimental	3

It will be seen at once that even in a relatively homogeneous group there were widely divergent and often antithetical points of view as to what principles should underlie the choice of plays for a theatre that was not dependent upon box-office success. Incidentally, I was rather amused by the fact that only twelve of the fifty-one took into account the capacities of the performers. For the practical director of a repertory theatre this would be almost the first thing to be considered in the selection of plays. I was also surprised that only five of this very advanced group saw the importance of encouraging the new and the experimental.

When we turn to the choice of plays the differences of opinion are even more striking. Of course, with each of 51 individuals selecting 10 plays, a total of 510 different choices was possible. There were not as many as that but there *were* 194, which is a good many. Of these, 96 were named only once; 35 twice, and 24, three times. For the purpose of comparison, I give in one column the plays that were named eight times or more, and in another the ten plays that (as of June 1, 1958) had had the greatest number of performances on Broadway:

24	*Death of a Salesman*	3,224	*Life with Father*
17	*Oedipus Rex*	3,182	*Tobacco Road*
16	*Hamlet*	2,327	*Abie's Irish Rose*
15	*The Glass Menagerie*	2,248	*Oklahoma!*
14	*Long Day's Journey into Night*	1,925	*South Pacific*
11	*The Cherry Orchard*	1,775	*Harvey*
10	*Desire Under the Elms*	1,642	*Born Yesterday*
9	*Our Town*	1,557	*The Voice of the Turtle*
8	*Othello*	1,444	*Arsenic and Old Lace*
	Major Barbara	1,404	*Hellzapoppin*
	Street Scene		
	The Importance of Being Earnest		
	Mourning Becomes Electra		

What strikes us immediately is that there is no correspondence whatever between the plays most favored by my hypothetical art theatre directors and those that have proved most popular with Broadway audiences. Furthermore, of the ten Broadway favorites, three are musical comedies and the remainder are comedies, several definitely on the broad side. The N.Y.U. list leans heavily upon tragedy. Only two of the thirteen plays could possibly be labeled comedies: *The Importance of Being Earnest* and *Major Barbara.*

These disparities seem to indicate that there is an unbridgeable gulf between art and commercialism in the theatre, and that the producers, after all, understand and cater to the public taste. But when we look at a few supplementary facts and attendant circumstances, the picture is not quite so clear. In the first place, all of the seven American plays on the N.Y.U. list were Broadway hits. *Mourning Becomes Electra* ran for 150 performances, which is quite a remarkable showing for a play—actually a trilogy—that took more than four hours to enact—twice as long as the playing time to which the American theatregoer is conditioned. The other six plays had runs ranging from over 300 performances to well over 700, though not one of them had the characteristics that are usually associated with good commercial risks. It seems evident that mercenary motivation is not necessarily an impediment to the communication of art—and also that art sometimes pays off!

Now, by way of appraising the astuteness of the Broadway experts, let us look briefly into the history of the first four plays on the Broadway list. *Life with Father,* which had an uninterrupted run of eight years in New York alone, during which time some three million people paid a total of about ten million dollars to see it, was two years in reaching Broadway. So dubious was the producer about its prospects that he decided to bring it to New York only after an encouraging tryout in a summer theatre in Skowhegan, Maine. *Tobacco Road,* second on the list, received a most unfavorable press and seemed doomed to immediate failure. I attended the first Saturday matinee, at which barely fifty people were present. After the performance I met the producer, who was steeped in gloom, as well he might have been. If he had had good business judgment, he would have closed the play that night. But he was inexperienced and stubborn; the cast was small, the operating expenses low, and Henry Hull, the star, enjoyed his part and was willing to make salary concessions—this was before costs had skyrocketed and Equity rules had tightened—so the play was kept on. Gradually business began to pick up; when the play finally closed in New York it had run for nearly eight years. Meanwhile, numerous road companies roamed the land. Many years later I made a trip to Cleveland and found that *Tobacco Road* had just completed its sixth return engagement there.

The history of *Abie's Irish Rose* is similar. It had the sort of reception that usually spells a quick finish. But the author (who, I believe, had produced the play herself because of her inability to find anyone else who would) insisted upon keeping it on. Like *Tobacco Road*, it had a small cast and there was no Equity or Dramatists' Guild control over salaries and royalties. I happen to remember very well that it ran for six years. For in 1925, when it had been running for three years, I remarked to a friend of mine, on the eve of my departure for Europe: "Here I am, going off for a year or more, and I haven't seen *Abie's Irish Rose*." "Oh, well," he said, "why not see it when you get back?" I followed his advice and saw it upon my return two-and-one-half years later. I often wonder how many of the dozens of plays that close every season, after a few performances, would develop into successes if the producer had the hardihood—and the cash!—to keep them running. If he liked it well enough to go through all the trials attendant upon production, and his backers had enough confidence in it to risk their money, may there not be thousands of others who have similar tastes? Of course this is sheer speculation, but it is far from improbable that many a potential *Abie's Irish Rose* or *Tobacco Road* has passed into oblivion because someone got discouraged too soon or ran out of dollars.

The story of *Oklahoma!* has been often told. The Theatre Guild, in financial difficulties, hoped to re-establish itself by producing a musical. But the problem of raising the necessary capital seemed insurmountable. Audition after audition was held for prospective investors, with most unsatisfactory results. It was pointed out that Lynn Riggs' play, *Green Grow the Lilacs*, on which the musical was based, had been a failure; that there was no appeal in a story about cowboys with no stars in the cast and not even a chorus line; that Oscar Hammerstein II, author of the book and lyrics, had not had a success in twelve years. Metro-Goldwyn-Mayer—shrewd appraisers of popular taste—who owned the motion-picture rights to the play, refused to invest in return for a share in the musical. Finally, just as the whole project was about to be abandoned, the necessary funds were painfully raised. The outcome bewildered everybody, including the producer and the authors. (It is interesting to note that *Oklahoma!*, *Life with Father* and *Tobacco Road* were respectively adaptations of a play and two books, none of which had had a great degree of popular success.)

For me, the N.Y.U. list contained many surprises and much food for rumination. I had expected *Oedipus Rex* and *Hamlet* to be among the first choices, and I was not surprised to find Williams, Shaw, Chekov and O'Neill ranking high too. But I had certainly not expected twenty-four of the fifty-one who handed in lists to select *Death of a Salesman*. (I do not say this in derogation of Miller's fine play: I simply was not expecting it.)

Perusal of the list suggests many other puzzling questions. Collectively Shakespeare, Molière and the Greeks are cited 108 times, more than 20 per cent of the grand total of 510 choices. Does this express a genuine excitement for their plays, or does it merely represent a conditioned genuflection of the college-bred to the classics? Ibsen and Chekov had 49 citations, yes, but why only 6 for Strindberg? Why does O'Neill outrun O'Casey, 50 to 8? In the new generation, Williams and Miller of course rank high; but Inge gets only 6 mentions. But what astonished me most—and I must say frightened me a little too—is that the dramatists who remade the American theatre in the 1920's and 1930's, and who for the most part are still alive and active, received almost no notice whatever! To cite a few examples; Kaufman & Hart and Maxwell Anderson received 4 mentions each; Hellman, Connelly and Odets 3 each; Lindsay & Crouse, Sherwood (winner of three Pulitzer prizes) and Behrman 1 each!

How is one to account for this neglect by drama students and theatregoers of dramatists whose work has had wide recognition and who have won for the American drama a foremost place in the world theatre? After much pondering, I have arrived at certain conclusions that—perhaps not altogether by coincidence—support the premise upon which this whole book is based: namely, that plays are written to be acted and the reading of a play can never have the impact that a performance of it has. Applying this to my group at N.Y.U., we find that—omitting the classics to which I have already alluded—the plays cited most frequently were mainly plays that they had *seen*. Most of the members of the class were in their late twenties or early thirties, which meant that their theatregoing had covered a period of not more than fifteen years or so. They had read Anderson, Sherwood, Odets, Hellman and the rest, but had never seen them performed. Why of all Shaw's plays did *Major Barbara*, by no means one of his best, receive the most votes? Because it had recently been revived in New York. So had *The Glass Menagerie*, *Desire Under the Elms* and *The Cherry Orchard*. *Death of a Salesman* had been done only ten years before, and *Long Day's Journey into Night* was currently running.

I hope that all this has thrown some light upon the great game of guessing what the public wants: a game which has no definable rules, which any number can play, and in which one man's guess is likely to be as good as another's. By way of further illustration I shall give a detailed account of the production of a play with which I was closely associated —because it happens to be one of my own.

XIX THE BIOGRAPHY OF A PLAY

I am telling this story because I know of no better way of demonstrating the inability of intelligent and experienced theatrical businessmen to gauge the values of a playscript. At the same time I think it will give some indication of what happens to a script in the course of its journey from the typewriter to the stage: in other words, what the process of communicating a dramatic creation entails.

Late in 1927 I returned to the United States after a lengthy sojourn in Europe. Though I am a native of New York, and had lived there most of my life, my long absence had given me a fresh perspective on the city and I decided to write a play about it. The background and subject matter had been in my mind for many years: a multiple dwelling, housing numerous families of varying origins; and a melodramatic story arising partly from the interrelationships of the characters and partly from their environmental conditioning. The setting was the façade of a "brownstone front"—a type of dwelling of which there are still thousands of examples in New York —and the sidewalk before it. As I visualized the scene, and as it was later projected, there were visible the two lower stories of the house and a suggestion of the third; the stoop and entrance hall; and the steps giving access to the cellar.

At one side of the house was a building in process of dem-
olition, also a familiar New York sight; at the other,
the entrance to a storage warehouse. These unoccupied structures I chose deliberately, in order to concentrate the action
on the apartment house and avoid the distraction of nonessen-
tial neighbors. The house was conceived as the central fact
of the play: a dominant structural element that unified the
sprawling and diversified lives of the inhabitants. This concept
was derived partly from the Greek drama, which is almost
always set against the façade of a palace or a temple. But
mainly I was influenced, I think, by the paintings of Claude
Lorrain, a French artist of the seventeenth century. In his
landscapes, which I had gazed at admiringly in the Louvre and
other galleries, there is nearly always a group of figures in the
foreground, which is composed and made significant by an impressive architectural pile of some sort in the background. In
fact, the original title of my play was *Landscape with Figures;*
but I felt that this was a little too special, so I borrowed again
from the terminology of painting and called the play *Street
Scene.*

Though the house is shabby and the street mean, the play is
not about slum dwellers or derelicts. This is not Skid Row,
but a lower-middle-class milieu, inhabited by workers of various sorts and even by a few intellectuals. There are an Italian
violinist, with a German wife, who gives music lessons; a
Russian-Jewish radical, whose daughter is a schoolteacher and
whose son is a law student; an Irish-American stagehand,
whose daughter works in a real-estate office; a shopkeeper,
with a taxi-driving son; a Swedish janitor; and assorted clerks
and artisans. There are also numerous visitors and passers-by:
policemen; a collector for a milk company; an ambulance
crew; an iceman; a social worker; moving-men; vagrants;
nursemaids; college girls; a postman; a doctor; delivery boys;
and nondescript persons of all ages and conditions. In all there
are some seventy-five characters, I suppose, and a cast of fifty

is required; many of the smaller parts can be doubled.

There is a central love story: a sort of Romeo and Juliet romance between the stagehand's daughter and the radical's son; and a main dramatic thread of murder, committed by the girl's father when he comes home unexpectedly and finds his wife with her lover. But there are numerous subplots and an intricate pattern of crisscrossing and interweaving relationships. The house is ever present and ever dominant, and the entire action of the play takes place on the sidewalk, on the stoop or in the windows. I give these details in order to make it clear that, whatever the play's merits or defects, it is an unconventional drama, in setting, in technique and in size of cast.

The play was completed early in 1928. I had been writing plays for fourteen years, and had had eight or ten Broadway productions, with varying success, so I was not unknown in the professional theatre. I had intended to market the play myself, but a surgical operation incapacitated me for several months, so I put the script into the hands of a very competent play agent, who began making the rounds with it.

The responses of the producers were emphatically and unanimously negative. I remember some of them. The Theatre Guild, which had produced my play *The Adding Machine*, said that *Street Scene* had "no content." Winthrop Ames, a man for whose judgment I had great respect, said that it was not a play. Arthur Hopkins, who had scored a great success with my first play, *On Trial*, told me that he found *Street Scene* unreadable. Others found it dull, depressing, sordid, confusing, undramatic. One producer opened the script, looked at the list of characters and read no further.

At length there was a show of interest. Sam H. Harris, who had also been associated with the production of *On Trial*, offered to take an option. I was pleased, of course, but rather wary; for I knew that Harris had already optioned more plays than he could possibly produce—a common practice, since it costs little to option a play, and it is an advantage to have numerous scripts to choose from—and, having had some bitter experiences, I had a feeling that he would never get around to doing *Street Scene*. So instead of giving him the usual six months' option, with the right to renew, I limited him to three months and no renewal.

It was fortunate for me that I had taken this precaution. For as Harris became more and more deeply involved in production activities, it was apparent that he could not take on *Street Scene*, and so the option lapsed. True, I had the script back on my hands, which was not very satisfactory; but it was only September, and the season was just beginning. Again my agent put the script in circulation. By now, all the leading producers had said no, and the approach had to be made to those in the second, third and fourth categories. But the lower echelons were as unresponsive as the upper had been. We were getting near the bottom of the roster, and I had about abandoned hope of a production, when my agent informed me that William A. Brady might be interested in doing the play.

I could hardly believe it. It would never have occurred to me to submit the play to him. In fact, I had almost forgotten his existence. In the golden pre-World War I era, he had made a fortune by producing a whole series of successful melodramas and farce-comedies, including plays by Dion Boucicault and Owen Davis. He was noted for his penuriousness, not only in the payment of actors' salaries, but in the quality of his productions. It was a standard joke on Broadway that Brady had only one set of scenery, which he had repainted for each new production, and that if he failed to find a play suitable to the scenery, he would commission one to be written. This was, of course, gross exaggeration; but there was no doubt that he was hardly the man to look to for a first-class production. Furthermore, the new era in the theatre had not favored him, and he had not had a success in twelve years. Long near the top of the Broadway ladder, he was now in his late sixties and completely overshadowed by his daughter, Alice Brady, and his wife, Grace George, both brilliant actresses, and by his son, William A. Brady, Jr., who had formed a very successful producing partnership with Dwight Deere Wiman, a multimillionaire who gave up industry for the theatre, which he loved passionately and to which he made many notable contributions. As Brady put it to me once: "They had me dead and buried." About all that remained of his former glory was the Playhouse, a theatre he had built in the days when construction was cheap, and which had long since paid off its cost.

It was with some misgiving that I went to see Brady. But he was obviously quite serious about producing the play. He was determined to make a "comeback," but no established author or important agent had been willing to bring him a script, and he seized upon *Street Scene* as a last desperate gamble. However, I was relieved to find that he seemed to grasp some of the values I had tried to put into the play. He was a crude and illiterate man, but far from stupid, and he had plenty of that indefinable sixth sense known as showmanship. He had seen, in his boyhood, a good deal of the teeming life of the poorer quarters of the metropolis; and somehow he associated the play, too, with the works of Boucicault, one of whose great successes was called *The Streets of New York*. I know little about Boucicault, beyond the reference to him in one of W. S. Gilbert's lyrics, so I cannot say what the connection was.

It was now late in October, and again I asked for a three months' limitation. Brady made no objection. In fact, he was anxious to get into production at once. The Playhouse was tenanted by a Brady (Jr.) and Wiman production, which was not doing well enough to satisfy the older Brady. His contract gave him the right to end the tenancy whenever he liked, but he did not wish to do so until he had a new tenant ready, and *Street Scene* was intended to meet that requirement. The fact that the play whose closing would be enforced was produced by his own son made not the slightest difference to him. After the contract was signed, I asked to see the stage in order to make sure that it was technologically suitable for the very special setting. While Brady and I were discussing the matter, young Bill emerged from the shadows and without any preliminaries said: "What are you doing, digging my grave?"

Afraid that Brady in order to save a few dollars would engage a third-rate director, I took the further precaution of insisting upon the right to approve the choice of a director. This clause was not in the original Minimum Basic Agreement of the Dramatists Guild, but at my urgence it has since been included, and now every dramatist has this necessary protection. After some discussion, we agreed upon a young director who had shown considerable talent in managing a good stock company—he has since become very successful in Hollywood—and casting began early in November.

Casting in the theatre is never very well organized, and is usually a trial for actors and for the director, since there are always twenty times as many applicants as there are parts, and the mere physical arrangements for interviewing present great problems, quite apart from the difficulty of making correct selections. But I have never seen anything comparable to the conditions under which *Street Scene* was cast. Brady had a small private office on the top floor of the Playhouse building, with a large, sparsely furnished anteroom, suitable for rehearsals. When word got around, as it quickly did, that there were fifty parts in *Street Scene*, the actors converged on the Brady office by the scores and hundreds. Brady's staff consisted of an elderly secretary, so there was no one to police the elbowing crowd that filled the anteroom to suffocation. Each time the door of the private office opened to dismiss an applicant, there was a mad rush to get in, for everybody was certain that in a cast of fifty there must be something for him and that everything depended on getting in first. Each hopeful came catapulting in, breathless and often in tears, with clothing and emotions in a state of disarray. It was hardly the best method for judging the qualifications of aspirants.

While I had the right of approval of the cast, I was aware of the importance of maintaining a harmonious relationship with the director, so though I had doubts about the wisdom of some of his selections, I thought it impolitic to make too much use of my veto power. Also, because of my long absence abroad and my subsequent illness, I was not very well acquainted with most of the actors who applied.

Brady was having his troubles getting the play financed. He had no money available, and his record for the past dozen years was not one that inspired the confidence of backers. He asked Brady (Jr.) and Wiman for a loan but was turned down (They had read and rejected the play. Seventeen years later it was Wiman who gave the musical version of *Street Scene* a handsome production.) Finally, Brady succeeded in getting backing from Lee Shubert, an old associate, who as a large-scale operator in the theatre played percentages. I do not know how much money was needed, but I am sure that the whole production did not cost ten thousand dollars. (Today rehearsal salaries alone, for a cast of fifty, would come to more than that.) With the financing arranged, Brady set the opening date for January 12, less than six weeks off. There was to be no tryout, because of the expense, so we were opening cold, which meant that all problems relating to script, cast and production had to be solved during the rehearsal period.

Suddenly the play, which had been stagnating for nearly a year, was being rushed into production. Knowing how much depended upon the setting, I thought it advisable to get that part of the production organized as quickly as possible. Brady was aware that none of the sets in his warehouse

THE BIOGRAPHY OF A PLAY 215

would do, so he was prepared to have a new one built. Accordingly, I began to search for a house that could be used for a model. I spent hours and hours roaming the streets of Manhattan, looking at brownstone fronts. There was certainly no shortage of them, but it was days before I found one (on West Sixty-fifth Street) that was exactly adapted to the stage business as I had described it in the play. I told Brady of my discovery and suggested that we engage a competent scene designer at once. Brady demurred; since the house was there, he said, it would be a simple matter for his stage carpenter, who was also a builder, to take a look at it, and reproduce it on the stage. It took me quite a while to persuade him that there might be something more to stage designing than a carpentry job based upon photographs and measurements. At length he agreed reluctantly to employ Jo Mielziner, then at the beginning of his brilliant career.

Preparations were now proceeding on all fronts. Then one day the director, after a morning of casting, announced that he was going to lunch and would be back in an hour. He did not return that day, and the following morning a telegram arrived to the effect that he had been suddenly called out of town and would get back as soon as he could. Of course casting had to be suspended. Next day, Brady informed me that he had learned that the director had not gone out of town but was rehearsing another play in a theatre down the block. He had never had much confidence in *Street Scene*, and when something that looked better was offered to him he simply switched over. (The other play opened two days after *Street Scene* and ran for eight weeks.)

Of course we were in desperate straits. Rehearsals were to begin in about ten days, the opening date had been set, the scenery was being designed and we had no director! A frantic search for a substitute was begun. Brady, in his frugality, proposed one mediocrity after another, but fortunately I was protected by the approval clause which I had had inserted in my contract. On the other hand, every one of the five or six first-rate directors who, at my suggestion, were reluctantly approached by Brady declined the job. Not one of them saw anything in the play or thought it had any possibility of success. We had reached an impasse, and it looked as though the production would have to be abandoned.

As a last-ditch attempt to get the play on, I volunteered to direct it myself. I told Brady that while I had worked briefly with amateur groups many years before, I had never directed a professional production; nevertheless, I thought I knew what the play was about, and that I might perhaps be able to convey to the actors what was required of them. Brady hesitated—as well he might have!— but he too wanted to get the play on, and when finally I told him that I would not ask for a director's fee unless the play were a success, the day was won.

It was no light task for a novice to undertake, with a cast of fifty, simultaneous action at three or four levels, crowd scenes, about one hundred entrances and exits in the first act alone (the average play has perhaps a dozen), innumerable sound effects and offstage cues. And no tryout for smoothing the mechanics and rectifying errors! But the very fact that there was so much to be done gave me no time to be frightened. So I plunged blindly ahead, hoping for the best.

The first thing I did was to eliminate most of the actors who had been tentatively engaged by the erstwhile director. Now that I had a free hand I was determined to make my own selections. Further, though Grace George, Bill Brady, Jr., and his wife, Katharine Alexander, an excellent young actress, all thoroughly disliked the play, and had done everything they could to talk Brady out of doing it, they had also managed to work some of their unemployed friends into the cast. (Several of Grace George's friends who had appeared with her in the pseudo-elegant "drawing-room" plays of the preceding decades declined the opportunity to be seen in a play that dealt with characters of inferior social position.) Brady, too, had taken on some old pensioners, who, to put it mildly, were decidedly "old-school." I felt sorry for them; but it was no moment for sentimentality, so I exercised my contractual rights and let them all out.

It was not easy to assemble a cast of fifty, in a very limited time, and with a very limited salary budget! Brady had a bad reputation among actors, not only because of his stinginess but because of his discourteous treatment of them, and I could get some of those I wanted only by assuring them that Brady had promised not to meddle in the direction of the play. He had agreed to this condition of mine, and in fairness to him, I must say that he faithfully adhered to it. Others wanted far more than Brady would pay, but I persuaded them to accept small salaries, with additional percentages if the receipts exceeded a certain amount. Brady readily agreed to this, for he had no expectation that the specified figure would ever be exceeded. The actors who had this arrangement eventually got two or three times what they had originally asked for, and I am sure that Brady never quite forgave me.

Somehow, the cast was assembled and rehearsals began in mid-December, on schedule. The Equity rules allow only twenty-eight days of rehearsal for any nonmusical play, no matter how large the cast or how complicated the production, and as it would have been folly to attempt to play to a first-night audience without at least two previews, I had to be prepared to give a performance before an audience in exactly twenty-six days. The task was not made easier by the regulations of the stagehands' union, which do not permit the use of scenery and properties unless a full stage crew is put on salary (and overtime). Because of these requirements, neither author, director nor actors see the scenery or the furniture and properties that are to be used until the dress rehearsal, which is usually a day or two before the actual public opening. However, since we were having no tryout, I told Brady I would have to have the set to work in for several days before the previews and he reluctantly agreed.

The first three weeks of rehearsals, however, were conducted on a bare stage, and as much time had to be spent in approximating the timing that would be required in the actual set as in training the actors in the interpretation of their roles. I was constantly saying something like this: "Now A enters at right and goes down the cellar steps, as B comes out of the house and on the stoop encounters C who has come on at left. While they greet each other D and E enter, respectively, left and right, and time their crossing so that they pass each other just to the right of the stoop. While they are making their exits, B comes down the stoop and goes off at left, while C enters the house, just as F appears at the first-floor window to the right of the stoop and A comes up the cellar steps and goes off right. At this point, G comes running on at left and up the stoop as C leans out of the second-story window to the left of the stoop, and H and I come on at right, engaged in earnest conversation."

In a way, it was fortunate that I was kept too busy to pay much attention to the surrounding psychological atmosphere, which was not good. Word had got around Broadway that a play practically everybody had rejected was now being produced by the discredited Brady with the additional handicap of a wholly inexperienced director. Everywhere I went I encountered pitying looks and skeptical grunts. The situation at rehearsals was not conducive to peace of mind either. Grace George and Katharine Alexander came in frequently and sat in the back of the theatre, whispering, whispering. Sometimes Katharine's little daughter came along and added her childish prattle to the sibilant chorus. They made no attempt to conceal their dislike of the play, and while they occasionally favored me with disparaging comments about the actors, there was never a word of encouragement.

Brady, who had been one of the pioneers of the film industry, still retained an interest in the studio buildings of the World Film Company at Fort Lee, New Jersey. These premises were now used mainly for the construction of scenery and it was there that the set for *Street Scene* had been built. Since the jurisdiction of the stagehands' union did not extend to the studio, it was possible to put up the scenery there without employing a stage crew. Of course, this meant that the entire cast had to be transported to Fort Lee, but apparently it was cheaper to hire a bus than to pay the stagehands. So, every day for a week, we all piled into a bus and in the bitter January weather ferried across the Hudson and scaled the Palisades to the old movie studio.

But we were all heartened when we saw Mielziner's strikingly realistic set, and even more when all the movement, including the surging crowd scenes, which we had theoretically rehearsed on the horizontal stage, fell neatly into place. A few things had to be corrected, but nothing fundamental. Brady seemed quite pleased and for the first time a slight feeling of optimism was possible. In fact, when the set was transferred to the Playhouse, just before the first preview, I received a shock of surprise. The sidewalk had been represented by a wooden platform, painted to simulate cement; but as the actors crossed and recrossed the stage countless times, the clicking of the women's heels destroyed any illusion that the pavement was real. I had been after Brady to put down a thin coating of cement, but he kept telling me that the expenditure of another seven hundred dollars was out of the question. When he informed me that he had ordered the cement job, I could hardly believe that I had heard aright. This was the first genuine compliment that the play had received!

Our first preview was on a Tuesday night. We had filled the house with an invited audience, drawn from various groups, in an effort to get a cross section of the New York theatregoing public: college students, office workers, hospital nurses, lawyers, shopkeepers, a sprinkling of actors and of personal friends. Needless to say, I was not without trepidation. But when the curtain rose, the solid-looking, skillfully lighted setting received a great round of applause; and when the action began it was evident that the attention of the audience was engaged. There was warm applause at the end of the first and second acts, and at the final curtain there were no less than nineteen curtain calls—not the usual thing, as any regular attendant at previews knows.

I was pleased and so was Brady. But late that night he called my home and told me gloomily that he had just had a talk with Lee Shubert, who had had the performance covered by his casting director—a former osteopath, known to me only as Doc Hunt. The play, Hunt had reported to Shubert, had no chance of success. I asked Brady how Hunt explained all those curtain calls. The explanation was simple; it was a friendly audience; there would be no paying customers. The second preview was very much like the first, except that there were twenty calls. There still seemed room for hope, in spite of the good doctor's prognostications.

The opening-night reception was even more enthusiastic: cheers, and so many calls that I lost count. On Friday, after the opening, the press was unanimously favorable. There were reservations, here and there, but the general tone was eulogistic. I was elated, of course, and later in the day I went to see Brady, expecting to find him in high spirits. Far from it: he was steeped in gloom. It seemed he had been making the rounds of the ticket agencies, which, at that time, used to buy up large blocks of seats for successful plays. Not one of them would undertake to buy a ticket. The play, they told Brady, was a "critics' success" without audience appeal; their clients were not interested in seeing a gloomy play about tenement-house life. (When the play was reviewed the following week by *Variety*, the skillfully edited trade journal of "Show Biz," which measures all entertainment activity in box-office terms, it was generously praised, but the reviewer said: "Whether this play which starts so interestingly will catch high public favor is questionable.") I was not cheered by this report, but there was nothing to do now but wait and see.

The Friday-night patronage was not very encouraging. Saturday matinee was better, and Saturday night was a sell-out. However, Saturday night in the theatre is always good, and the favorable reviews were bound to arouse a certain amount of curiosity. When the box office opened on Monday morning a line formed, and for a solid year it never broke. After a few weeks Brady added a midweek matinee, and for six months we played nine performances a week (twelve during Easter week: a matinee every day). There was never an empty seat, and always as many standees as the fire laws allowed. The ticket agencies now began clamoring for seats and grumbling because they were not getting enough.

That is by no means the end of the story. Once the play was established, I began urging Brady to organize a Chicago company. He brushed aside the idea. True, he said, the play was packing the house but that was because it afforded New Yorkers the pleasure of recognition; people outside New York would simply not be interested. It took me a whole year to persuade him. When a second company was finally sent to Chicago, it was an instantaneous success, and though the stock-market crash had affected theatrical business everywhere, the play ran in Chicago for four months and then made a successful tour, as did the New York company at the conclusion of its run of 601 performances. Later I organized another company which played on the Pacific Coast.

I then began a campaign for a British production. But Brady, who was making many thousands weekly, was unwilling to risk the small amount required to take up his option on the British rights. It was obvious to him that this play of local American life could have no appeal to foreigners. Thereupon I produced the play in London myself, in association with a London manager. The first-night reception was comparable to the one in New York, the press was equally laudatory, and the play ran for about five months, unusual in London, where plays with large casts are under a handicap because of the limited seating capacity of the theatres. The play has also been produced and well received in Argentina, Australia, Austria, Belgium, Canada, Denmark, France, Germany, Greece, Holland, Hungary, Japan, Mexico, Norway, Palestine, Poland, Scotland, South Africa, the Soviet Union, Spain and Sweden.

Meanwhile, the motion-picture companies, in the course of their routine coverage of all Broadway productions, had sent their story scouts to see the play. These experts, from the vantage point of seats purchased at high prices from ticket agents, came to the conclusion that the play had no audience appeal, and so reported to their employers. After the play had run for six months, however, and had been awarded the Pulitzer Prize, some of the bolder spirits in the motion-picture industry began to surmise that audience appeal might be injected by going inside the house and showing what went on in the various apartments. But when it became known that I took the position that, if the play were filmed, its form should be adhered to, what little interest there was quickly dried up. At length Samuel Goldwyn, who had long wanted to film a New York story, put in a bid for the rights, and a deal was concluded. But when it came to the closing of the contract, Goldwyn's attorney advised him not to sign it, because I was insisting upon the insertion of a clause that guaranteed the integrity of the play. A conference was called for the purpose of dissuading me. But I had known Goldwyn a long time, and I knew that, like Brady, he was a first-rate showman. I pointed out to him that he was foolish to pay a very large sum for the rights to *Street Scene*, unless *Street Scene* was what he wanted to do, and that that was all I was asking of him. He replied that of course he wanted to do *Street Scene*, brushed aside his lawyer's objections and signed the contract. He then engaged me to write the screen play, and the resultant picture was an almost exact reproduction of the play. It was very successful, both here and abroad, and Goldwyn has since told me that it is one of the most satisfactory pictures he ever made.

One more episode will bring the story full circle. With the development of television, a great demand was created for dramatic material. It occurred to me that *Street Scene*, with its variegated characters, would lend itself admirably to a series of episodes, all centering upon a multiple dwelling house and its occupants. An agent who was fired by the idea undertook to find a producer for it. He did not succeed. The reason is clearly stated in a letter, written in 1954, by one of the largest producers of television shows. It is an interesting document, written in the pontifical style that is characteristic of the upper echelons of big business, but as it is too long to reproduce in full, I shall merely quote a few significant paragraphs. After acknowledging that the play has merit and stating that in his opinion there is "a need for a television series which will dramatize the daily incidents of urban life," the writer goes on to say that there are, however, "many serious objections to the treatment of this property as presented in the existing prospectus." The letter then proceeds:

> Foremost among these objections is the squalor of the setting, the lower class social level of all the chief characters, and the utterly depressing circumstances which they all find themselves in. . . .
>
> We know of no advertiser or advertising agency of any importance in this country who would knowingly allow the products which he is trying to advertise to the public to become associated with the squalor, depression, continuous frustration and general "down" quality of the present conception of *Street Scene* week after week.
>
> On the contrary, it is the general policy of advertisers to glamorize their products, the people who buy them, and the whole American social and economic scene. If you will glance at the advertisements in your favorite magazine, listen to radio or television, for any one night, you will see the confirmation of this. The American consuming public as presented by the Advertising Industry today is middle class, not lower class; happy in general, not miserable and frustrated; and optimistic, not depressed.

Which is where we came in—twenty-five years earlier!

XX NOTHING SUCCEEDS BUT SUCCESS

How are we to account for the apparent inability of seasoned specialists to arrive at even approximately valid judgments, not only of the intrinsic merits, but of the commercial prospects of the material in which they deal? It would be easy enough to charge the producers with stupidity, timidity and mismanagement, and to support the indictment with many damning instances. But it would be a gross injustice to put the sole responsibility for the chanciness and instability of play production upon managerial inefficiency.

Producers are not all alike, and in the theatrical business there are no uniform industrial "policies," such as one finds in the monopolistically controlled, mass-production broadcasting and motion-picture industries. On the contrary, most theatrical producers are aggressive individualists, and it is the very dissimilarity of their tastes and standards that has created a collective theatre which is characterized both by exasperating confusion and by stimulating variety. At one extreme there are crude, semiliterate speculators, to whom play production is merely a gambling game in which one sometimes hits the jackpot; at the other are true idealists, who, when they can afford it, will take risks on plays whose chances of financial success seem very slight. And there are many gradations in between. What further complicates the whole situation is that examples of all types may be found in the ranks of both the most successful and the most unsuccessful. The irrational determinant is what is called showmanship; but that quality is as intangible and as undefinable as genius. Besides, there is showmanship in the production of *The Demi-Virgin*, as well as in the production of *Long Day's Journey into Night*.

Many factors over which the producer has little or no control enter into the determination of a play's success or failure. Some have already been mentioned; first-night accidents, for example: a crucial mechanical error, or the sudden inability of a leading actor to remember his lines. News of a great catastrophe, a sudden threat of war, or a bad stock-market break may drastically affect the mood of the first-night audience and hence the reception of the play. If a trifling play opens immediately after an important one it is almost certain to suffer by comparison; just as a second-rate play will benefit if it follow a succession of fifth-rate ones.

It often happens that a promising play fails because of miscasting or bad direction. Frequently the producer is guilty of errors in judgment, but not always, for the fault may lie more with the dramatist than with the producer. Besides, even the best director is not always at the top of his form; and good actors sometimes give very bad performances. Again, the producer may overload the production with costly actors; or, on the other hand, he may parsimoniously engage inferior actors. In the first instance, the play is forced to close because it cannot pay its way; in the second, because the production is not good enough. Here, too, the producer may be said to have used bad judgment. Yet many mediocre plays have won popular favor because of the performances of stars; and many plays have survived a shaky start because low running costs made it possible to keep them on until they found their audiences.

But there are two peculiar conditions affecting the popular response to plays, about which neither the producer nor anyone else in the theatre can do anything. The first is the exaggerated importance which attaches to the opening-night reception of a play. To all the other hazards of play production must be added the crucial one of the official New York première; out-of-town performances and previews are rarely decisive. In most instances, it is equivalent to staking everything you have on one throw of the dice.

There are many special features about an opening night, not the least of which is the composition of the unique audience. It consists of various elements which always include: (a) a large number of newspaper employees—sometimes as many as 150— who are there, not primarily as theatregoers, but in the course of their professional duties; (b) a generous sprinkling of friends and relatives of author, actors and producer, who usually want the play to succeed for personal reasons; (c) a certain number of investors, who are inclined to judge what they see in terms of potential box-office receipts; (d) a good many who come to be seen rather than to see, often unemployed actors who wish to publicize their availability; (e) theatrical agents, dramatists, producers, directors and Hollywood scouts, who want to keep in touch with what is happening in the theatre, and whose interest in the production is mainly professional; (f) an indeterminable number of theatre lovers, who have come simply in hope of entertainment or aesthetic pleasure.

Obviously, this is not the typical theatre audience, which normally is composed preponderantly of members of the last group mentioned. Whether it is "worse" or "better" than the typical audience is debatable. It is worse in the sense that many of its members are present because of duty or of some personal interest, often unfriendly, or are jaded by continual theatregoing, and not easy to please. It is better in that most of those present are experienced in the perception of theatrical values, and are exceptionally appreciative of the various skills that enter into a stage performance. It is often said that a play never has a more alert audience than on its opening night in New York. But the point is that, whether better or worse—or better *and* worse—it is this atypical audience that, more often than not, decides the fate of the play.

Chiefly decisive are the newspaper reviews of the play, again because of the fierce concentration upon a single performance. Reviews of exhibitions of painting and sculpture appear sporadically and probably have very little effect upon the attendance at art galleries, for most gallery visitors are not likely to read the reviews, since admission is usually free and it costs them nothing to go and form their own judgments. Besides, the show ordinarily stays on for a specified time regardless of attendance. Book sales are undoubtedly affected by reviews, but there is great diversity here, both temporally and geographically. Books are not necessarily reviewed on the day of publication—many are never reviewed at all—nor are the reviews confined to one locality. On the contrary, hundreds of reviews appear in publications throughout the land, and while one may be more influential than another, there is certainly none that is decisive. Further, on the date of publication, the book has already been widely distributed among booksellers and proprietors of lending libraries, and it is from them that many book buyers seek guidance. Even if time is required to overcome adverse reviews, it costs nothing to keep the books on the shelves while the public demand develops.

Not so in the theatre. Operating costs cannot be met for long if there is no substantial demand at the box-office, unless there has been an enormous advance sale. Since the degree of immediate public response is determined almost entirely by the newspaper reviews which appear on the day after the opening, the importance of critical opinion is apparent. Strangely enough, while a bad press almost invariably spells failure, a good press does not always spell success; for as everyone in the theatre knows, lasting success is the product of what is quaintly known as "word-of-mouth," that is, recommendation of the play by large numbers of those who have seen it. Good notices will start an immediate rush to the box-office, but if audiences are disappointed the demand will soon diminish. On the other hand, bad notices will keep people away, and so not only do the losses pile up, but there is no way of recruiting a sales force of contented customers. It is no wonder then that for everybody concerned, the most nerve-racking hours in a play's history are those that must elapse between the fall of the first-night curtain and the appearance of the first reviews.

It can hardly be denied that dramatic criticism serves a useful purpose. Even if it did not, it would still be true that, in a free society, anyone has a right to express his opinion of a play, no matter how unfavorable or how harmful that opinion may be. When producers, dramatists and actors sound off about the critics—as they frequently do—it is chiefly because they are only too well aware of the drastic consequences of adverse reviews. The weight that the critic's opinion carries is considered more important than the nature of his comments or his qualification for the job.

As far as qualification goes, there are good, bad and indifferent critics, just as there are good, bad and indifferent producers, dramatists and actors. But here an important distinction must be made. An incompetent producer will soon be out of business; an incompetent dramatist's plays will not usually survive; an incompetent actor will have trouble finding jobs. But an incompetent critic is not necessarily discharged—perhaps because of the indifference or the friendship of his employer, perhaps because he has a sensational or amusing journalistic style, or because of other reasons that have nothing to do with his fitness to be a critic. Therefore he may, for years, be in a position to do immeasurable damage to the careers of those who depend upon the theatre for their livelihood. This is not theoretical: it has been known to happen.

If the review of a play were recognized for what it is, namely the expression of a single individual's opinion, it would be unreasonable to take exception to it. But this is not the case, for the critic is identified with the important newspaper that employs him, and this gives his opinion a vast authority. I do not know how often I have recommended a play and been told that "the papers said it was terrible." Usually, I find that the "papers" were one paper, and that the unfavorable opinion was, of course, the sole judgment of one man, perhaps well qualified, perhaps not. If my friend had happened to read another paper, he might have been prompted to go to the box office. Even three or four unfavorable notices represent only the reaction of three or four men. Yet the disturbing fact is that three or four men can call the turn, and make it impossible for a play to find whatever audience it may potentially have.

This situation is due to the fact that because of the high cost of theatregoing and the competition of other forms of entertainment, people are reluctant to buy tickets for a play without some assurance that they will not be wasting their time and money. Dramatic criticism was always influential, but thirty or forty years ago there were many people to whom theatregoing was a regular habit, and who were not deterred by the cost of tickets or the rival attractions of movies, television and night-club floor shows. Further, the number of newspapers has steadily declined, while the population has steadily risen. When my first play was produced, there were fifteen or sixteen daily newspapers in New York. Today, half that number serve a population that has doubled. And since only three or four of the existing papers are widely read by theatregoers, it is clear that, as I have said, three or four reviewers can decide the fate of a play. Intelligent reviewers are disturbed by this state of affairs; for, recognizing their own fallibility, they feel that the responsibility imposed upon them is too heavy, particularly since there seems to be no general agreement as to the function of the critic.

Indeed, in view of the weight that his opinion carries it is not easy to say just what his function should be. Should he, in his evaluation of a play, be guided solely by his personal likes and dislikes? But suppose he has an antipathy to naturalistic plays, or to verse plays, or to musical comedies or to war plays, or perhaps even to the theatre itself? Should he regard the theatre merely as a form of entertainment and judge a play merely in terms of its capacity to divert? Or should artistic excellence be his only criterion? And if so, shall the level of excellence be determined by classical or by contemporary standards? Should criticism, in other words, be what Anatole France called "the adventures of a soul among masterpieces"? Should he attempt to identify himself with the audience and appraise the play from the point of view of the average theatregoer? (But is there an average theatregoer? And if there is, can the critic prejudge his response any better than the dramatist, producer or backers can?) Or should his aim be to ascertain the intention of the dramatist and to judge the play on the basis of how well that intention is realized, even though, on the one hand, he is confronted with the expert expression of a trivial or ignoble idea; or on the other, with the fumbling execution of an exalted and inspiring theme? Since each critic has his own approach to his task, it is easy to see why dramatic criticism collectively is, like most things in the theatre, a hit-or-miss affair; and why it is impossible for those who are vitally affected by it to know exactly what to expect.

One of the most puzzling aspects of the prevalent method of reviewing plays is that it combines reporting with criticism. For some inexplicable reason, the opening of every play is regarded as a news event, and receives the same amount of attention and space, whether it is the masterwork of a great dramatist or an odious bit of hackwork. It is as though the newspaper gave equal linage and prominence to a Presidential address and to the irresponsible remarks of a ward politician. Consequently, the critic must rush from the theatre to his typewriter and hammer out his review in time to meet the deadline for the early-morning editions. Even if the newspapers are correct in treating every opening as a newsworthy happening that must be immediately recorded, it would be a simple matter to have it covered by a qualified reporter, who could supply the readers with all the facts about the producer, the dramatist, the director, the cast, and right on down to the house electrician and assistant stage manager. The report might also include a list of the celebrities present, what the ladies were wearing and perhaps a noncritical synopsis of the play, as well as a description of the audience's response, seldom mentioned by the critic. This would relieve the critic of the pressure of time and the burden of factual reporting, and would permit him to prepare a more carefully considered review at his leisure, perhaps next day, perhaps two days later. This again is not theoretical; it describes a practice that is quite common in many European countries. Anyhow, as things stand now, the knowledge that the fate of a play may depend upon the wholly unpredictable judgment of the dramatic critics is detrimental to the morale of everyone connected with the production, and often creates a state of nervousness and tension that prevents actors from doing their best. As for the producer, he can only keep his fingers crossed and hope!

A second imponderable and uncontrollable determinant of the public reception of plays is inherent in the psychology of the American people. There is in the United States, and perhaps not only in the United States, an interest in success for its own sake, rather than as an indication of quality or performance. Everybody, it seems, loves a winner, without much regard to how the victory was achieved or what it connotes.

This curious obsession with success is strikingly apparent, for example, in the world of sports. Baseball, generally recognized as the "national game," arouses the populace to a high degree of excitement and partisanship. Cities in which there is no major-league team bid competitively for a franchise; if one is obtained civic jubilation mounts to fever pitch and finds expression in public celebrations, and in the heaping of honors upon the arriving players. The ball park is filled to capacity, and the press hails every victory of the local heroes over an opposing team as an exploit unmatched in the annals of history. This state of affairs continues as long as victories predominate. But when the team begins to lose more games than it wins, interest cools, attendance falls off, the stature of the idols diminishes, and attention is focused upon the clay feet rather than upon the laurel crowns. Even in cities with long-established teams, attendance fluctuates with the team's showing. A long winning streak produces an immediate increase in the number of spectators, a losing streak an immediate decrease. Apparently most baseball fans would rather see a one-sided or sloppily played game which the home team wins than a close and exciting contest of skill which it loses. If two teams are tied for first place on the last day of the six-months' season, and the final game is decided by a margin of one run, the winners are proclaimed "champions" and hailed as supermen, while the miserable runners-up are regarded as unworthy second-raters. "Wait till next year!" the losers cry, plaintively and apologetically, well aware that the only thing that really counts is winning.

Some years ago I happened to be visiting a large mid-Western university on "Homecoming Day," when the alumni flock back to the campus to see one of the big football games of the year. A faculty friend invited me to attend the game, played in the university stadium, which has a capacity of nearly 100,000. The home team lost, and as we shuffled along in the gloomy crowd my host said ruefully: "I'm afraid this is going to cost our library building fund a lot of money."

The same emphasis upon success is evident in the public response to the arts. People do not buy books, they buy "best-sellers." If the bookseller's stock is temporarily exhausted or the lending library has a waiting list, the demand zooms, for everybody wants to be on the band wagon. When a book is selling, its publisher's advertisements play up the fact that five editions have been exhausted and a sixth is on the presses, rather than that a distinguished literary critic has spoken well of it. Two of the best and most widely read literary sections in America—those of the *New York Times* and the New York *Herald Tribune*—have as a regular feature a best-seller list, which tabulates current books in the order of public demand, with no reference either to their contents or their quality. It has been said that these lists, compiled from reports of leading booksellers, are not always accurate, for the bookseller who is overstocked may sometimes report a book that is not "moving," in the hope that its appearance on the best-seller list will stimulate sales. Could there be better proof of the pervasiveness of the success fixation?

In the musical field it is the highly publicized soprano or symphonic conductor who is likely to draw the crowds, rather than the work that is being performed. It need hardly be pointed out that fame is not always synonymous with excellence, or that a modest performance of a new or rarely played composition may be more rewarding than even the most brilliant rendition of one that has become hackneyed through constant repetition. Again, a piano virtuoso who has been honored abroad is accorded a ticker-tape parade to the accompaniment of the cheers of thousands who have never heard him play, and who would probably be bored to tears if they did. Is he greatly superior to this or that contemporary who is struggling for recognition too, but has never set foot on foreign soil? Who knows or cares? Our hero is a sensational success, so he must be heard at any cost.

A few years ago, an exhibition of the paintings of Vincent Van Gogh was overrun by thousands of people who knew nothing about them, but who had read that these once-neglected works were now almost priceless. It had also become known that the painter had cut off his ear and given it to a prostitute. While this is not exactly an indication of success, it has the sensational and spectacular qualities that so often go with success. I was in the Borghese Gallery in Rome once, looking at Titian's *Sacred and Profane Love*, when a guide came along with an American in tow. The tourist, clearly a man of importance, was evidently in a hurry, and paid little attention to the guide's rhetorical exposition of the qualities of the picture. But when the guide remarked: "And for this painting the gallery has refused one hundred thousand pounds," the man's interest was instantly engaged. "Pounds!" he exclaimed, looking at the picture for the first time. "Say, he must have been some painter!" Another time, while looking at a small Raphael in the Grand Gallery of the Louvre, I felt a gentle tug at my sleeve. Looking round, I saw a sweet-faced old lady, who was pointing to the opposite wall. "The *Mona Lisa*'s over there," she said.

So it is in the theatre, which is what concerns us here. People do not go to see plays; they go to see hits. They do not go to see acting; they go to see stars. Spread the word that tickets for a play are unobtainable and the demand for them becomes frenzied; people stand tensely in line for an hour to book seats for performances six months off. Meanwhile, in the adjoining theatre, a worth-while play that, for one reason or another, did not immediately catch on, is dying of inanition. Often, when asked whether he enjoyed a play, the theatregoer will reply: "Oh, yes, I liked it very much"; only to add, as though he had been a victim of misrepresentation, "But the house was half empty!" At a dinner party, I heard an intelligent, well-to-do businessman, who has himself dabbled a little in playwriting, say: "I go to the theatre a lot. Of course, I don't see everything that's produced, but I manage to get to all the hits."

Variety, the hard-boiled trade journal of the entertainment industry, recognizes the importance that attaches to success. Every week it lists all the plays current on Broadway and on tour and states the number of performances, the money capacity of the theatre, and the amount of actual receipts. Reviews of new plays, often shrewd and well written, never fail to estimate the chances of box-office success. For years *Variety* featured what it called a "critics' box-score." This was a rating of the New York dramatic critics solely on the basis of the correspondence between their evaluations of the plays reviewed and the verdict of the public as measured by box-office receipts. "Percentages" were arrived at by the same method used in determining the batting averages of baseball players, that is, the ratio of "hits" to times "at bat." In the theatrical scoring, the critic was credited with a "hit" for correct predictions of failure as well as of success. The test was: did he guess right? At the end of the season, the critics were ranked according to their ability to appraise plays in financial terms. This extraordinary tabulation was eventually discontinued, largely, I believe, because the more responsible critics objected to it. Nevertheless, there is a general tendency to judge a critic's soundness on some such basis. In the cities where plays are usually tried out, the dramatic critics, who often are experienced and discerning, cannot help being aware that their judgments of plays will be re-examined in the light of the New York verdict. The more forthright among them are not likely to be influenced by this consideration; but there are others who provide an escape hatch for themselves by suggesting that the play could succeed "if the necessary work is done before it reaches New York," the implication being that if it does succeed, the necessary work has been done; whereas if it fails, it has not.

It is not only *Variety* that stresses the success aspect of productions. Newspaper stories and feature articles dealing with the theatre are almost always about the current successes and the personalities associated with them, and often they include references to earnings, even though the plays may be mediocre and the personalities dull. If the editor replies that he publishes what interests his readers most, I can only say that this seems to prove that what interests his readers most is success.

No doubt this preoccupation with success can be variously explained by psychologists; but whatever the explanation, the effect upon the theatre is disastrous. It seems more and more to be the rule that a play is either an outright success or an outright failure. The play with a limited but genuine appeal cannot survive, because its potential audience has time and money only for the hits.

Almost everyone who works in the theatre will agree that this is an unhealthy situation. No dramatist, producer or actor who is not motivated solely by monetary considerations—and most of the good ones are not—would see any inevitable correlation between the quality of his work and its material success. In fact, nearly everyone cherishes most what he regards as gallant failures that never received the recognition they deserved. As Aldous Huxley has said: "Success—'the bitch-goddess, Success,' in William James's phrase—demands strange sacrifices from those who worship her."

XXI THE NONCOMMERCIAL THEATRE

Though New York is the only really important production center of the American theatre, and the careers of dramatist, actors and directors are made chiefly on the stages of Broadway, its thirty-odd playhouses and sixty or seventy annual productions represent only a tiny fraction of the total theatrical activity in the United States. No study of the American theatre would be complete without a survey of the varied forms of this widespread activity.

There are two main types of theatre: the professional and the nonprofessional; usually the former is commercially operated, and the latter is not. But there are many exceptions to this general rule and much overlapping; for example, professional groups are often subsidized in one way or another, and many amateur groups employ professional directors and sometimes professional actors.

The professional theatre comprises, in addition to Broadway, the "road," or what is left of it; summer theatres; a scattering of more or less permanent stock companies and community theatres; and what has become known as the "off-Broadway" theatre, which, as its name indicates, is a complex of theatrical activity that lies, both geographically and operationally, outside the Broadway area.

The road, by which is meant the cities that are visited by touring companies, either prior or subsequent to the New York run of a play, has shrunk alarmingly. In an earlier chapter I detailed the route of a typical road company of forty years ago. Today such a tour is inconceivable, and it is a generation since many of the towns listed have seen a professional performance of a play. Tryout tours are now usually confined to a few cities on the Eastern seaboard: half a week in New Haven, Princeton or Wilmington, a week or two in Boston, Washington, Baltimore or Philadelphia. The post-New York tour has become more and more restricted, not only because of the enormous increase in all costs, but because, due to the growing popularity of winter vacations and the development of aviation, more and more people from all over the United States do their playgoing in New York. Only the most successful Broadway plays now go on tour, and if the cast is large and the production elaborate, the tours seldom pay. Because of the excessive cost of meals and hotel accommodations, many actors refuse to go on tour unless their New York salaries are substantially increased. The number of cities that can be profitaby visited keeps on diminishing. The "one-night stand" has almost disappeared, except for a few cities that have vast auditoriums, where the receipts are large, but where playing conditions are far from ideal. Since there are few large cities between St. Louis and San Francisco or Los Angeles, the vast territory between the Mississippi and the Pacific Coast hardly ever sees a touring company. The same is true of practically the whole region south of the Mason and Dixon line, and of New England north of Boston. The significance of the tours then is that they make professional productions of the latest Broadway hits available to the inhabitants of twenty or thirty large cities, and that, in so far as they are profitable, they contribute to the commercial success of the plays.

Summer theatres, which are mainly professional, have increased in number and in popularity. They are usually situated in rural areas, principally in the Northeastern states, and cater chiefly to urban vacationists. The season is brief—not more than eight or ten weeks as a rule—and the prevailing tendency is to produce light comedies, with small casts and simple scenic requirements. Sometimes a new cast is engaged for each production, but more frequently a resident company is augmented weekly by a different visiting star. Of late, there has been an increase in the number of "package shows," organized groups of players, headed by a star, performing a single play, in a circuit of theatres. When this system is employed, the theatres, of course, become merely booking outlets for touring companies. Perhaps twelve or fifteen of the hundred or more summer theatres in operation are expertly managed, employ good actors and directors and maintain a fairly high level of professional excellence. The Westport Playhouse in Connecticut, the Cape Playhouse in Massachusetts, Elitch's Gardens in Denver and the Bucks County Playhouse in Pennsylvania are conspicuous examples. But in most of the theatres neither standards nor achievement are of a very high order. The shortness of the season and the narrow margin of weekly profits makes it advisable to keep costs down. Further, a weekly change of bill does not allow adequate rehearsal time, as the productions often make painfully evident. But people on holiday are inclined to be indulgent, and to tolerate in a converted barn what they would indignantly reject in a Broadway theatre. A few of the theatres are enterprising enough to undertake the production of new plays, and occasionally one of these shows sufficient promise to warrant a New York presentation: for example, *Life with Father* and *The Fourposter*. Some of the theatres augment their income by taking on paying "apprentices," or by operating "schools" of rather dubious value. However, the summer theatres do serve a very usual purpose, in giving aspiring novices an opportunity to acquaint themselves with the discipline of the theatre and the skills of play production: the building, painting and handling of scenery, the making of costumes, lighting, make-up, and so on. Also young actors are enabled to play to audiences and to appear in a variety of parts, a type of experience that is not easy to acquire in the American theatre.

Little need be said about the few and widely scattered winter stock companies and the professional community theatres. The former, in general, follow the familiar pattern, and present plays of established Broadway popularity or standard classics of the world drama. Sometimes, like the more lively summer theatres, they encourage young writers by producing their plays. There are several community theatres, such as the Cleveland Playhouse and the Pasadena Community Playhouse, that have long records of worth-while achievement. But their influence is mainly local, and limited even locally, for I know of none that is fiancially self-supporting. All are subsidized in one way or other: they either have wealthy contributors, operate schools, or depend upon the willingness of their workers to accept meager salaries. These theatres are sometimes excellent training schools and have provided Broadway with many first-rate actors and technicians. But the very fact that these talented individuals have chosen to come to New York in search of greater rewards and wider audiences seems to prove that the community theatres have no deep cultural roots and little professional prestige.

The off-Broadway movement is vital, healthy and promising. As we have seen, there have been, in the past forty or fifty years, various peripheral groups—the Provincetown Players, the Washington Square Players, the Civic Repertory Theatre and others—that have made valuable contributions to the American theatre. But in recent years, they have increased in number and in scope, until at present there are probably more theatres operating outside the Broadway area than in it; and collectively they constitute an important adjunct to Broadway. It is hard to single out individual producing groups, for they come and go, and none as yet has established permanence. The list of plays performed is impressive, for it includes works by Shakespeare, Jonson, Ibsen, Chekov, O'Neill, O'Casey, Williams and Miller, as well as by such esoteric dramatists as Sartre, Joyce, Pirandello,

Beckett and Ionesco. Many of the productions have been characterized by skillful staging, fine acting and interesting technical innovations.

But while the merits of the off-Broadway theatre are unquestionable, it can hardly be said to put the Broadway theatre to shame, as some of its more enthusiastic supporters seem to think. On the average, off-Broadway and on-Broadway show about the same range. Triumph matches triumph, and ineptitude, ineptitude. On the technical side, Broadway certainly has the edge. Its theatres, antiquated and inadequate though they are, undoubtedly make better provision for the requirements of a production and the conveniences of an audience than do the cellars, lofts, hotel ballrooms and churches that do duty as off-Broadway theatres. At best, one is glad to make allowances in order to see an unusual play, vividly presented; at worst, physical shortcomings aggravate the torture inflicted by the clumsy enactment of an impossible script.

Like the community theatre, the off-Broadway theatre is almost never self-supporting. Sometimes it owes its existence to the bounty of some wealthy individual, but mainly it has to depend upon indirect subsidies. These consist of reduced rentals by landlords with unmarketable property on their hands; relaxation by the theatrical unions of their featherbedding requirements and their minimum-wage scales; royalty concessions by dramatists; and, principally, the willingness of high-salaried actors to accept nominal pay, for a limited period, in order to play parts that interest them. Nearly all these concessions, of course, are made upon the understanding that the enterprise is a nonprofit one. As soon as it becomes profitable, the concessions are revoked and the costs go up. In fact, they go up anyhow. An off-Broadway producer must now reckon his production costs in terms of thousands of dollars, instead of hundreds, as he was able to do only a few years ago. This has necessitated an increase in the price of seats, and the gap between the Broadway and the off-Broadway scale has narrowed considerably. In short, there is no escaping the operation of the iron laws of economics, and to keep his theatre alive, the off-Broadway producer too must think in terms of dollars and cents. And in fairness it should be said that many a Broadway producer has a favorite play that he would be glad to present on a nonprofit basis, if he could book a theatre for the mere cost of its overhead, cut royalty payments in half, rid his payroll of unnecessary employees and get stars to work for cigarette money. Meanwhile, he, like all theatre workers who esteem the dramatic art, applauds the accomplishment of the off-Broadway theatre as not only admirable in itself, but as an important contribution to the education of audiences and the creation of a demand for better plays and finer productions.

Coexistent with the professional theatre is the nonprofessional, or, as it is usually called, the amateur theatre. Its personnel includes both amateurs in the sense of persons who engage in an activity merely for the love of it, and amateurs in the sense that they lack talent or training. The two categories are not, of course, mutually exclusive. The number of amateur groups that put on plays, more or less regularly, has been estimated at 25,000 or more. If this figure is correct and the average number of performances per year is conservatively estimated at 10, we arrive at the staggering total of 250,000 performances! An average attendance of 200 (again a low figure) would bring the annual amateur theatre audience to 50,000,000, which is probably ten times the number of those who attend professional performances. It would be impossible to estimate how many *individuals* are included in each group, because most theatregoers see more than one play in a year, and many attend both professional and amateur performances.

The amateur groups comprise almost every type of social organization: universities, schools, churches, labor unions, professional societies, fraternal orders, clubs of every sort, prisons, racial and ethnic associations. The plays produced are infinitely varied. The catalogue of one of the several agencies engaged in the business of leasing amateur rights lists some three thousand titles, under such categories as Catholic Plays, Chinese Plays, Hallowe'en Plays, High School Plays, Lincoln Plays, Melodramas—Old Gay '90 Type, Mock Trials, Negro Plays, Plays with a Majority of Women, Puppet Plays and Revue Sketches. Most of the plays listed were written during the past fifty years, for the copyright period is only fifty-six years; hence any play written prior to the twentieth century is in the public domain and may be performed without permission or payment of royalty.

Amateur productions are presented for a variety of reasons. While those who organize and participate in them are usually motivated by an interest in the theatre, there is often a secondary or supplementary motive. Schools and colleges are likely to produce plays for their educational and cultural values, as well as for entertainment. (I do not mean that education cannot be cultural, or culture educational; but there is a great difference between an activity that is intended to increase knowledge and one that is intended to develop aesthetic perception.) Sometimes the productions are part of training courses. Religious groups tend to produce plays that foster piety; racial groups, plays that emphasize special characteristics and keep traditions alive. Many groups of all sorts produce plays in order to raise money, either for the promotion of their own activities or for some philanthropic cause. Because the cost of most amateur productions is trifling, substantial sums are sometimes realized by the sponsoring organizations. And often play producing is merely a form of social and recreational activity.

Since the great majority of those engaged in amateur theatricals have no professional aspirations and no particular aptitude for the theatre, it is not surprising that the general level of achievement is not very high. One could hardly expect secondary-school students, busy professional men and women, or employees of an insurance company to put on a performance that attracts anyone but friends and well-wishers. But it does not follow that these activities are futile or deplorable. On the contrary, not only do they serve the healthy purpose of providing a leisure-time occupation that entails both teamwork and self-expression, but each helps, in a small way, to keep the theatre alive.

At the other end of the scale there is a substantial number of university and well-established community or "little theatre" groups that maintain high standards, both in the selection and in the performance of plays. Many universities have a full program of drama courses that includes instruction in acting, designing, directing and playwriting. Young dramatists are sometimes in residence, and production of their plays is made a student project. Frequently faculty members are pressed into service for the more mature parts in plays, and I have seen a few university performances that were superior to many professional ones.

But the sad truth is that, for the most part, college and little-theatre productions have little to commend them, not merely because of lack of talent and of skill, but for reasons that are, theatrically speaking, quite extraneous. For one thing, the success psychology often permeates the campus too, and though no investment is at stake, the director of the college theatre is likely to incline toward Broadway hits, rather than toward the experimental or limited-appeal play that has not made the grade. Again, the director, either because of innate timidity, or because he regards himself as the guardian of the students' morals, or fears the disapproval of conservative parents, or of the legislators who supply the college funds, is likely to avoid doing plays that are unconventional in theme or in language. The same is true of little-theatre directors, who hesitate to offend the sensibilities of the townsfolk, or of some contributor to the maintenance of the organization.

Actually, there is no sharp cleavage between the commercial and the noncommercial theatres. Each has its peculiar characteristics, but there is a great similarity in merits and in defects. They serve to complement each other, and to merge in that strange and complex entity which is the American theatre.

XXII THE ACTOR

All the conditions that have been discussed play a part in determining what shape the theatre takes and how it works, and therefore vitally affect the communication of drama, and to some extent its creation. But important though they are, these factors are mainly social, rather than artistic: environmental accidents, that have little or no relationship to the drama as an art. Inherent in the nature of drama, irrespective of external conditions, is the need for interpretative elements to bring the play script to life and to present it to the audience for which it is intended. Hence any inquiry into the theatre as an institution would be incomplete without examining the character of these elements and their functions in the communicative process.

Since plays are written to be acted, the actor may be said to be not only first in importance, but indispensable. Whether the play be a duologue, in which the performers simply sit and talk, or a pantomime that depends entirely upon physical movement, it is the actor who is mainly responsible for conveying to the audience the dramatist's meaning. The business of the actor is to perform what is written by the dramatist; but it is also the business of the dramatist to write what can be acted. Failure to meet this requirement accounts for the inability of many great poets and novelists to write for the theatre.

It is not surprising that some of the world's greatest dramatists were themselves actors (Sophocles, Shakespeare, Molière). Many others have written plays with specific actors in mind. But even when the dramatist creates without thought of particular actors, it is imperative that he have some awareness of what the actors will be doing and how his dialogue will sound when it is spoken on the stage. If he does not, his play will not effectively express what he is trying to say.

Every established dramatist knows how much he owes to fine actors who have vividly made evident the values of his play. Unless he is unusually fortunate he has also seen those values lost because the actors were miscast or were lacking in skill. Few theatregoers can differentiate a poor play and a poor performance. Even drama critics often put the blame on the dramatist, when it is the actor who is at fault; or praise an actor unduly because he has been assigned to a showy part. People who see plays performed by stock companies, or even at the end of a long original run, when the actors are jaded, often find that the play does not measure up to what they had been led to expect. One of the reasons for the decline of the road in the United States is that the producers sent out inferior companies, in the belief that they could trade upon the plays' New York reputation. As long as there was no competition, the audiences in other cities took what was offered them; but when talking pictures came in, with their star-studded casts, theatregoers were no longer willing to pay to see slovenly performances by incompetent actors, no matter how good the play.

One thing is certain: the actor can never be *better* than the part he plays, for his function is to interpret the character that the dramatist has created. If he embroiders the part or gives it deeper meanings than the dramatist had conceived, then he is creating something new and, in effect, becomes a dramatist himself. Actors are always trying to improve their parts, so that they may appear to better advantage, and they frequently do so by the introduction of distractions and irrelevancies that are detrimental to the play as a whole. A simple example: if one actor strikes a match while another is saying something important, the effect of the speech may be entirely lost, for in the theatre the eye is far more alert than the ear. (A late-comer will always draw the attention of the audience, no matter what is being said on the stage.) Of course, the devices used by some actors to make themselves noticed are usually far more subtle and complex than the one I have mentioned.

On the other hand, the better the part, the greater is the variety of interpretations to which it lends itself, as must be evident to anyone who has seen a great play performed by several companies. *Hamlet*, of course, provides the obvious illustration. No wonder they all want to play Hamlet. For this character is so complicated, and has been the subject of so much discussion and controversy, that no one actor could possibly realize everything that is implicit in the script. Therefore each actor is able to discover his own set of meanings and to give a more or less individualized characterization. I have seen *Hamlet* performed at least twenty times, and in half a dozen languages. No two interpretations were remotely alike, yet each had some special features of interest, and justification for each could be found in the text, just as ministers of religion often find diametrically opposite meanings in Biblical passages. So Hamlet has appeared on the stage as a poet, a philosopher, a suicidal melancholic, a madman, a psychopath, a lover, a scheming politician, an incestuous-minded son, a modern swashbuckler, and even as a woman.

Every play is not *Hamlet;* but any really good part can be played in different ways. I have seen many Lady Macbeths, Candidas and Hedda Gablers, but no two alike. I saw performances of *The Cocktail Party* and of *The Chalk Garden*, first in New York and later in London. Each play was splendidly acted in both places, and while the essential qualities of the plays were of course preserved, the relative values and emphases were substantially, and interestingly, altered. An even more striking instance was *The Glass Menagerie*, which I saw when it was first performed by Laurette Taylor and later, when it was revived by Helen Hayes, both superb actresses. As Miss Taylor interpreted the character of the mother—impractical, daydreaming, fumblingly living on memories of the past—she became the rather pathetic and sentimentalized figure of a faded gentlewoman. As played by Miss Hayes, the absurdities and futilities of the character were stressed, and one was moved to laughter rather than pity. It would be hard to say which performance was more interesting. Yet each of these fine artists could be said to be following the advice attributed to Epictetus: "Remember that you are an actor in a play, the character of which is determined by the playwright. For this is your business: to play admirably the role assigned to you; but the selection of that role is another's."

Unfortunately for the dramatist, and therefore the theatre as a whole, it is not always easy to find actors who can play "admirably" the roles assigned to them. This is particularly true in the American theatre, for a number of reasons, which should be briefly noticed. In the first place, there are no permanent companies in the United States, so that actors do not have the opportunity to work continuously in a variety of roles, and under a director who is able to study their capabilities and to help in their development. Each production is a new enterprise and the procedures for interviewing actors are so haphazard and unorganized that casting is often a matter of chance or luck.

Again, because the number of available actors is always far in excess of the number of parts to be filled, and the sorting out of candidates is a laborious and hazardous process, many directors depend upon what is called "type casting," which means that the actor is chosen because of certain physical characteristics that seem suitable to the part, or because his past performances have been identified with a certain type of role. This has led actors to "specialize" in playing a particular kind of character. I am always astonished when an actor says to me: "I understand that there is a doctor (or a housemaid or a plumber or a grand duchess) in your play. I played one in So-and-So and in Such-and-Such." As though any doctor (et cetera) as portrayed by any dramatist were exactly like any other!

The economic factor enters too. Ideally, every part, no matter how small, should be played for everything that is in it. In the great repertory theatres of Europe it often is. I have seen performances by the Moscow Art Theatre, for example, in which the leading actors of the company played very small parts. But the American producer dare not further increase his budgetary problems by engaging high-priced actors for minor roles. Further, prominent actors usually feel that they suffer a loss of prestige by appearing in a minor part. It is told that two actors were discussing the announced intention of a famous actress to organize a repertory company. "Isn't it wonderful!" said one. "One night Jane will be playing a big star part, and the next night she'll just come on carrying a tray." "If Jane comes on carrying a tray," said the other, "you can be sure that the head of John the Baptist will be on it."

But the main trouble is that the majority of so-called professional actors are deficient in talent or in training, and only too often in both. This is not said in derogation of actors. There are many mediocre and incompetent teachers, doctors, lawyers and engineers too; but in these professions a fairly rigorous course of instruction, and the ability to measure up to certain qualifying standards are prerequisites to practice. In the American theatre there are no such requirements for actors. Any young man or woman who through personal connection, salesmanship or just sheer luck succeeds in getting a part that calls for the delivery of only one line is eligible to membership in Equity, and as long as he or she continues to pay the nominal dues is a professional actor. A handsome face, a winning manner, a neat figure often count for more than genuine talent and years of preparation. The sad truth is that the acting profession is overloaded with those who have no real vocation for it: youngsters who are attracted to the theatre by its "glamour," or by the opportunities it offers for exhibitionism and the gratification of vanity; and immature or frightened individuals who are unwilling or unable to face the realities of life and who seek escape through identification with the fictitious characters they portray. (This second category often includes many excellent actors.) An incompetent painter, composer or dramatist does not impede the progress of his abler colleagues; but the hundreds and hundreds of incompetent actors who clog the labor market deprive qualified competitors of employment and lower the general standards of the theatre by creating a state of chaos in the casting of plays.

In defense of the actor, it should be said that while his incompetence frequently is indicative of lack of talent, it may also be due to lack of adequate training. Acting is a severe discipline that includes many skills: diction, voice production, bodily grace, timing, teamwork, make-up, characterization. The mastery of these skills is a long and costly process. There are many good schools in which acting is taught: some in universities, some associated with community or summer theatres, some existing independently. But, as in all other professions, theory and classroom exercises must be supplemented by actual experience before the novice is equipped for practice. The young lawyer or the young doctor acquires the rudiments of his science in law school or medical school, but it is his apprenticeship in the courtroom or the hospital that finally qualifies him for his lifework. But while there are many courtrooms and hospitals, there are relatively few theatrical organizations in which the fledgling actor can have a chance to try his wings. In the days

when stock companies flourished, many of them were training schools for actors. But today such institutions are almost
nonexistent. How then is the aspirant to learn? The answer is
that only too often he never learns, and either gives up in
frustration, or struggles on as best he can, to the impediment
of his own career and to the detriment of the dramatist, producer and theatregoing public. Actors constantly complain,
and with considerable justice, that without practical experience
it is almost impossible for them to get parts; and that if they
cannot get parts it is impossible to get experience. This is another of the seemingly insoluble problems that arise from the
unstable conditions of the professional theatre in the United
States.

Like any art, the art of acting is encumbered with many
traditions, many styles and many theories. But unlike the purely
creative arts, its various manifestations directly affect the art
of the drama, as must be apparent to anyone who has seen Shakespeare played by actors who have not learned to read blank
verse, or a modern play in which actors employing different
techniques produce an effect that is disconcertingly inharmonious.

What is the correct approach for the actor? Should he completely submerge himself in the part and seek only to project
the dramatist's conception? Or should he attempt to enhance
the vividness of the protrayal by injecting into it something of
his own personality? Both the dramatist and the drama student
would be inclined, I think, to take the first view. Yet a meticulously correct interpretation of a part can sometimes result in
a dull performance; whereas many successful actors owe their
popularity to their individual charm or magnetism and to the
fact that they adapt every part they play to their unique personalities. Bobby Clark as Bob Acres, Bert Lahr as Argan, and
W. C. Fields as Micawber have pleased audiences, whatever
Sheridan, Molière and Dickens might have thought of them had
they had the privilege of seeing their performances.

Again, should the actor give a performance in which every

detail, every intonation and gesture has been carefully thought out and is always executed with the same precision; or should he play the part as he "feels" it at the moment of performance? In recent years, the tendency in the American theatre has been toward the latter approach, mainly because of the influential positions occupied by former members of the Group Theatre, an organization completely dedicated to the famous Stanislavski "method." There is no doubt that a merely "technical" performance may be rigid and lacking in emotional color, and that a certain amount of spontaneity can produce a sense of freshness that communicates itself to an audience. Sometimes, for example, the excitement that attends an opening night will stimulate "inspired" performances that are never again repeated.

But the general advisability of a general application of the "method" must be regarded with some skepticism. There is considerable difference between the ensemble performances of the Moscow Art Theatre company, whose members work together, year after year, and who study a play for many months before they give a public performance, and the average catch-as-catch-can Broadway company, composed of actors who may never even have met before, and who must somehow attempt, in the very inadequate rehearsal time, to put together a stable and cohesive performance. Further, not every teacher of the "method" is a Stanislavski, nor is every pupil a Moskvin or a Chekova. Improvisation may add color and vitality to the performance of a company of technically expert actors, accustomed to give-and-take, and able to adapt themselves easily to modulations of pattern. But in an aggregation of casuals, nothing can be more disconcerting than sudden or unexpected deviations from the established routine. It is significant that many of the most vociferous advocates of the "method" are actors who lack the skill and the self-control that are required for a steady and well-constructed performance.

The dramatist then, in the process of creation, must remember that the communication of his play is dependent upon actors;

and that the effectiveness of communication may be greatly enhanced by the ability and insight of the performers or greatly diminished by their incompetence and stupidity. The theatre is at its best when the dramatist expresses himself in terms that give the actor an opportunity to utilize his talents to the full, and the actor employs all the art at his command to convey what the dramatist has tried to express.

XXIII THE DIRECTOR

No theatregoer, however illiterate or unsophisticated, can be unaware of the participation of the actor in the presentation of a play, for there he is, ever present, the living medium through which the dramatist's characters and plot are made visible and audible. I suppose that most theatregoers are also aware that someone invented the story and wrote the dialogue; but for the majority he is a shadowy and secondary figure. Ask a hundred people to name the author of the play they saw last night, and not one in ten will know the answer. When Alan Jay Lerner and Frederick Loewe appeared as guests on a television program, the announcement of their names brought no response from the studio audience. It was only their identification as librettist and composer of *My Fair Lady* that evoked thunderous applause. Of course, if Rex Harrison and Julie Andrews, the stars of the show, had been announced the ovation would have been instantaneous. At a London dinner party, a lady said to me: "I never fail to see Gladys Cooper; she always says such witty things."

But if only one theatregoer in ten knows or cares who wrote the play, it is safe to say that not one in a hundred knows who directed it, or is even conscious of the fact that it was directed at all. This is not surprising, nor altogether deplorable, for the mechanics of play production are most effective when they are least apparent. In a well-directed play the movement is so easy and graceful, the flow of words so smooth and natural, that it all seems to be something that is happening spontaneously, instead of the precise execution of a carefully conceived and minutely detailed pattern.

Yet for all his anonymity the director is nearly as indispensable to the communicative process as is the actor. It is almost impossible to imagine a company of actors preparing a play for performance without the guidance of a director. They would not know what to do, where to go, how to speak their lines, and the production would be a hopeless muddle, completely lacking in form and in cohesion. Many years ago, in New York, a group of musicians formed a "conductorless" orchestra, which made a number of public appearances. Not only were the performances mediocre, but I suspect that during rehearsals the concertmaster or some other member of the orchestra indicated the tempi and co-ordinated the several sections. And musicians, of course, are not required to move about, to assume fictional identities or even to memorize the notes they play. No experienced actor or dramatist underestimates the importance of the director, for the reception of the play may very well depend upon the kind of job he does.

The number of stage directors in the contemporary theatre is small, and very few ever rise above mere competence. First-rate directors are rare indeed. One reason is that since the advent of talking pictures, the experienced stage director has found Hollywood far more attractive than Broadway, not only financially, but in terms of prestige. Many actors have given up the stage for the movies too. But the actor must forego one of his chief rewards: the direct response of his audience; whereas in Hollywood, the anonymous stage director becomes a dominant and well-publicized figure. Consequently, most American and English stage directors today are either producers, dramatists or actors. Dramatists usually, though by no means invariably, direct plays of their own authorship. Actors, on the other hand, seldom direct plays in which they themselves appear, for this duality creates many difficulties.

Exactly what does the director do? His first task is to cast the play, and, speaking as a director, I should say that if he casts it well, he has taken a long stride toward the accomplishment of his mission. Casting is a slow and difficult process, not only because of the chaotic conditions described in the preceding chapter, but because it takes a special kind of perception to relate the candidate's personality and ability to the part he is required to play. Familiarity with the actor's previous appearances is, of course, helpful; but past performance is not a certain guide, for actors may be better or worse than they have seemed in a particular part. Unless the director is completely convinced of the actor's fitness for the part, a reading, or series of readings, is almost essential. Since most actors are acutely self-conscious and suffer far more from office fright than they do from stage fright, reading is always an ordeal, and some flatly refuse to undergo it, upon the ground that no mere reading in a room or even on a stage can convey what weeks of work and study will produce. Of course that is true; but no sensible director expects a reading to be a performance: in fact, he would be inclined to be wary if it were. What he looks for is the coloration of the actor's personality and his attack upon the part. In my own experience, no actor who has not shown an instinctive grasp of the essence of a character upon a first reading has ever given a really satisfactory performance. Intelligence is not necessarily a handicap to an actor, but in acting, as in any other art, sensitivity and perceptiveness count for more than intellectuality, and the best actors arrive at their interpretations through their feelings rather than by a process of cerebration.

In casting a play the director must do more than select a suitable actor for each part; he must consider the parts in relation to each other, and assemble a company that plays in the same key and seems to belong in the same milieu. Every theatre-goer has been jarred upon occasion (though without knowing why, perhaps), by the disharmony that results from the inter-play of actors who are not attuned to each other. Highly touted "all-star" revivals are often disappointing, because they offer an aggregation of soloists, each playing in his own style, rather than a concerted ensemble. If the director is neither the producer nor the author, his selections usually are subject to the approval of both; and when, as is often the case, there are two authors and several producers, the conflict of opinions end in "compromise" choices that are not always happy ones. In the theatre, as in other fields of activity, the best decisions are not likely to be arrived at in committee.

Another important part of the director's preliminary work is to familiarize himself with the physical layout of the scenes in which the action is to take place. Ideally, he should work from the beginning with the scene designer, in order that he may be certain that the settings are suited to the required busi-ness of the play; that sight lines are unobstructed; that means of access are advantageously placed; that furniture and prop-erties can be arranged so that they can be most effectively used; and that a dozen other physical and technical details have been properly organized. When a satisfactory ground plan has been worked out, he proceeds to use it as a basis for his pattern of the stage movement that is involved in "putting the play on its feet."

When it comes to the actual business of staging a play, meth-ods vary widely. It may be said that in general there are three categories of directors: author's directors, actor's directors, and director's directors. The author's director tends to use the ac-tors as instruments to bring out the values of the play script, much as the musical director uses the instruments of the orches-tra. The actor's director tends to treat the script as material to be used by the actors for the display of their talents. The director's director employs both script and actors for the exhibition of his mastery of the tricks of stagecraft. Of course, every director cannot be neatly stowed into one or another of these pigeonholes; in fact, many directors show traces of all these tendencies. But as a rule it is not hard for the practiced spectator to see where the emphasis has been placed.

The director who is primarily concerned with the script is likely to concentrate upon the story line and the interrelationships of the characters. He plans his production so that it highlights the significant points of the drama, and traces the course of its development clearly and cleanly. This does not mean that the actor is subordinated, but simply that he is directed always to stay within the bounds of the character the dramatist has created, and to use the play script as a touchstone to test the veracity of whatever he says and does. If the play is good, if the actor has artistic integrity as well as skill, and if the director knows his business, this type of production can be deeply convincing and aesthetically satisfying.

The actor's director—himself often an actor or former actor —is inclined to study each part in terms of the histrionic opportunities it offers. He sees the play as a succession of scenes, each with a point to be made, with whatever means are most effective; so that the intention is likely to be focused upon what the actor is doing rather than upon the progression of the plot. To put it another way, the points that are made are theatrical rather than dramatic. When the play is weak and the actors are good, a combination that is far from rare, this method works very well, for the deficiencies of the script are concealed by the skillful performance of the actors. Many plays, of course, are deliberately designed as "vehicles" for popular actors. And it is not uncommon for stars to choose plays that have little or no substance but that make ample provision for a parade of their accomplishments. (In my early days in the theatre, the mother of two clever and well-known young actresses suggested that I write a play for them. One was a serious actress, she said, and would require some emotional scenes. The other was better at comedy, and would do very well with some funny lines. One had a good Cockney accent, the other could manage a brogue; so in the first act they would be in lowly surroundings, suitable to the use of dialects, and of course would dress in rags. By the end of the play, their circumstances would be vastly improved, and they would talk like ladies and wear beautiful clothes. She was quite surprised when I declined what was obviously a fine opportunity for a young dramatist.) When the play is a fine one, however, the overstressing of the actor's skill is likely to obscure or dilute the dramatist's creation. The actor's director, too, tends to spend a great deal of time in giving technical instruction to the actors, whereas the author's director is likely to feel that it is not his job to teach acting, and that once he has made clear to the actors what they are expected to convey, it is up to them to find the required technical means—just as a businessman does not undertake to teach his secretary stenography, or a housewife to tell a plumber how to repair a leak. Sometimes the director-teacher welcomes the opportunity to demonstrate how well he could play the part himself.

The cult of the *régisseur*, or the director who directs for the sake of directing, is of comparatively recent growth. Usually he is a "showman" who is interested chiefly in producing sensational effects by the use of any device that comes to hand or that he can invent. The play is something to hang a production on, the actors puppets to be moved about to suit the exigencies of the game. Two of the most famous of these practitioners were Max Reinhardt and David Belasco, who for decades filled the stages of Europe and America with tasteless and pretentious demonstrations of what can be done with scenery, lights, costumes, mobs, eccentric staging, photographic literalism, tawdry fantasy and every other trick in their bottomless bags. (They have their current counterparts; so that, every now and then, one is invited to see not somebody's play, but So-

and-so's "production" of somebody's play.) The enormous popularity of Reinhardt and Belasco is simply one more proof that
there is no accounting for tastes. But it is also proof that there
is room in the theatre for every type of production. In fact, a
superlative production might very well comprise the interpretative, the histrionic and the spectacular.

Whatever the director's approach, he must, in staging the
play, translate the play script into terms of acting and stage
mechanics. The devising of appropriate stage business is by no
means easy. Stage movement to be effective cannot be haphazard. In a well-staged play each movement should have significance, either as indicative of character or of emotion; as
part of the physical action of the play; or as a means of high-
lighting a particular point in the dialogue. There are no close-
ups in the theatre; but the director can bring an actor into focus
by manipulating him on the stage. The dramatist's stage di-
rections, which are seldom more than general indications of
movement, are usually ignored by the director, even when he
himself is the dramatist. He cannot rely upon vague generalities,
for the actor must be told, down to the smallest detail, when to
stand, when to sit, when to walk or turn, when to listen or
not listen.

Almost no play can be staged exactly as it is written, and it
is this well-known fact that accounts for the ceaseless reiter-
ation of Dion Boucicault's aphorism: "Plays are not written;
they are rewritten." Like so many other aphorisms, this one is
hardly even a half-truth. Of course, dramatists rewrite, but so
do novelists and poets. But authentic works of art are usually
altered only in matters of detail; the basic conception and the
substance are seldom changed. Plays that are substantially rewritten are usually contrived pieces: farces or melodramas, or
plays made to order for a star and remade to suit.

If the play is a sound one, the changes that are made in the
course of rehearsals—usually at the suggestion of the director
—are for purposes of clarification and greater dramatic effec-

tiveness. In theory, every moment of a play should be both intelligible and interesting. Few productions ever reach this goal, but it is the aim of the director to get as close to it as possible. The reader of the play script, like the reader of the novel, may skim over the dull passages and reread the obscure ones, but in the theatre there is no way of evading boredom and no turning back the page. Hence, even the first rehearsal may reveal lapses that were not apparent in the text; and the first performance before an audience is bound to. Some dramatists (and I am one of them) deliberately overwrite their plays, first for the purpose of giving the actors fuller conceptions of their characters than need be made explicit in performance; and second because it is easier to cut than to pad, and it is useful to be able to test out material before deciding what to discard. Again, an actor, by a look or a gesture, may convey what the dramatist had found it necessary to express in words. A serious line may evoke laughter because of some quirk of phrasing or connotation, and a line intended for a laugh may fall flat because it has not been sufficiently prepared for, or because the order of the words is wrong. These discoveries are made, bit by bit, as the rigid material of the script becomes plastic in the director's hands.

The director, too, if he is to do his job properly, must be something of a psychologist. His relationship to the actors is a quasi-parental one. He must win their confidence, allay their recurrent misgivings, know when to praise and when to crack the disciplinary whip. The layman cannot be aware how important backstage morale is to the spirit of a production, and morale depends to a great degree upon the director. The audience may properly be unaware of his existence, but during the crucial production period he reigns supreme.

XXIV THE DESIGNER

In the western theatre, since its beginnings in ancient Greece, some form of scenic investiture has usually been regarded as an essential element in the production of a play. For two thousand years scenery was architectural in character, and served merely as a suggestion of the locale or background of the play, and perhaps, too, as a sounding board for the actors' voices. The permanent and solid structures on the stages of the antique theatre (simple in Greece, more elaborate in Rome) represented the formalized façade of a temple or palace, or whatever other setting was appropriate to the action of the play. Even in medieval times the religious plays were staged either within the church or outside, with its exterior for a background. When the plays were presented on a platform in the marketplace, temporary structures were used to denote heaven, hell, Noah's ark or what not.

It was not until the late Renaissance that painted scenery began to be used to any great extent. Improvements in the science of painting, and the development of the stage proscenium led to the use of backcloths, often painted in perspective to give an illusion of depth; and also of painted "wings"—side pieces, placed one behind another, partly to mask the offstage areas, and partly to demarcate passageways for the entrance and exit of the actors.

Many references to these devices still may be found in theatrical lingo, e.g., "in the wings"; "upper left"; or "in one," meaning the stage area nearest the audience, or before the first entrance. It is worth noting that this new scenic technique did not reach England until the seventeenth century, a very fortunate circumstance indeed, for if Shakespeare's plays had not been performed, perforce, on the almost bare stage of the Elizabethan theatre, we might have been deprived of the many beautiful passages that describe nonexistent scenes. ("How sweet the moonlight sleeps upon this bank!" "But, look, the morn in russet mantle clad, walks o'er the dew of yon high eastern hill." And many, many more.)

The growing popularity of opera and of court masques led to ever greater ornamentation, until at times it became fantastically elaborate. There was no attempt at "realism" or verisimilitude. The backdrop and wings were partly utilitarian, partly decorative, and at most merely suggestive of the play's setting. The modern theatregoer is so accustomed to the representational "box set" that it is hard for him to realize that this is a comparatively recent innovation: as recent, in fact, as the late nineteenth century. Even the interior scenes in the "well-made" plays of Sardou were performed in sets with open wings, sometimes with furniture painted on the backdrop; and it is only in the past few decades that musical comedies were done in any other way. This is still the standard production formula for the Gilbert and Sullivan operettas.

Two influences are, I suppose, mainly responsible for the introduction of realistic scenery: one dramaturgical, the other technological. The development of realistic drama, with its emphasis upon the creation of an illusion of actuality and its great reliance upon the use of properties and stage effects, necessitated the invention of an entirely new type of scenery. If, as in *A Doll's House*, the action turns upon the dropping of a letter through the slot in a door, there must be a door with a slot in it. Nor can Peter Pan fly in through the window unless the window is there. Greek and Elizabethan plays contain, at most, a bare identification of the locale; but the texts of many modern plays include detailed descriptions, not only of the architectural features of the setting, but of the decorative scheme, and of every article of furniture, down to ornaments, crockery and even books.

On the technical side, the substitution of electricity for gaslight made possible a whole new range of effects that had never even been dreamed of before. By the use of dimmers and of colored silks and gelatin frames, the quality and intensity of light can be delicately varied to suggest the time of day or, more important still, to help create an atmosphere or mood appropriate to the stage action. Other mechanical devices, such as the turntable, the wagon stage and the elevator stage, have made it possible to change scenes with amazing rapidity and to produce effects that are often startling. Finally, extraordinary illusions can be created by the use of projection, which, in essence, is the enlargement of colored slides upon a translucent screen; really a development of the old magic lantern.

These revolutionary changes, both in the form of drama and in the machinery for its production, greatly enhanced the importance and prestige of the scenic designer. Once a subordinate figure in the theatre, he has become, in the course of the past fifty years, one of its chief functionaries. The contemporary dramatist and producer are likely to use as much care in the selection of the designer as in the selection of the director or the leading actors. For while realism is still dominant in the drama, and the emphasis is still upon the meticulously faithful representation of an interior—outdoor scenes that include natural objects are seldom convincingly imitated—there is a growing tendency toward greater fluidity in dramatic technique, and correspondingly a greater degree of stylization in scenery. There is a vast difference between the photographic reproduction of a Childs Restaurant in David Belasco's staging of *The Governor's Lady*, and the flexible and suggestive setting provided by

Jo Mielziner for Miller's imaginative *Death of a Salesman*. When the play is a classic, for which there is no prescribed setting, the designer is inclined to give free rein to his inventiveness— and sometimes to let it run away with him.

For along with the cult of the *régisseur*, there has grown up the cult of the designer. This is not surprising, for it is very human to take pride in what one does and sometimes to attach undue importance to it. Once, at the tryout of an important play, I happened to be sitting beside the costume designer. As the curtain fell on the second act, I said: "Well, what do you think?" "I think," she replied, "that her dress should be let down another inch." On another occasion I was standing backstage at a performance of *Street Scene*, just before the sound of murderous shots sends a crowd of forty rushing onto the scene. Suddenly I heard one of the young actresses exclaim: "Heavens! I'm wearing the wrong shoes!"

An extreme example of the exaggeration of the designer's (and director's) function is to be found in the writings of Edward Gordon Craig, son of the famous Ellen Terry. Craig, though he had a background of practical stage experience, spent most of his life theorizing about the theatre, and making designs for hypothetical productions. His considerable influence does not seem to be justified either by his achievements or by the soundness of his ideas. While he is certainly right in his contention that most people go to the theatre to *see* plays performed, his preoccupation with the mechanics of production at times becomes nonsensical. He even advocates reducing the actor to the status of a puppet, and having plays performed by "über-marionettes," whatever they may be. He conceives the designer-director as a kind of superman, "capable of inventing and rehearsing a play; capable of designing and superintending the construction of both scenery and costume; of writing any necessary music; of inventing such machinery as is needed and the lighting that is to be used."

No experienced producer or dramatist will deny that the

designer can make a very important contribution to the effectiveness of a production. But when the scenery becomes an end in itself, when it cries out for recognition, and detracts attention from the business of the stage, it can be more of a hindrance than a help. Many a play has been seriously damaged by settings that were overelaborate or that were designed to please the eye of the spectator rather than to make adequate provision for the exigencies of the drama. It is all very well for the rising curtain to reveal a charming or intricate scene that evokes a spontaneous round of applause, but mere scenery cannot hold the interest of an audience for long, and if the play is dull the graphic art of a Michelangelo could not save it. Worse still, a play that is not dull may be made ineffective if the eye is distracted by a cluttered stage, if too vivid colors make the actors fade out, or architectual form is achieved by sacrificing sight lines. One of the most frequent sources of conflict between the designer and the director is the lighting of the production. Since painted canvas looks best when it is not too brightly lighted, the designer's tendency is to keep the lights down. On the other hand, the director knows, as do the dramatist and the actor, that dim lighting is not conducive to close attention on the part of the audience, except when the stage is purposely darkened to create tension; and that, even more importantly, the full effect of the performance cannot be attained unless the actors' faces are well lighted. This is particularly true of comedy scenes, which simply cannot be played in half-light. Sometimes a kind of seesaw game takes place, in which the designer instructs the electrician to lower the readings on the lamps, and the director, in turn, orders them raised.

At best, scenery, costumes, lights, properties and all the physical paraphernalia of the stage are background material whose purpose it should be to enhance the values of the play and to assist the actors in their task of interpretation. A play well written, well cast and well rehearsed is a solid entity that stands on its own feet and does not depend upon external accouterments, though they should and can contribute greatly to the interest and aesthetic pleasure of the audience. But I have seen, on a bare stage, under a single naked work light, performances whose magical quality seemed to evaporate in the thick ambiance of the final production. In designing, as in every art, the finest effects are achieved by an economy of means, and by devices that are not obstrusive or self-evident.

The healthy tendency away from realism in the creation of plays has been accompanied by a tendency away from the conventional proscenium or "picture-frame" stage and toward the more plastic arena theatre with its apron stage (really a return to the antique amphitheatre), and the central-staging type of theatre which is very like the one-ring circuses of Europe. These new styles in production present interesting challenges to the actor and to the director, and perhaps even more to the designer, calling for the full use of his imaginativeness, intelligence and technical knowledge. Fortunately, there are many contemporary designers who possess all these qualities in good measure.

XXV THE AUDIENCE

Of all the factors that contribute to a complete theatrical performance, none is more necessary or important than the audience. For the dramatist has not succeeded in communicating the play he has created until an audience has assembled for the purpose of viewing it. The mere presence of an audience in a theatre is convincing evidence not only of the attractive power of enacted drama, but of the astonishing and unique human capacity for deliberate and voluntary self-discipline. Every time I go to see a play, I am struck afresh by the amount of social organization that is involved in the performance. Even passing over the construction and maintenance of the building itself, we find in the pattern of the production an amazing complex of personal relationships and co-ordinated skills. The more easily the performance flows, the more, we may be sure, it depends upon the split-second timing, the nicely balanced give-and-take and the unity of purpose of dramatist, actors, director, designer and technicians.

The audience is an even more amazing phenomenon. After all, the theatre workers are pursuing their chosen careers, and often their livelihood depends upon the success of their efforts. They have special reasons, therefore, for concentration of their energies and for submission to discipline. But the members of an audience are under no such compulsion. For the most part, they are drawn to the theatre by nothing stronger than a desire for entertainment, using that word in its broadest sense. The reader picks up his book and puts it down at will, wherever he happens to be. The art lover wanders into the gallery at almost any hour of the day, and stays as long as he chooses. Further, the reader takes his pleasures in solitude; for the art lover a companion or two suffices.

Not so the theatregoer. At a very specific time, he must take himself, at considerable expense and often at great physical inconvenience, to a specific place, to join a gathering of five hundred or a thousand fellow-theatregoers, nearly all strangers to him, and linked to him only by momentary similarity of purpose and willingness to submit to immobile captivity for the "two hours' traffic of our stage." Apart from this unity of purpose, the audience is almost certainly a heterogeneous assemblage indeed, composed of individuals varying widely in age, occupation, religion, race, education, intelligence and taste. The coming together of this motley gathering is both accidental and purposeful; ordinarily, neither its exact composition nor its exact response to the performance is predictable.

Yet this crowd, like any crowd, takes on an identity and a character of its own, which is not wholly like that of any of its component members. In certain respects everybody in the audience will react in the same way. For example, if the theatre is overheated, if the seats are too uncomfortable, if the actors are only half audible or half visible, nobody will enjoy the play, no matter what its merits. But in quite another category is the operation of the mores, those indefinable but very real criteria that somehow express the collective sense of what is fitting to be seen and heard in public. Obviously, there is a vast difference between private and public behavior; and people will be outraged to hear in a theatre the use of language and the mention of subjects which may be conversational commonplaces at their dinner tables. When Clyde Fitch's play *The City* was posthumously produced, the general opinion was that it was not one of his best. Yet people flocked to see it apparently for the shock value of hearing "God damn" spoken for the first time on the New York stage. At much less trouble and expense, they could have stood at any street corner and heard far stronger language used by the passers-by. Marc Connelly and I once speculated on what the audience reaction would be to a play in which the characters discussed their physical disabilities and hygienic problems in the manner familiar to the readers of advertisements in the mass-circulation magazines designed for "home" consumption.

Again, the moral judgments and intellectual concepts of the audience are likely to vary greatly from those of its individual members. An audience is almost certain to react hostilely to a character who is guilty of dishonesty, cruelty, non-comic drunkenness or non-comic marital infidelity, even though many of its members may not be entirely guiltless of one or more of these offenses. On the other hand, a *comic* treatment will evoke laughter even from those who have had painful experiences. Patriotic, pious and moral platitudes and clichés are often greeted in the theatre with approval and even applause by persons who would reject them in cold type or in private conversation. On the other hand, an audience may respond to poetic beauty or spiritual perception that is far above the general level of feeling or even of comprehension. Of course, the appeal of the theatre is primarily emotional rather than intellectual and the effect of a play is to increase sensitivity and to blunt the power of judgment. Theatregoers who read a play after seeing it often wonder why they were moved to laughter or to tears, or why they accepted situations or ideas that will not bear examination. (Sometimes they discover points that they missed in the theatre; but that is likely to be due to inattentiveness or to an inadequate performance.)

For me the most fascinating thing about an audience has always been the kind of gyroscopic balance it maintains between objectivity and participation. A play is most effective when the performance creates an illusion of reality so strong that it enables the audience to identify itself in some way with the characters and to share their joys, sorrows and perplexities. Yet this "voluntary suspension of disbelief" is never so complete that it destroys the audience's awareness that it is all pretense. It knows that the walls of the elegant salon are painted canvas, that the liquor that flows so freely is cold tea, that grandfather's beard is held in place with spirit gum, that the baby carried so tenderly is only a doll, that the falling snow is torn paper, that the lethal gun is loaded with blank cartridges, that the dead hero will arise in a moment to take his curtain call, and that the beautiful weeping heroine who kneels beside him has just divorced her third husband. Stated in these terms, the whole business of the theatre seems ridiculous. Yet it is not so, and the audience is only too glad to give itself up to the enjoyment of what it knows to be only make-believe. In fact, that is the very purpose for which it has come to the theatre. There is nothing more amazing than to see an audience that has been torn to shreds by the enactment of an emotional scene burst into thunderous applause the moment it is over, thus expressing acknowledgment of the skill of the actors, and perhaps of the dramatist, who have aroused it to this high pitch of excitement.

One of the best ways to judge the effect of a performance is to sit in a stage box, with one's back to the stage, and watch the audience. The changing expression of the faces and the movement of the bodies are a clear index to how the play is being received. "Sitting on the edges of their seats" is a literal description of audience behavior in moments of tension, and while "rolling in the aisles" is certainly figurative, it suggests the contortions of people who are in the throes of uncontrollable laughter. Smiles, tears, clenched hands, wide eyes all reflect the changing moods induced by the stage proceedings. Sexual allusions sometimes produce disapproving looks, sometimes self-conscious giggles or smirks; telling lines prompt an interchange of knowing looks between companions; and tender scenes are conducive to hand-holding. If there are coughs, yawns and restless squirmings you may be certain that the interest is slackening and that, for one reason or another, the contact between stage and auditorium has been broken. In fact, the nonrespiratory cough is an almost infallible danger signal: an attentive spectator does not cough.

Audiences are singularly obtuse about some things, singularly observant about others. Important information must usually be conveyed two or three times before it is fully grasped, as most dramatists are well aware. Yet frequently an audience will anticipate the point of a joke or the significance of a situation (as actors say: "They're way ahead of us") and after a performance or two, lines that were carefully written and rehearsed are eliminated. Incredible happenings are sometimes readily accepted, while trivial flaws are instantly detected. I once saw an actor—obviously an understudy pressed into service at the last moment—read his entire part from various documents that he kept bringing forth. It was not until the last act that the audience became aware of what was going on. In *Counsellor-at-Law* there is a climactic scene near the end of the play which hinges on a telephone call. On the morning after the first preview at least twenty people called up to say that Paul Muni had dialed only six times instead of the required seven. No reader is very much disturbed by typographical errors or even the omission or repetition of a word. But very often an actor's mispronunciation of a word or the substitution of an incorrect one will break the mood of the audience or even produce a titter. A smudged collar, a protruding slip or a lipstick smear may provide a focus of attention that is fatally distracting. Actors almost invariably check their zippers before making an entrance. And any accident in the audience itself will destroy the spell: an explosive sneeze, an ill-timed guffaw, a drunken altercation, to say nothing of people suddenly bolting out of their seats and up the aisle, or having epileptic fits—not infrequent occurrences.

It is this element of audience participation and this constant interplay across the footlights—figuratively speaking, for footlights are almost obsolete—that keep the theatre boiling and give each performance a touch of adventuresomeness. For no two performances of any play are ever exactly alike. Audiences vary with the season, the weather, the day of the week, the day's news. Any actor will tell you that Monday audiences are usually quiet; that Saturday-night audiences are relaxed and out for a good time; that Wednesday matinee audiences do not respond to humor but adore all the little homey touches; that benefit audiences are hard to please; that Sunday-night audiences are impervious to subtleties; and so on. These generalizations are undoubtedly a little too broad, but they are based upon long experience. And anyone who stands backstage during a performance is almost certain to hear an actor say, as he comes off: "They're laughing at anything tonight," or "They're sitting on their hands out there." Many times I have seen an actress almost in tears because she did not get the accustomed round of applause on her exit. The longer a play runs, the less perceptive is the audience. The reason is clear: the first audiences consist mainly of seasoned theatregoers, who are sophisticated and "theatre-wise" and therefore quick on the uptake. Audiences in which "out-of-towners" predominate are quite different from audiences of New Yorkers. If a play is a great success the audience is often "sold" on it well in advance. An actor in a great hit said to me: "You know, we used to wait for that first big laugh about two minutes after my entrance. Well, by the third week they began laughing the minute I came on. By the second month they laughed when the curtain went up. And after that, they were laughing as they came down the aisles to their seats." On the other hand, an audience may be oversold, and theatregoers who have waited months to see a play may find themselves disappointed in watching a tired performance, or hearing lines that have lost their luster through familiarity.

For the actor, as for any interpretive artist, the immediate response of the audience is of paramount importance. He has direct personal contact with it, in a way that no creative artist who does not also happen to be a performer can. His performance is necessarily ephemeral, forever wasted if it is not appreciated at the moment of execution. This is not to say that he finds no satisfaction in the characterization itself, which at its best demands the employment of imagination and many skills. But we have seen that for any artist expression is not enough; there must be communication too. And for the actor true communication exists only when he stands physically in the presence of an audience and wrests recognition from it by the display of his talents. That is why there are very few actors who do not prefer the stage to the television or motion-picture screen. Broadcasting and the movies may offer more security and greater financial rewards, but acting for a camera can never be the same as acting for an audience. Besides, a filmed performance is frozen and unalterable, whereas a stage performance is always fluid and vibrant, slightly modulated at each repetition to attune it to the mood of the audience, and having its minor defects, like the small irregularities that distinguish a bit of handicraft work from the smooth cold flawlessness of a factory job.

The dramatist, of course, has no such personal communion with the audience. When the curtain rises, he must depend upon the actors—and all his other associates in the production—to reveal what he has created. If he happens to be in the theatre during a performance he can see and hear for himself how his work is being presented and how it is being received. He is elated when the play is going well, disheartened when it is going badly. But the fact that it is going at all represents the accomplishment of what he desired from the beginning: the communication to others of what he had expressed. The communication may be incomplete because of faulty expression, of feeble interpretation or of imperfect apprehension. But, for better or worse, he must have an audience. If there can be no drama without a theatre, then certainly there can be no theatre without an audience. The audience then is more than a mere passive recipient. In a vital, living theatre, the role of the audience is functional and creative.

XXVI CENSORSHIP

One more influence that vitally affects the communication of drama must be considered. Wherever the theatre exists, it is subject to pressures and regulations which, to a greater or less degree, restrict what may be said or done upon the stage. This restriction, which is loosely called censorship, is of the greatest concern to the dramatist, for while he is free to write whatever he pleases, he is limited in the stage presentation of his plays to what is legally permissible and socially acceptable. Almost anything may, at one time or another, meet with the censor's disapproval, but usually the nature of the objectionable material is political, religious or moral.

Strictly defined, censorship is an act of prior restraint by a governmental agency: in other words, the official banning of a play before it is performed in public. But by extension censorship also includes the enforced closing of a play after production. Nonofficial influences and pressures, too, though they may not be properly classifiable as censorship, often have effects that are decidedly restrictive. The censorship situation throughout the world is far from uniform or even constant: it varies from country to country, and even in different areas within a particular country, and is affected by all sorts of social and political conditions.

Of one thing we may be certain: wherever there is a dictator, there is a censor. Censorship is an inevitable concomitant of any form of totalitarianism, for a totalitarian regime can survive only by the ruthless suppression of all opposition, and this includes the expression of ideas that are considered inimical to the ruling power or at variance with its basic philosophy. Under dictatorship the art of the drama withers and dies, since originality and spontaneity are not encouraged, and what is demanded of the dramatist is slavish conformity to the prevailing political doctrine. Modern Germany affords a vivid example. The German theatre of the 1920's was vigorous and creative. With the advent of Hitler and the imposition of censorship, and of course the banishment of "non-Aryans" and opponents of Nazism, the theatre became dull and insignificant, given over almost entirely to mediocre productions of the classics and to crude propaganda. When Hitler fell, the censorship was relaxed, some of the exiles returned, and the theatre came to life again; though it cannot be said that as yet there have been many notable new plays.

In the Soviet Union, theatrical activity, as we have seen, is widespread, and the quality of productions is often very high. But the art of the drama has sunk to a pitiably low level. It could hardly be otherwise when the censor is in full control, and the dramatist knows that if he wants his plays produced, creative self-expression must give way to strict adherence to the "party line": a line whose erratic movements are not easy to follow, so that the play that was orthodox in its inception may, by the time it is finished, require drastic alterations. Even when there is no question of "correctness," other considerations may result in proscription. In Moscow I learned that Pudovkin, one of the great Russian film directors, had been working for two years on a movie that dealt with collective farming; but, my informant said, it would never be released. When I asked him why, he replied tersely: "Too much poetry, and not enough tractors."

At the Moscow Art Theatre I saw a play called *Days of the*

Turbins, which dealt with the civil war in the Ukraine. The Turbins were a family of Ukrainian nationalists who were resisting the Bolsheviks. For once the characters were credible human beings instead of stereotypes, and in a superbly acted scene, in which drunkenness creeps up on them, they pledge their allegiance to the old regime and, to my great astonishment, end by singing the Tsarist national anthem. (In the end, of course, they are converted to Communism.) I asked one of the American newspaper correspondents how this scene had got by the censor. He told me that there had been great controversy about it. At the dress rehearsal the censor had ordered the singing of the hymn deleted, but the director had pleaded with him, pointing out that the singers were drunk, and that after all, they did finally see the light and abandon their erroneous beliefs. At length the censor yielded and allowed the song to stay in—but only on condition that it was sung off key.

Where there is political freedom there is usually freedom from censorship too. It is therefore surprising to find that censorship of plays still exists in Great Britain, a country justly celebrated for its democracy and its liberal political institutions. Before a play can be publicly performed in England, it must be read and licensed by the Lord Chamberlain, whose control of the stage derives historically from the functions of the Master of the Revels of Tudor days. Originally this officer was charged with checking riotous behavior in the theatres and disciplining the actors, who were once legally classified as "rogues and vagabonds"; he also had power to delete seditious or blasphemous utterances from plays. Gradually his authority was increased, and in Queen Victoria's reign he became a sort of guardian of public morals, with the right to prohibit arbitrarily the performance of any play that offended his sense of propriety. Repeated attempts have been made to abolish this antiquated licensing system, but it is still in full force.

Among the plays that have at one time or another been refused licenses in England are *Oedipus Rex, Ghosts, Monna*

Vanna, The Cenci and *Mrs. Warren's Profession.* It is said that a license was almost denied to *The Mikado,* on the ground that it might offend the Imperial Japanese Government. Certain subjects are altogether taboo; thus, for example, until very recently no play that dealt with homosexuality could obtain a license from the Lord Chamberlain. As is usually the case when an antiquated or absurd law is enforced, means of evasion or violation are easily found. The English device is ridiculously simple. Since the Lord Chamberlain's authority is limited to public performances, the producer organizes a "club" which gives "private" performances for its "members." Membership fees are equivalent to the price of two tickets. Thus the dignity of the law is upheld and the morals of English theatregoers are saved from corruption.

But even where there is no licensing system or official censorship, the broad police powers of the state sometimes are used to suppress plays. For example, in 1937, when political feeling everywhere in Europe was running high, and there were clashes in the Place de la Concorde between rightists and leftists, the Parisian police forced the Comédie-Française to withdraw its production of *Coriolanus,* because its treatment of the problem of dictatorship was regarded as inflammatory and an incitement to riot.

The career of a play of my own is very much to the point. In 1934 I wrote an anti-Nazi play called *Judgment Day.* It was set in an unspecified Balkan country, but it was actually a thinly disguised dramatization of the notorious Reichstag fire trial. When it was produced in New York, most people were not yet awake to the dangers of Hitlerism, and the play was pooh-poohed as exaggerated and alarmist. In 1937 a London producer applied to the Lord Chamberlain for a license to perform the play. At first he met with a refusal, upon the ground that the German Embassy would protest. The producer pointed out that the scene of the play was not Germany, and that any protest would be tantamount to an admission of guilt. This argument evidently

impressed the official—by this time Hitler was no longer regarded as merely a bad imitator of Charlie Chaplin—and he
granted the license, with the delightful observation that if the
Germans did protest, the British Government could always reply: "Why, is that how justice is administered in Germany? We
had no idea"!

At any rate the play was produced in London, received a very
favorable press, and had a good run, as a result of which I was
offered productions in Norway, France and Holland. Only one
materialized, and that had a brief life indeed. On the opening
night in Oslo, a large Fascist contingent in the audience created
so great a disturbance that the play had to be withdrawn. In
Paris, my producer was summoned to the Quai d'Orsay and
reminded by an official in the Ministry of Foreign Affairs that
while no censorship existed in France, and he was free to produce
anything he liked, the police did have the power to close any
play that might endanger public order. My producer took the
hint and abandoned the planned production. In the summer of
1938, I happened to be in Holland on the very day that the
Burgomaster of Amsterdam forbade the opening of the play,
which was in the final stages of rehearsal. Similar action was
taken in the Hague and in Rotterdam, where productions were
also in preparation. The suppression of the play was a front-
page story in all the Dutch papers, and a deputy arose in Parlia-
ment to inquire if Holland was now being ruled by foreign
ambassadors. But with the Nazi war machine poised on the
border, it was considered impolitic to offend the Germans, and
the ban held. (No megalomaniac can be placated or appeased,
and when Hitler was ready to launch his westward drive, he
ruthlessly bombed Rotterdam and overran Holland just the
same.)

The censorship situation in the United States is one with which
I happen to be particularly familiar, because for more than
twenty-five years I have been a member of the board of directors of the American Civil Liberties Union, and chairman of

its affiliate, the National Council of Freedom from Censorship. I have also served on the anti-censorship committees of the Authors' League of America and of the P.E.N. Club. Censorship is an involved subject, and not easy to describe, partly because of the complex American structure of federal, state and municipal governments, and partly because of the activities of nongovernmental agencies.

However, a few generalizations can be made. There has never been a theatrical censorship, nor any sort of play-licensing system, either nationally, or, as far as I know, in any of the states. But almost every state has "obscenity" laws which may be, and sometimes are, invoked against theatrical performances. Since there is no general uniformity either in the language of these statutes, their application by trial courts, or their interpretation by appellate courts, it is impossible to predict either the incidence or the outcome of criminal prosecutions against plays. Actually, such cases rarely come to trial, and I know of none in which there has been a conviction. A New York State law provides that in the event of a conviction on the ground of obscenity, the license of the theatre in which the production was given may be revoked; and it may be that, upon occasion, the theatre owner has refused to book a play rather than incur the risk of losing his license. But it is stretching a point to call this censorship. There is also a state law in New York, enacted as the result of pressure from religious organizations, which prohibits the representation upon the stage of any member of the Trinity. Yet *The Green Pastures*, in which "de Lawd" was the principal character, had a long run in New York without interference, perhaps because many prominent clergymen thought it conducive to the promotion of religious belief. If there is any law anywhere that regulates the political content of plays—and I doubt that there is—it is certainly inoperative.

On the municipal level, the picture is far less clear. With a few exceptions, there are no civic censors or play-licensing agencies, but not infrequently the performance of plays is controlled by direct police action or by improper use of the theatre-licensing power. These arbitrary administrative acts are frequently over-ruled by the courts, but since in cities outside New York they relate mainly to touring companies, which usually are booked only for a week, it is not easy to get court relief before the company has to move on. The situation is worst in Boston, where a minor police official is empowered not only to excise from plays anything he happens to find objectionable, but even to ban the play in its entirety. For example, *Strange Interlude* was not per-mitted to play in Boston, though it had had a long New York run and had been awarded the Pulitzer Prize. However, the pro-ducers put up a large tent just outside the city limits, to which the citizens of Boston swarmed. When the Chicago police com-missioner forced the withdrawal of Sartre's *The Respectful Prostitute*, the University of Chicago invited the company to ap-pear upon its campus, over which the municipal police have no jurisdiction.

New York, as the only important play-producing center, is, of course, the crucial city. Here there has been comparatively little interference with the performance of plays. Occasionally, overzealous mayors or police commissioners have forced plays to close, usually by threatening the theatre owner with revoca-tion of his license—a gross abuse of a function that is merely administrative. But on the whole the New York stage has been happily free from censorship, a fact that is partly responsible for its variety and vitality. Numerous attempts have been made in both the state and the municipal legislative bodies to establish a theatrical censorship, but they have always been defeated, thanks mainly to the vigorous opposition of all the important groups in the theatre; for however inharmonious their relationships may be in other respects, all stand together in their determination to keep the theatre free. Hence they have opposed, too, various suggestions that have been made from time to time for the set-ting-up of a "play jury" composed of prominent citizens who would pass upon the fitness of plays to be seen; or the adoption of a "code" such as exists in the motion-picture and broadcasting industries.

Nearly all responsible theatre workers believe that there is no place for censorship in a democracy whose constitution guarantees the right of freedom of expression, or in a theatre that has importance as a cultural institution. They take the sensible view that the best regulator of the theatre is public taste, and that the mores will determine what may or may not be properly seen and heard on the stage. This view is expressed by Shaw, with his usual brilliance, in his famous preface to *The Shewing-up of Blanco Posnet:*

The persistent notion that a theatre is an Alsatia where the king's writ does not run, and where any wickedness is possible in the absence of a special tribunal and a special police, was brought out by an innocent remark made by Sir William Gilbert, who, when giving evidence before the Committee, was asked by Colonel Lockwood whether a law sufficient to restrain impropriety in books would also restrain impropriety in plays. Sir William replied: "I should say there is a very wide distinction between what is read and what is seen. In a novel, one may read that 'Eliza stripped off her dressing-gown and stepped into her bath' without any harm; but I think if that were presented on the stage it would be shocking." All the stupid and inconsiderate people seized eagerly on this illustration as if it were a successful attempt to prove that without censorship we should be unable to prevent actresses from appearing naked on the stage. As a matter of fact, if an actress could be persuaded to do such a thing (and it would be about as easy to persuade a bishop's wife to appear in church in the same condition) the police would simply arrest her on a charge of indecent exposure. The extent to which this obvious safeguard was overlooked may be taken as a measure of the thoughtfulness and frivolity of the excuses made for the censorship.

The force of this argument is ignored by those who prophesy the abuses that would result from the abolition of motion-picture censorship boards and the revocation of the motion-picture and broadcasting "codes." The theatre, in the absence of any such restraint, operates within the limits of prevailing public standards of propriety, which often differ from private standards, and which also vary widely with time, place and circumstance. For example, I remember a producer telling me how worried he was because the play he was doing contained some words which, though pretty well known to everybody, are not usually uttered in public, and he had been unable to persuade the author to delete them. I told him I thought his fears were groundless for I was sure that the words would not be spoken on the opening night—and of course they were not!

Nevertheless, the theatre is one of the favorite whipping-boys of individuals who, though seemingly well able to protect their own morals, feel an imperative call to safeguard the morals of others. Most frequently, the outcries against the theatre and the demands for its regulation emanate from the pulpit. The church still considers it its duty to discipline its once subservient offspring, like many another staid parent who can never quite accept the fact that the child has attained manhood and chooses to live a life of its own. No one can object to a minister of religion announcing that a particular play, or even the theatre as a whole, does not conform to his own beliefs or moral standards; nor from dissuading theatregoers to attend, either by the use of argument or by threats of punishment, in this life or in the next. But it is quite another matter when he attempts to proscribe what he considers offensive, not only for those who share his beliefs, but for those (almost always the majority) who do not.

Too often the charges hurled against the theatre are inspired by emotion and a flair for sensationalism rather than by ascertainable facts. A good many years ago, the papers on Monday morning, when news is usually scarce, carried a front-page report of a sermon delivered by a well-known clergyman, celebrated for his "liberalism" and his advocacy of unorthodox causes, in which he stated that the entire New York stage was given over to "filth" and that something must be done about it at once. Incensed, I challenged his statement and invited him to defend it in a public debate. He accepted, and the debate was held in his church. He made a fine, ringing speech against pornography and the use of the theatre for its dissemination; but when I insisted that he be specific and enumerate the plays that he considered offensive to morality, he admitted that he had not seen a single current play, but had based his denunciation upon the report of a female parishioner in whose judgment he had great confidence.

In recent years there has been a growing threat to freedom of expression, in all the arts, from "pressure groups," a generic term for organizations of all sorts—ecclesiastical, professional, economic, nationalistic, racial, patriotic—which attempt, by persuasion or threats of reprisal, to suppress anything that might be regarded as even remotely detrimental to the special interests of the group. Often this pressure is exerted by the salaried executives of these organizations, as alleged spokesmen for a membership that usually does not know what is being done in its name, and might disapprove if it did know. The monopolistic motion-picture and broadcasting industries have been particularly susceptible to these pressures and have adopted policies that exclude, from the screen and from the air, practically anything that could conceivably give offense to any organized group. It is greatly to the credit of theatrical producers (and of book publishers, too) that they have continued to behave as stubborn individualists, and, in general, have resisted the attempts of pressure groups to supervise and control them.

A few examples of pressure-group activity will illustrate both its breadth and its absurdity. When a play was produced in which a character grimaced because the arsenic spray had not been entirely removed from an apple he was eating, the apple-growers' association demanded the deletion of this incident, and offered, as a reward for compliance, free distribution of apples to the theatre patrons. In another play, the appearance of a comic hotel maid who performed her duties in a perfunctory manner prompted the hotel-workers' union to put a picket line in front of the theatre. Most incredible of all, the public relations office of the American Bar Association requested that changes be made in a play that allegedly was unfair to lawyers. The play was Miller's *The Crucible* and the lawyers who were maligned were those who appeared in the Salem witch trials in 1698. Another tendency—sporadic, but nevertheless dangerous—is indicated by the attempts of veterans' organizations to prevent the performance of plays, not because of their subject matter, but because their authors, or even their performers, are charged with holding incorrect political opinions. It is to the credit of the theatre that, unlike the motion-picture and broadcasting industries, it has taken a firm stand against political black-listing.

Thus, while threats to the freedom of the stage are ever present, and occasionally successful, the American theatre as a whole is an unrestricted institution and nowhere in the world is the communication of drama less impeded by censorship than in the United States.

XXVII THE LIVING THEATRE

Every week a Jeremiah or a Cassandra arises to prophesy the doom of the theatre; every month some critical high priest administers to it the last rites. Yet the "fabulous invalid"—as Kaufman and Hart called it, in the play they wrote on the subject— lives on. And will live on!

This is not to say that all is well with the theatre. Indeed, the frequently asked question "What is wrong with the theatre?" invariably educes a long list of grievances, supplemented by an abundance of proposed remedies. One may as well ask "What is wrong with humanity?" or "What is wrong with society?" for the theatre is both a human creation and a social institution, and as we have seen, its form and its operation are determined by the nature and the cultural pattern of the society within which it functions. It is a product of human intelligence, imaginativeness, craftsmanship, stupidity, crassness and avarice; and of social organization, enterprise, inefficiency and wastefulness. No wonder then that even its most ardent well-wishers often view it with despair and disgust.

In the preceding chapters many of the ills and shortcomings of the theatre have been described or touched upon. Many are perhaps irremediable; but there are many, too, for which a cure can be sought and found. And it seems fitting to conclude this survey of the contemporary theatre with a sort of general diagnosis, a few therapeutic suggestions, and a very tentative attempt at prognosis. The book has dealt mainly with the American theatre, and so will this recapitulation of the principal points I have tried to make. But many of the conclusions will, I think, be found applicable to the theatre in other countries, particularly countries that are highly industrialized.

The Broadway theatre receives first attention because it is located in the principal city and cultural capital of the United States, and because it is the center of activity for practically all the foremost professional theatre workers: dramatists, actors, directors, designers. Therefore it more or less sets the tone for the rest of the country and, in the eyes of the world, typifies the American theatre.

Two conditions are largely responsible for the undeniable vitality of the Broadway theatre. The first is that it operates in a free and democratic society, and is unhampered by censorship and governmental control. The dramatist is free to write as he chooses, the producer to present what pleases him. Secondly, the theatre is small business, not big business. Its entrepreneurs are individuals whose exercise of personal taste in the selection of plays, and whose concentration upon particular productions, are in striking contrast to the prescribed standards and mechanized procedures of big business. Consequently, the plays that are offered to the public represent a wide variety in taste and quality, ranging from the often horrendous to the occasionally magnificent. Almost always, of course, the aim is box-office success, but the determining factor is individual judgment, and there is little or no pandering to outside agencies, such as sponsors or pressure groups, or to a hypothetical mass audience that includes large numbers of young children and of the mentally retarded. Nor, it may be proudly said, is there any organized black-listing of theatre workers for their political beliefs or personal behavior. Nothing worse could happen to the theatre than to have it come under the monopolistic domination of a small group, no matter how great its efficiency or how high the standards of its component members.

But individual enterprise has its shortcomings too, and these are nowhere more clearly exemplified than in the theatre. Aesthetic judgment is not always accompanied by business acumen, and vice versa. Some producers have both, but some have neither. Some of the most brilliant are also the most egocentric and least willing to submit to organizational control; some are selfishly indifferent to the common good; a few are crooks. Therefore, it has never been possible for producers to form an association with power to discipline its members and to devise effective means for correcting some of the most grievous defects of the theatrical business.

Concerted and co-operative action by the producers could reduce costs, increase the revenue of theatres and win back thousands of theatregoers who have been alienated by the high price of tickets, the difficulty of getting them and the discomforts of theatregoing. The establishment of a central ticket office where seats for all current plays were available, over the counter or by mail; a vigorous campaign against the black market in tickets; the use of modern advertising and promotional methods; low-priced late afternoon performances for students, would all combine to entice people to the theatre and to put it within the reach of those who cannot now afford it, and of those who would go more often if they did not have to pay speculators twice the box-office price. A collective warehouse for the storing of scenery and properties, to which any producer could have access, would greatly diminish the wastefulness of buying new equipment for each new production.

A little boldness in making capital expenditures would help too. If theatres were properly air-conditioned they could remain open all summer, thereby substantially reducing the overhead expenses and greatly increasing employment. The installation of bars and refreshment rooms, wherever possible, would be another source of considerable revenue. Another badly needed improvement is the equipment of theatres with adequate switchboards and permanent stage-lighting systems, which would eliminate the present antiquated and costly system of removing all the lamps every time a play closes, and immediately replacing them with exactly the same type of lamps. All these are merely examples of what might be accomplished within the existing framework through unity of purpose, long-range planning and investment in improvements.

Of course there is a crying need for new theatres that are comfortable, modern and well equipped. Innovations in theatre construction can greatly improve visibility and audibility, and at the same time increase the seating capacity, thus at once making the play available to more spectators and increasing the revenue. The question is: who is going to put up the capital required for the construction of modern theatres? Unfortunately, from a strictly business point of view, it is not a particularly good risk.

On the operational side, the theatrical unions too could alleviate the economic burden by abandoning the wasteful and dubious practice of "featherbedding." Often a play that is hanging in the balance could survive if the payroll were not loaded with workers who are not needed. If plays were able to run longer, the resultant increase in employment would more than offset the superfluous jobs that were eliminated. Moreover, there would be a marked improvement in the present strained, and often hostile, interrelationships among different groups of theatre workers. Going even farther, it would be highly desirable if, during the first weeks of a play's run, dramatists and high-salaried actors made concessions that enabled the producer to keep the play on at a cost that was not prohibitive. It might also be possible, under proper safeguards, to work out some form of profit sharing that would compensate dramatists, actors and directors for reducing their weekly percentages or salaries. But there is little likelihood of the adoption of any such plan as long as producers are chiefly concerned with making a quick killing, and theatre workers with immediate gains.

At best, these proposed changes affect only the economics of professional play production, and do not touch basic artistic considerations, or the development of the theatre as a cultural and social institution. If the theatre is to realize its potentialities as an instrument of the national culture, it cannot depend almost solely upon business operations that are concentrated in one city on the Eastern seaboard, particularly operations that make practically impossible the survival of any play that is not an instantaneous popular success; operations, too, that make no provision for the training of theatre workers or for continuity of employment.

There is only one way to remedy these defects, and that is by the establishment of decentralized permanent repertory theatres, such as one finds in many European countries. Theatres of this sort serve many important purposes. They become an integral part of the cultural life of the community and a source of civic pride; they add to the general cultural stock-in-trade by keeping alive meritorious plays of limited appeal; they elevate standards of popular taste by offering examples of the best drama of all periods; they become training schools for actors, directors and designers.

Since the need for such theatres is generally recognized by those to whom the fostering of the theatre is a matter of vital concern, it may well be asked why they do not exist. The answer is simple: a good repertory theatre, offering a varied bill of fine productions of fine plays, at popular prices, cannot be economically self-sustaining; and, so far, no subsidy has been available.

There are two possible sources of subsidy: governmental grants and private endowment. The repertory theatres of Europe are usually supported by national or municipal governments, either in continuance of the tradition established by court theatres, or, as in the Soviet Union, as instruments of a totalitarian cultural and educational program. In the United States, however, in the absence of any such tradition or program, the militant opposition of taxpayers and the artistic innocence of most legislators are obstacles that are almost insurmountable. From time to time there is talk of the establishment of a national theatre in Washington, but the prospects are very remote indeed. I know of no city that supports a theatre or that even has such a project under consideration. It was the lifelong dream of Mayor La Guardia in New York to establish a great art center that comprised an opera house, a concert hall, a theatre and an art museum; but the dream never became a reality. When a Masonic hall, known as Mecca Temple, fell into the hands of the city through a tax default, La Guardia seized the opportunity to set up the New York Music and Drama Center, as a quasi-public enterprise. For a number of years this organization has presented a miscellaneous program of opera, ballet and drama, much of it of good quality. But the theatre is ill equipped, there are no city funds available, no permanent company or permanent policy has ever existed, and the enterprise has been kept alive only by recourse to expedients of doubtful artistic value. When, some years after La Guardia's death, plans were announced for the building of the Coliseum, on the very site selected by La Guardia, I wrote to Commissioner Moses, reminding him of the Mayor's vision, and urging the inclusion of a theatre in the structure. He replied, of course, that no money could be obtained for anything of the sort; so instead of the temple of the arts envisaged by La Guardia, there arose an architectural monstrosity, dedicated to the display of dish-washing machines and motorboats.

Even if public funds were provided for the support of theatres, there would always be the danger that their management would be entrusted to incompetent political appointees and that there would be political control of the artistic program. The Federal Theatre Project, as we have seen, was made possible only as an economic measure for the relief of unemployment, and before it was fairly established became the victim of political sabotage. There would be danger of censorship too, for many lawmakers regard the theatre as sinful, irreligious and Communistic—terms that, in legislative parlance, are often interchangeable.

To supply the needed underwriting, then, the theatre must look to the munificence of wealthy individuals and grants from heavily endowed foundations, ever increasing in number, as wealth accumulates and men decay. It is high time that the theatre came in for its share of private and institutional subsidy. Opera companies, symphony orchestras, public libraries and art museums have always depended upon subsidies—could not, in fact, exist without them. But the theatre has always been the stepchild among the arts; though it is hard to understand why a company performing a repertory of fine plays should be expected to pay its own way, while a company performing a repertory of operas or an orchestra performing a repertory of symphonies is not. Is it because actors were for so long regarded as vagabonds? Or because, in the United States, the theatre has always been associated with commercial enterprise?

Whatever the reasons may be, there are hopeful signs that a change of attitude is taking place. Recently, some of the foundations have shown a tentative interest in supporting struggling community theatres and providing training for talented newcomers. In Stratford, Connecticut, the Shakespeare Theatre, emulating its British and Canadian forerunners, has been enabled through endowment to erect a charming playhouse and to establish what promises to be a fine Shakespearean repertory company. Here and there, throughout the country, local companies are being helped by well-to-do theatre lovers. In New York, Mrs. Vivian Beaumont Allen has contributed three million dollars for the construction of a repertory theatre in the new Lincoln Art Center—after the federal government refused to contribute to the project unless plans for the erection of five splendid theatres were canceled! These may be taken as evidence of a growing recognition of the theatre's need for some help with its financial problems. And as the cities of the West grow in population and in wealth, it may be that they will discover that a fine theatre can be as bright a civic ornament as a major league baseball club.

The shortcomings of the professional theatre are matched by those of the nonprofessional theatre, particularly the universities. While nearly every institution of higher learning has drama-study courses and engages in play-producing activities, the organization, equipment and quality of instruction and achievement are, in general, far below those of other branches of study, including the other arts. Many colleges have faculties and even schools of painting, music and architecture, while the drama courses are unco-ordinated and scattered among English and speech departments or reduced to the status of extracurricular activities, for which the students receive no academic credit. Very few have well-rounded drama departments. Harvard has a fine School of Business Administration, but no school of the theatre; Columbia has a School of Journalism but no school of the theatre; Michigan has a fine School of Medicine (and a first-class hospital), and though it has an excellent playhouse, drama instruction is woefully impeded by lack of autonomy and lack of a concerted program. So it goes throughout the country. Only a few universities have adequate theatres, though they are handsomely equipped with laboratories, gymnasiums and, of course, football stadiums.

Yet a university is an almost ideal location for a theatre. Many of these institutions have student populations of fifteen thousand or more—enough to pack a large metropolitan theatre for several weeks—almost all of whom are potential theatregoers. A campus theatre, once built, costs little to operate, and it can not only provide entertainment and enlightenment for the student body, but serve as a training school for practitioners of all the varied arts and techniques of the theatre, and as a testing ground for the work of young dramatists (or old ones, for that matter!). Unfortunately, there are few universities that come anywhere near the fulfillment of these functions. Again, it is often because of the old prejudices against the theatre: it is frivolous; it is immoral; it has no place in the higher education—while of course home economics and salesmanship do. Productions are likely to be either ritualistic performances of obsolete classics or unactable closet-dramas, or inferior reproductions of Broadway successes. Seldom is there a well-planned and expert creation of a living theatre that incorporates and co-ordinates every phase of dramatic production from the writing of the play to its stage presentation before a receptive and informed audience. The universities have yet to learn that the best cure for the commercialism of the professional theatre, which they so often decry, is the inculcation of higher standards of taste in the audiences of the future. Fortunately, there are numerous college presidents and teachers who are attempting to extend and improve dramatic activities.

For in the end it is the audience that calls the tune. With theatre, as with government, the people get the kind they deserve. If they stay away from the polls or support unworthy candidates, they can hardly complain about corruption and inefficiency in government; if they stay away from the theatre or support feeble plays, they can blame only themselves if mediocrity and vulgarity prevail. This is not to argue that the theatre should exist only on a lofty intellectual plane. In fact, the pedantic highbrows who would make of it an austere temple, frequented only by an aesthetic elite, serve it no better than do the idle pleasure seekers to whom it is merely a place for brainless diversion. The range of the theatre should be broad enough to satisfy every taste, but upon whatever level it functions, its vitality and effectiveness will depend largely upon the alert and active participation of the audience.

If there is one question that is asked more often than "What is wrong with the theatre?" it is "What is the future of the theatre?" No answer that is not purely speculative is possible. Could it have been intelligently answered a century ago, unless the prophet had been able to foresee the rise of industrialism and of totalitarianism; the effect of the theories of Marx, Darwin and Freud upon society and upon the thinking of men; the revival of the art of the drama throughout the Western world, and particularly the development of realism; the sweeping technological advances that included the invention of the motion picture and television? Prophecy would be even less reliable in a world that is seething with political upheavals and economic crises, and bewildered by a succession of startling scientific discoveries; a world that is bemused, at one and the same time, by visions of space conquest and fears of total annihilation. The theatre is fluid: it assumes the shape of the society that contains it.

But there is one prediction that can be safely made: whatever the shape of society, the theatre will never die. As long as the world lasts and its inhabitants continue to dream, there will be a theatre; for the theatre is dreamland, the land of make-believe. All the world is a stage in far more than the Shakespearean sense, and one man in his time plays many parts, not only in actuality, but in imagination, expressing and satisfying in self-dramatization his fears, hopes, longings, loves, hatreds, aspirations, guilt feelings; overriding the restrictions of reality with the free play of fantasy; fooling himself with vicarious gratifications. In the theatre he is able to sit back and indulge in the luxury of being fooled by experts. There is nothing else like the theatre and nothing can ever take its place in answering the needs of the human spirit.

INDEX

.